Isabel Maddison

Handbook of British, continental and Canadian universities

With special mention of the courses open to women. Second Edition

Isabel Maddison

Handbook of British, continental and Canadian universities
With special mention of the courses open to women. Second Edition

ISBN/EAN: 9783337204754

Printed in Europe, USA, Canada, Australia, Japan

Cover: Foto ©Andreas Hilbeck / pixelio.de

More available books at **www.hansebooks.com**

Handbook

OF

British, Continental and Canadian

Universities

WITH SPECIAL MENTION OF THE

Courses Open to Women

COMPILED FOR THE

GRADUATE CLUB OF BRYN MAWR COLLEGE

BY

ISABEL MADDISON, B.Sc. (Lond.), Ph.D. (Bryn Mawr).

SECOND EDITION

NEW YORK
THE MACMILLAN COMPANY
1899

PREFACE.

THE many graduates of Bryn Mawr College who have continued their studies abroad, have strongly felt the need of a handbook defining the position of the different foreign universities in regard to the admission of women to their courses, and giving particulars of the lectures, degrees, entrance requirements, etc., of foreign universities and colleges. Accordingly, in 1896, the Graduate Club of Bryn Mawr College published a Handbook of Courses Open to Women in British, Continental and Canadian Universities containing all the information on the subject which it was possible, in a necessarily limited space of time, to collect. The funds necessary for the purpose were secured through the interest and assistance of the President of Bryn Mawr College.

In 1899 it was decided to publish a new edition of the Handbook, and as it was found that practically all European universities and colleges were open to women and that the majority of the facts collected were as valuable to men students as to women students, the title was slightly modified. The information given in the Handbook has been obtained from the authorities of the different universities and collected from the calendars and other official publications. The facts gathered from these different sources have been put together in a condensed form, and it is hoped that the alphabetical arrangement adopted will be found convenient for reference.

The attention of women students is called to the work of the Council to Accredit Women for Advanced Work in Foreign Universities, a committee of the Association of Collegiate Alumnæ.

PREFACE.

The Editor wishes to express her gratitude to all those whose kindness in supplying information made the compilation of the book possible, and to acknowledge her indebtedness to the "Minerva Jahrbuch der Gelehrten Welt."* It is intended to issue a new edition of the Handbook yearly, and the Editor will be grateful for corrections of the errors almost unavoidable in a book of this kind and for suggestions which may tend to make the next issue more serviceable.

The Graduate Club of Bryn Mawr College is glad to allow members of other colleges to make use of its collection of official programs and calendars; particular books will be lent for a few days to applicants prepaying postage.

All communications in regard to the Handbook, and all requests for programs and calendars, should be addressed to MISS ISABEL MADDISON, Bryn Mawr College, Bryn Mawr, Pennsylvania.

* Published by Karl J. Trübner, Strassburg.

AUSTRIA-HUNGARY.

AUSTRIA.

(See also Hungary.)

The universities of Austria, like those of Germany, are state institutions. They are supported by the Government and are directly subject to the Austrian Minister of Education.

With the exception of the university at Czernowitz, which has no Faculty of Medicine, the eight universities of Austria

Addendum.

Information has been received that the Université Nouvelle de Bruxelles has been closed in consequence of lack of money.

while declaring that there could be no question of a general admission of women to academic courses, he yet made provision for particular cases. Certain courses might, as an exception and with the express sanction of the Minister, be given especially for women, and advanced women students might in addition be allowed to attend the courses held for men, provided that they could in every case obtain the consent of the faculty in question, in conjunction with that of the academic senate and the individual professors, with whom work was desired. In no case were women to be allowed to register as students in the universities, but were to be considered as hearers.

PREFACE.

The Editor wishes to express her gratitude to all those whose kindness in supplying information made the compilation of the book possible, and to acknowledge her indebtedness to the "Minerva Jahrbuch der Gelehrten Welt."* It is intended to issue a new edition of the Handbook yearly, and the Editor will be grateful for corrections of the errors almost unavoidable in a book of this kind and for suggestions which may tend to make the next issue more serviceable.

The Graduate Club of Bryn Mawr College is glad to allow members of other colleges to make use of its collection of official programs and calendars; particular books will be

AUSTRIA-HUNGARY.

AUSTRIA.

(See also Hungary.)

The universities of Austria, like those of Germany, are state institutions. They are supported by the Government and are directly subject to the Austrian Minister of Education.

With the exception of the university at Czernowitz, which has no Faculty of Medicine, the eight universities of Austria comprise the Faculties of Philosophy (Arts and Science), Law, Medicine and Theology. Courses of lectures, seminary and laboratory work in different subjects are provided by the several faculties, and the degree of Doctor is given to matriculated students who have fulfilled certain stated requirements.

The entrance requirements for men are similar to those of German universities; the candidate for admission must hold the *Maturitätszeugniss* of a gymnasium or a certificate that he has already attended a university.

In 1878 the admission of women to the Austrian universities was regulated by a decree of the Minister of Education; while declaring that there could be no question of a general admission of women to academic courses, he yet made provision for particular cases. Certain courses might, as an exception and with the express sanction of the Minister, be given especially for women, and advanced women students might in addition be allowed to attend the courses held for men, provided that they could in every case obtain the consent of the faculty in question, in conjunction with that of the academic senate and the individual professors, with whom work was desired. In no case were women to be allowed to register as students in the universities, but were to be considered as hearers.

In March, 1897, these regulations were revised, and the following new regulations are now in force: any woman who is a native of Austria and over eighteen years of age is admitted as a regular hearer to the philosophical faculty of an Austrian university, provided she has passed the *Reifeprüfung* of an Austrian State gymnasium or of a foreign gymnasium considered equivalent to this by the Minister of Education. The Dean of the Philosophical Faculty decides on the admission of candidates, but in case of refusal further application may be made to the Minister.

Women hearers are under the same regulations as men in regard to registration, matriculation, payment of fees, discipline, attendance at lectures, the *Abgangszeugnis* and admittance to the philosophical *Rigorosen* (examinations).

Women who have attended certain schools other than those mentioned above, approved by the Minister of Education, are admitted as *ausserordentliche Hörerinnen* to the philosophical faculties but must, except in special cases, register for more than ten hours of lectures weekly. Permission to attend separate lectures is given to women in exceptional cases only, under the regulation of 1878.

A noteworthy decree putting Austrian women who have studied medicine at any foreign university on the same footing as men in regard to obtaining Austrian degrees in medicine was published on May 19th, 1896. Women who have passed the *Reifeprüfung* of an Austrian gymnasium, are over 24 years of age and have studied for at least ten semesters at a foreign university considered suitable by the Minister of Education, may proceed to take all the final examinations in medicine, omitting those in Natural Science, and to obtain diplomas on exactly the same conditions as men.

The university libraries are open to women.

The academic year is divided into two semesters, the first, or winter semester, which begins on October 1st, and ends on the Thursday before Palm Sunday, and the second, or summer semester, which begins on the first Thursday after Easter and ends about July 30th.

The system of university fees is in general the same in Austria as in Germany. (See under Germany.)

CRACOW, Galicia, Austria.

JAGELLONISCHE UNIVERSITÄT.

UNIWERSYTET JAGIELLOŃSKI W KRAKOWIE.

This university, founded in 1364, is under the same regulations as all the universities of Austria; see above. In the winter semester of 1898–99, 107 women were attending courses in the university.

Enquiries may be addressed to the secretary, LEON CYFROWICZ.

Professors and Lecturers.

ARTS.

LANGUAGES.—INDO-IRANIAN: *Docents* v. Mankowski, Rozwadowski.

CLASSICAL: *Professors* Miodonski, Morawski, Sternbach.

ENGLISH: *Reader* Dziewicki.

GERMANIC (Polish, Slavonic): *Professors* Creizenach, Malinowski, Graf Tarnowski, Tretiak; *Docents* Studzinski, Windakiewiez, v. Zdziechowski.

ROMANCE: *Professor* Kawczynski; *Reader* Rongier.

COMPARATIVE PHILOLOGY: *Professor* de Courtenay.

PHILOSOPHY: *Professors* Pawlicki, Straszewski; *Docent* Ziembicki.

HISTORY: *Professors* Lewicki, Graf Mycielski, Smolka, Zakrzewski; *Docents* Czermak, Krzyzanowski.

ART AND ARCHÆOLOGY: *Professors* Bienkowski, Sokolowski; *Docent* Graf Mycielski.

PEDAGOGY: *Professor* Straszewski; *Docent* Kulczynski.

SCIENCE.

MATHEMATICS AND ASTRONOMY: *Professors* Kepinski, Karlinski, Rudzki, Zorawski.

PHYSICS: *Professors* Natanson, Witkowski; *Docent* Birkenmajer.

CHEMISTRY: *Professors* Bandrowski, Godlewski, Olszewski, Schramm; *Docent* Jentys.

MINERALOGY: *Professor* Kreutz.

GEOLOGY: *Professor* Szajnocha.

BIOLOGY: *Professors* Hoyer, Wierzejski; *Docent* Garbowski.

BOTANY: *Professors* Janczewski, Rostafinski.

GEOGRAPHY: *Professor* Szwarcenberg-Czerny.

AGRICULTURE: *Professor* v. Lubomeski; *Docents* Ajdukiewicz, Jentys, Klecki.

ENGINEERING: *Docent* Ajdukiewicz.

LAW AND POLITICAL SCIENCE.

Professors Brzezinski, Cyfrowicz, Czerkawski, Fierich, Górski, Kasparek, Kleczynski, Krzymuski v. Radwan, Leo,

Madeyski, Milewski, Piekosinski, Rosenblatt, Ulanowski, Zoll; *Docents* Estreicher, W. L. Jaworski, Makarewicz, Rostworowski, Wróblewski.

MEDICINE.

Professors Browicz, Bujwid, Cybulski, Domanski, Jakubowski, W Jaworski, Jordan, Klecki, Korczynski, v. Kottanecki, Lazarski, Obalinski, Parenski, Pieniazěk, Poniklo, Reiss, Stopczanski,
Trzebicky, Wachholz, Wicherkiewicz, Zarewicz; *Docents* Baurowicz, Bossowski, Braun, Leprowski, Korczynski, Krynski, Raczynski, Rosner, Sroczynski, Zulawski.

THEOLOGY.

Professors Chotkowski, Gabryl, Gromnicki, Knapinski, Morawski, Pelczar, Spis, Trznadel, Wadolny.

CZERNOWITZ, Buckowina, Austria.

K. K. FRANZ-JOSEFS-UNIVERSITÄT.

This university, founded in 1875, is under the same regulations as all the universities of Austria; see pp. 1-3.

Enquiries may be addressed to the secretary, DR. ANTON NUSSBAUM.

Professors and Lecturers.

ARTS.

LANGUAGES. — CLASSICAL: *Professors* Hilberg, Wrobel.
ENGLISH; *Reader* Romanovsky.
GERMANIC (Slavonic, etc.): *Professors* Kaluzniacki, Sbiera, Smalstocki, v. Summersberg; *Docent* Wolkan.
ROMANCE: *Professor* Gartner.
PHILOSOPHY: *Professor* Wahle.
HISTORY: *Professors* Herzberg-Fränkel, Zieglauer v. Blumenthal; *Docents* Kaindl, Milkowicz

SCIENCE.

MATHEMATICS: *Professor* Puchta.
PHYSICS: *Professors* Handl, Tumlirz.
CHEMISTRY: *Professor* Pribram.
MINERALOGY: *Professor* Scharizer.
ZOOLOGY: *Professor* Zelinka.
BOTANY: *Professor* Tangl.
GEOGRAPHY: *Professor* Löwl.

LAW AND POLITICAL SCIENCE.

Professors Ehrlich, v. Halban, Hauke, Hiller, Kleinwächter, v. Hörmann zu Hörbach, Ritter v. Roschmann-Hörburg, Skedl; *Docents* Kryspin, v. Wolan.

THEOLOGY.

Professors C. Popowicz, E. Popowicz, v. Repta, Tarnawski, Wojucki; *Docents* Gaina, Stefanelli.

GRATZ, Styria, Austria.

K. K. KARL-FRANZENS-UNIVERSITÄT.

This university, founded in 1586, is under the same regulations as all the universities of Austria; see pp. 1-3.

Enquiries may be addressed to the secretary, JOSEF HÜTTER.

Professors and Lecturers.

ARTS.

LANGUAGES. — ORIENTAL: *Professor* Kirste.
CLASSICAL: *Professors* Goldbacher, Ritter v. Karajan, Meyer, Picher, Schenkl.

ENGLISH : *Professor* Luick.
GERMANIC : *Professors* Schönbach, Seuffert ; *Docent* Zwierzina.
SLAVONIC : *Professors* Krek, Strekelj.
ROMANCE : *Professors* Ive, Schuchardt.
COMPARATIVE PHILOLOGY : *Professor* Meyer.
PHILOSOPHY: *Professors* Ritter v. Meinong, Spitzer, Strzygowski ; *Docent* Martinak.
HISTORY : *Professors* Bauer, Krones Ritter v. Marchland, Loserth, v. Zwiedineck-Südenhorst ; *Docents* Mayer, Mell.
ART AND ARCHÆOLOGY : *Professors* Cuntz, Gurlitt, v. Meinong, Pichler, Strzygowski.

SCIENCE.

MATHEMATICS AND ASTRONOMY : *Professors* Dantscher Ritter v. Kollesberg, Frischauf, v. Hepperger ; *Docent* Streissler.
PHYSICS : *Professors* Hann, Pfaundler, Streintz, Subic, Wassmuth ; *Docent* Henrich.
CHEMISTRY: *Professors* Schrötter, Skraup.
MINERALOGY : *Professor* Doelter.
GEOLOGY : *Professors* Hilber, Hoernes ; *Docent* Penecke.
BIOLOGY : *Professors* Böhmig, v. Graff ; *Docent* Ritter v. Heider.

BOTANY : *Professor* Haberlandt ; *Docent* Palla.
GEOGRAPHY : *Professor* Richter.

LAW AND POLITICAL SCIENCE.

Professors Freiherr v. Anders, Freiherr v. Canstein, Gumplowicz, Hanausek, Hildebrand, Lubec, Luschin Ritter v. Ebengreuth, Mischler, Freiherr v. Schwind, Steinlechner, Tewes, Thaner, Vargha ; *Docents* v. Glanvell, Sperl.

MEDICINE.

Professors Anton, Birnbacher, Bleichsteiner, Börner, Borysiekiewicz, Drasch, Ebner, Eppinger, Escherich, Habermann, Hoffer Edler v. Sulmthal, Hofmann, Holl, Jarisch, Klemensiewicz, Kratter, Kraus, Möller, Müller, Nicoladoni, Prausnitz, Freiherr v. Rokitansky, Rollett, v. Rosthorn, Schindler ; *Docents* Emele, Hammerl, Kossler, Laker, Rossa, Sachssalber, Steinbüchel v. Rheinwall, Tobeitz, Zoth.

THEOLOGY.

Professors Gutjahr, Klinger, Michelitsch, Ritter v. Scherer, Schlager, Stanonik, A. Weiss, J. Weiss.

MUSIC.

Docent ———.

INNSBRUCK, Tyrol, Austria.

K. K. LEOPOLD-FRANZENS-UNIVERSITÄT.

This university, founded in 1673-4, is under the same regulations as all the universities of Austria ; see pp. 1-3.

Enquiries may be addressed to the secretary, WILLIBALD STRICKER.

Professors and Lecturers.

ARTS.

LANGUAGES. — ORIENTAL : *Professor* Flunk.
INDO-IRANIAN: *Professor* v. Schröder; *Docent* Walde.
CLASSICAL : *Professors* Müller, Zingerle ; *Docent* Radinger.
ENGLISH : *Professor* Fisher.
GERMANIC : *Professors* Seemüller, Wackernell ; *Docent* Schatz.

ROMANCE: *Professor* Demattio ; *Docents* Farinelli, W. v. Zingerle ; *Reader* Genelin.
COMPARATIVE PHILOLOGY : *Professor* F. Stolz.
PHILOSOPHY : *Professors* Hillebrand, Ueberhorst.
HISTORY : *Professors* Friedrich, Hirn, Kaltenbrunner, v. Ottenthal, Pastor, v. Scala ; *Docent* Mayr.

ART AND ARCHÆOLOGY: *Professors* Reisch, Semper.

SCIENCE.

MATHEMATICS AND ASTRONOMY; *Professors* O. Stolz, Wirtinger; *Docent* Schober.
PHYSICS: *Professors* Czermak, Exner, Klemencic; *Docents* Hammerl, Radakovic, Tollinger.
CHEMISTRY: *Professor* Senhofer; *Docent* Hopfgartner.
MINERALOGY: *Professor* Cathrein.
GEOLOGY: *Professor* Blaas.
BIOLOGY: *Professors* Heider, v. Dalla-Torre-Thurnberg-Sternhof.
BOTANY: *Professor* Heinricher.
GEOGRAPHY: *Professor* Ritter v. Wieser.

LAW AND POLITICAL SCIENCE.

Professors Carnevale, Dantscher Ritter v. Kollesberg, Demelius, Galante, Hruza, John, Lentner, Myrbach v. Rheinfeld, Pacchioni, Puntschart, Ritter v. Sartori-Montecroce, Schiffner, Vinzenz, Wahrmund, Waldner; *Docents* v. Eccher, Payr, Zanetti.

MEDICINE.

Professors Dimmer, Ehrendorfer, Hochstetter, Ipsen, Juffinger, Kerschner, Klotz, Lode, Loebisch, Loewit, Loos, Lukasiewicz, Mayer, Nevinny, Pommer, Rille, Freiherr v. Rokitansky, v. Tschurtschenthaler Edler v. Helmheim, Victor Ritter v. Hacker, v. Vintschgau, Wildner; *Docents* Lantschner, Malfatti, Posselt.

THEOLOGY.

Professors Flunk, Gatterer, Hofmann, Hurter, Michael, Nisius, Noldin, Rinz, Straub; *Docents* Lercher, Müller.

LEMBERG, Galicia, Austria.

K. K. FRANZENS-UNIVERSITAT.

C. K. UNIWERSYTET IMIENIA CESARZA FRANCISZKA I.

This university, founded in 1784, is under the same regulations as all the universities of Austria; see pp. 1–3.

Enquiries may be addressed to the secretary, MARCELI CHLAMTACZ.

Professors and Lecturers.

ARTS.

LANGUAGES.—SEMITIC: *Professor* Sarnicki.
CLASSICAL: *Professors* Cwiklinski, Kruczkiewicz; *Docent* Jezieniecki.
ENGLISH: *Instructor* Kropiwnicki.
GERMANIC: *Professors* Colessa, Kalina, Pilat, Werner.
ROMANCE: *Docent* Porebowicz; *Instructor* Amborski.
PHILOSOPHY: *Professors* Graf Dzieduszycki, Raciborski, Skórski.
HISTORY: *Professors* Dembinski, Finkel, Gruszewski, Szaraniewicz, Wojciechowski; *Docent* Hirschberg.
ART and ARCHÆOLOGY: *Professor* Boloz-Antoniewicz.
PEDAGOGY: *Docent* Danysz.

SCIENCE.

MATHEMATICS AND ASTRONOMY: *Professors* Laska, Puzyna.
PHYSICS: *Professors* Fabian, Zakrzewski.
CHEMISTRY: *Professors* Lachowicz, Radziszewski.
MINERALOGY: *Professor* Dunikowski; *Docent* Niedzwiedzki.
GEOLOGY: *Professors* Niedzwiedzki, Siemiradzki, Zuber; *Docent* Teisseyre.
BIOLOGY: *Professor* Dybowski; *Docents* Nussbaum, Piotrowski, Wielowiejski.
BOTANY: *Professor* Ciesielski; *Docents* Szyszylowicz, Zalewski.
GEOGRAPHY: *Professor* Rehmann.
HYGIENE: *Docent* Szpilman.

LAW AND POLITICAL SCIENCE.

Professors Abraham, Bálasits, Balzer,

Bobrzynski, Glabinski, Gryziecki, Janowicz, v. Ochenkowski, Pietak, T. Pilat, Roszkowski, Starzynski, Stebelski, Szachowski, Till; *Docents* Chlamtacz, Dobrzanski, Dolinski, L. Pilat, Winiarz.

MEDICINE.
Professors Beck, Gluziuski, Kadyi, Lukasiewicz, Niemilowicz, Obrzut, Prus,

Rydygier, v. Sobieranski, Szymonowicz; *Docents* Baracz, Gatryszewski, Piotrowski, Schramm, Wehr, Widmann, Ziembicki.

THEOLOGY.
Professors Bartoszewski, Bilczewski, Fijalek, Filarski, Jaszowski, Kloss, Komarnicki, Sarnicki; *Docent* Narajewski; *Instructor* Redkiewicz.

PRAGUE, Bohemia, Austria.
K. K. DEUTSCHE KARL-FERDINAND-UNIVERSITÄT.

This university, founded in 1348, is under the same regulations as all the universities of Austria; see pp. 1–3.

Enquiries may be addressed to the rector, DR. ANTON KURZ.

Professors and Lecturers.

ARTS.
LANGUAGES.—SEMITIC: *Professor* Grünert.
CLASSICAL: *Professors* Holzinger Ritter v. Weidich, Keller, Rzach, Schubert.
ENGLISH: *Professor* Pogatscher; *Reader* Just.
GERMANIC: *Professors* Hauffen, Kelle, Lambel, Sauer.
ROMANCE: *Professors* Cornu, Rolin; *Reader* Vielmetti.
COMPARATIVE PHILOLOGY: *Professor* Ludwig.
PHILOSOPHY: *Professors* Freiherr v. Ehrenfels, Marty, Willmann; *Docent* Arleth.
HISTORY: *Professors* Bachmann, Fournier, Jung, Swoboda, Weber, Werunsky.
ART AND ARCHÆOLOGY: *Professors* Klein, Neuwirth, Schultz.
PEDAGOGY: *Professor* Willmann; *Docent* Toischer.

SCIENCE.
MATHEMATICS AND ASTRONOMY: *Professors* Bobek, Pick, Weinek.
PHYSICS: *Professors* Jaumann, Lecher, Lippich, Spitaler; *Docent* v. Geitler Ritter v. Armingen.
CHEMISTRY: *Professors* Brunner, Garzarolli Edler v. Thurnlackh, Gintl, Goldschmiedt; *Docent* Mayer.

GEOLOGY: *Professors* Laube, Pelikan.
BIOLOGY: *Professors* Hatschek, Lendlmayr, Ritter v. Lendenfeld; *Docent* Cori.
BOTANY: *Professors* Molisch, Schiffner; *Docent* Nestler.
GEOGRAPHY: *Professor* Lenz.

LAW AND POLITICAL SCIENCE.
Professors Finger, Frankl, Franz, Krasnopolski, Pfersche, Pfaff, Rauchberg, Schreuer, Schuster, Singer, Ulbrich, Ullman, Freiherr v. Wieser, Zuckerkandl; *Docent* Spiegel.

MEDICINE.
Professors Bayer, Chiari, Czermak, Dittrich, Epstein, Gad, Ganghofner, Hueppe, Huppert, Jaksch, Ritter v. Wartenhorst, Mayer, Petrina, A. Pick, P. J. Pick, Pohl, Pribram, Rabl, Rex, Schenkl, Singer, Steinach, Weil, Wölfler, Zaufal; *Docents* Boennecken, v. Frey, A. Fischel, R. Fischel, W Fischel, Hering, Herrnheiser, Knapp, Münzer, G. Pick, Pietrzikowski, Ramnitz, Spietschka, Waelsch, Wiener, Winternitz.

THEOLOGY.
Professors Elbl, Hauer, Kurz, Rieber, Schindler, Schneedorfer, Zaus.

MUSIC.
Professor Adler; *Reader* Schneider.

PRAGUE, Bohemia, Austria.
K. K. BÖHMISCHE KARL-FERDINAND-UNIVERSITÄT.
C. K. ČESKÁ UNIVERSITA KARLO-FERDINANDOVA.

This university, founded in 1882–3, is under the same regulations as all the universities of Austria; see pp. 1–3.

Enquiries may be addressed to the rector, PROFESSOR REINSBERG.

Professors and Lecturers.

ARTS.

LANGUAGES. — ORIENTAL: *Professor* Dvorák.
CLASSICAL: *Professors* Kvicala, Král, Novák; *Docent* Vysoky.
ENGLISH: *Reader* Sládek.
GERMANIC: *Professors* Gebauer, Kraus, Mourek, Pastrnck, Polívka; *Docent* Máchal; *Readers* Brábek, Kolář, J. Krejci.
ROMANCE: *Professor* Jarnik; *Readers* Malecek, Mohl.
COMPARATIVE PHILOLOGY: *Professor* Zubaty; *Docent* Kovár.
HISTORY OF LITERATURE: *Professor* Frida; *Docent* Vlcek.
PHILOSOPHY: *Professor* Durdík, Masaryk; *Docents* Cáda, Drtina, F. Krejci.
POLITICAL ECONOMY: *Professor* Braf; *Hon-Docent* Bloman.
HISTORY: *Professors* Emler, Goll, Kalousek; *Docents* Novotny, Pekar, Pic, Zibrt.
ÆSTHETICS: *Professor* Hostinsky.
ARCHÆOLOGY: *Docents* Chytil, Matejka.
PEDAGOGY: *Docent* P. Durdik.

SCIENCE.

MATHEMATICS AND ASTRONOMY: *Professors* Gruss, Studnicka, Weyr; *Docent* Sucharda.
PHYSICS: *Professors* Kolácek, Strouhal; *Docent* Novák.
CHEMISTRY: *Professors* Belohoubek, Brauner, Rayman.
MINERALOGY: *Professor* Vrba.
GEOLOGY: *Professors* Pocta, Velenovsky, Woldrich; *Docent* Barvir.
GEOGRAPHY: *Professor* Palacky.
METEOROLOGY: *Professor* Augustin.
BIOLOGY: *Professors* Celakovsky, Fric, Hansgirg, Vejdovsky, Velenovsky; *Docent* Mrazek.
ANTHROPOLOGY: *Professor* Niederle; *Docent* Matiegka.

LAW AND POLITICAL SCIENCE.

Professors Belohradsky, Braf, Celakovsky, Hanel, Henner, Herrmann, Heyrovsky, Kaizl, Ott, Prazak, Randa, Rieger, Storch, Stupecky, Talir, Zucker; *Docents* Bloman, Horácek, Tilsch, Trakal, Vancura.

MEDICINE.

Professors Chodounsky, Deyl, Eiselt, Hlava, Horbaczewski, Janosik, Janovsky, v. Jirus, Kabrhel, Kasparek, Kaufmann, Kuffner, Maixner, Maydl, Mares, Michl, Neureutter, Nessel, Pawlik, Reinsberg, Rohon, Rubeska, Schöbl, Schwing, Spina, Thomayer; *Docents* Formanek, Frankenberger, Haskovec, Hnatek, Honl, Kimla, Kukula, Mitvalsky, Pecírka, Pesina, Scherer, Schrutz, Slavik, Svehla, Velich, Vesely.

THEOLOGY.

Professors Kaderávek, Krystufek, Pachta, Pechácek, Sedlácek, Sykora, Tumpach, Vrestal; *Docent* Tippmann.

VIENNA, Austria.
K. K. UNIVERSITÄT.

This university, founded in 1365, is under the same regulations as all the universities of Austria; see pp. 1–3. The Medical Faculty is large and important, and for this reason the subjects lectured on by the different professors are stated below.

A *Verein* of women students has just been instituted, and a sum of money has been bequeathed for the purpose of founding scholarships for women students.

Enquiries may be addressed to the secretary.

Professors and Lecturers.

ARTS.

LANGUAGES.—CHINESE: *Docent* Kühnert.
SEMITIC: *Professors* Bickell, Heinrich, Müller; *Docents* Bittner, Hoffner, Wahrmund.
EGYPTIAN: *Professor* Reinisch.
CLASSICAL: *Professors* Gitlbauer, Gomperz, Hauler, Marx, Schenkl, Ritter v. Schneider; *Docents* Jurenka, Kalinka, Mekler.
ENGLISH: *Professor* Schipper; *Docent* Kellner.
GERMANIC (Slavonic, etc.): *Professors* Heinzel, Jagic, Jirecek, Minor; *Docents* Jellinek, Kraus, Much, Murko, Nagl, v. Resetar, Vondrak, v. Weilen.
ROMANCE: *Professors* Meyer-Lübke, Mussafia; *Docents* Alton, Friedwagner.
COMPARATIVE PHILOLOGY: *Professor* Meringer; *Docent* Sklenar.
PHILOSOPHY: *Professors* Jodl, Mach, Müllner; *Docents* Höfler, Jerusalem, Kreibig, Reich, Stöhr.
HISTORY: *Professors* Bormann, Büdinger, Dopsch, Mühlbacher, Pribram, Redlich, Szanto; *Docents* Fellner, Hartmann, Kretschmayr, Steinherz, Uhlirz, Wilhelm, Ritter v. Zitkovszky.
ORIENTAL HISTORY: *Professors* Karabacek, Krall.
ART AND ÆSTHETICS: *Professors* Freiherr v. Berger, Riegl, Wickhoff; *Docents* Dietz, Dollmayr, Ritter v. Schlosser, Wallaschek.
ARCHÆOLOGY: *Professors* Kubitschek, Reisch, v. Schneider; *Docents* Heberdey, Hornes, Reichel.
PEDAGOGY: *Professor* Vogt; *Docent* Höfler.

MUSIC: *Professor* Adler; *Docent* Rietsch.

SCIENCE.

MATHEMATICS: *Professors* Ritter v. Escherich, Gegenbauer, Kohn, Mertens; *Docents* Blaschke, Daublebsky v. Sterneck, Sersawy, Tauber, Zindler, Zsigmondy.
ASTRONOMY: *Professor* Weiss; *Docents* Hillebrand, Schram.
PHYSICS: *Professors* Boltzmann, Exner, Jäger, v. Lang; *Docents* Lampa, Moser, Smoluchowski, Tuma.
CHEMISTRY: *Professors* Herzig, Lieben, Lippmann, Weidel; *Docents* Blau Fossek, Natterer, Pomeranz, Schacherl, Vortmann, Wegscheider, Zeisel.
MINERALOGY AND PETROGRAPHY: *Professors* Becke, Berwerth, Tschermak.
GEOLOGY: *Professors* Diener, Fuchs, Pernter, Reyer, E. Suess, Waagen; *Docents* Edler v. Arthaber, E. E. Suess, Wähner.
GEOGRAPHY: *Professors* Penck, Tomaschek; *Docents* Paulitschke, Sieger.
BIOLOGY: *Professors* Brauer, Grobben, Hatschek; *Docents* Pintner, Schneider, Werner.
BOTANY: *Professors* Beck Ritter v. Mannagetta, Fritsch, Wettstein, Wiesner; *Docents* Burgerstein, Krasser.
ETHNOGRAPHY: *Docent* Haberlandt.
METEOROLOGY: *Docent* Trabert.

LAW AND POLITICAL SCIENCE.

Professors Adler, v. Bawerk, Bernatzik, v. Czyhlarz, Friedmann, Gross, Grünhut, v. Heinlein, v. Inama-Sternegg, F. Klein, Lammasch, Lustkandl, A. Menger, K. Menger, Menzel, Mitteis, Pfaff, v. Phillipsberg, v. Rechtenstamm, v. Schey, v. Seidler, Stooss, Unger, v. Zallinger; *Docents* Brockhausen, Burckhard, Ehrenzweig, Feilbogen, Gross, Gruber, Grünberg, v. Herrnritt, v. Juraschek, Komorzynski, Landesberger, Lenz, Löffler, Meyer, Pineles, Pollak, Schmid, v. Schrattenhofen, Schwiedland, Singer, Strisower, Tezner, Walker, v. Wretschko.

MEDICINE.

ANATOMY : *Professors* Dalla-Rosa, Paltauf, Schenk, Toldt, Weichselbaum, Zuckerkandl; *Docent* Kretz.

PHYSIOLOGY : *Professors* Exner, Fuchs; *Docents* Beer, Kreidl, Latschenberger.

HISTOLOGY : *Professors* Ebner Ritter v. Rofenstein, Schaffer; *Docent* Rabl.

CHEMISTRY : *Professors* Ludwig, Mauthner; *Docent* S. Fränkel.

MEDICINE : *Professors* Chvostek, Oser, Winternitz; *Docents* Biach, Drozda, Hammerschlag, Heitler, Herz, Klein, Kolisch, v. Limbeck, H. Lorenz, Mannaberg, Obermayer, Ortner, Pal, Pick, Schlesinger, Schwarz, Sternberg, Strauss, Weiss, Ritter v. Weismayr.

SURGERY : *Professors* Albert, Englisch, Ritter v. Frisch, Gussenbauer, Hochenegg, Hofmokl, A. Lorenz, Ritter v. Mosetig-Moorhof, Weinlechner; *Docents* Büdinger, Ewald, Fieber, Frank, Fränkel, Habart, Schnitzler, E. Ullmann, Zuckerkandl.

OBSTETRICS : *Professors* Braun, Breus, Chrobak, Lott, Schauta ; *Docents* Braun v. Fernwald, Felsenreich, Herzfeld, Jurié Edler v. Lavandal, Lihotzky, Ludwig, Peters, Wertheim, v. Weiss.

PHARMACY : *Professor* Vogl; *Docent* Paschkis.

PATHOLOGY : *Professors* Ritter v. Basch, Gaertner, Knoll, Neusser, Nothnagel, Schrötter Ritter v. Kristelli, Ritter v. Stoffella d'alta Rupe; *Docents* Biedl, Kovacs, Schütz.

DISEASES OF THE EAR: *Professors* Politzer, Urbantschitsch; *Docents* Bing, Gomperz, Pollak.

DISEASES OF THE EYE : *Professors* Bergmeister, Fuchs, Ritter v. Reuss, Schnabel ; *Docents* Bernheimer, Elschnig, R. Gruber, Klein, Königstein, Müller, Salzmann, Topolansky, Wintersteiner.

DISEASES OF CHILDREN: *Professors* Frühwald, Kassowitz, Monti, Freiherr v. Widerhofer ; *Docents* Eisenschitz, Foltanek, Fronz, Ritter v. Hüttenbrenner.

SKIN DISEASES : *Professors* Finger, Ritter v. Hebra, Kaposi, Lang, Mracek, Neumann, Edler v. Zeissl ; *Docents* Ehrmann, Grünfeld, Ritter v. Hebra, Kohn, Riehl, Schiff, Spiegler, K. Ullmann, Vajda.

NERVOUS DISEASES : *Professors* Benedikt, Frankl Ritter v. Hochwart, Fritsch, Freiherr v. Krafft-Ebing, Obersteiner, Wagner Ritter v. Jauregg ; *Docents* Freud, Holländer, Redlich, Freiherr Steiner v. Pfungen.

DISEASES OF THE THROAT : *Professors* Chiari, Stoerk ; *Docents* Grossmann, Hajek, Koschier, Rethi, Roth.

BALNEOLOGY : *Professor* Clar.

HOSPITAL PRACTICE : *Professor* Stern.

MEDICAL JURISPRUDENCE: *Professors* Haberda, Kolisko.

HISTORY OF MEDICINE: *Professor* Puschmann ; *Docents* Neuburger, Ritter v. Töply.

HYGIENE : *Professors* M. Gruber, Kratschmer ; *Docent* Schattenfroh.

THEOLOGY.

Professors Bauer, Ehrhard, Grimmich, Laurin, Neumann, Pölzl, Reinhold, Schäfer, Schindler, Swoboda.

BELGIUM.

There are in Belgium five universities, the state universities of Ghent and Liége, the free universities of Brussels and Louvain, and the new university of Brussels. In 1883 women were admitted on the same conditions as men to the universities of Brussels, Ghent and Liége and also allowed to take the state examinations. The new University of Brussels has been open to women since its foundation. The Catholic University of Louvain, however, does not admit women.

Each university comprises the Faculties of Arts, Science, Law and Medicine, and each of these Faculties provides instruction and grants upon examination the degrees of Candidate and Doctor to students who have fulfilled certain requirements.

Examinations are also held and degrees conferred by state commissions, made up of examiners chosen in equal numbers from among the professors of the state universities and the free university. These commissions are of two kinds, the central commission and special commissions. The central commission is accessible to any student who desires to present himself for examination, the special commissions, instituted for certain separate "faculties" or colleges which do not constitute a university, are accessible only to students of the faculties for which they were established.

No student is admitted to the examination for the degree of Candidate, unless he present a certificate, stating that he has followed certain specified courses of study. Such certificates may be given by the directors of private schools or even by private teachers. They testify, however, to a prolonged preparation, and since this enactment was passed in 1890 the number of women students in the universities has greatly diminished. Students who cannot produce the necessary certificate must pass an entrance examination.

No student is admitted to the examination for the degree of Doctor unless he has obtained the degree of Candidate or a degree considered equivalent to this.

To obtain the degree of Candidate in Philosophy and Literature, the student is required to study for four semesters and to pass two examinations. The course of study is definitely prescribed but foreigners are allowed to substitute equivalent work. It is advisable for a foreigner to have his diplomas certified by some member of the Belgian embassy. For the degree of Doctor of Philosophy two additional years of study are required, and one or two more examinations must be passed.

The year is divided into two semesters, beginning respectively on the first Thursday in October and on the last Monday in February.

The fees charged by the state and the free universities are approximately the same. Upon registering at the university each student is required to pay 15 fr. ($3). In addition he must register for the courses that he desires to take; for such registration a fee of 200 fr. ($40) or 250 fr. ($50) a year is charged for attending all the courses required for the different degrees. The fee for attending one particular course is 40 fr. ($8) to 80 fr. ($16) a year.

BRUSSELS, Belgium.

UNIVERSITÉ LIBRE DE BRUXELLES.

This university, founded in 1834, and independent of Church and State, consists of the Faculties of Arts, Science, Law, Medicine and Pharmacy, and a Technical School.

In 1897 the Special School of Social and Political Science was definitely organised. All the courses are open free to the public, but regular students must hold a Doctor's degree in one of the faculties of a Belgian University or a foreign degree equivalent to this, or must pass a preliminary examination. A two years' course is prescribed for the degree of Licentiate in any branch of Political Science, and an additional year's work is required before the degree of Doctor can be obtained.

Women are admitted to all lectures, examinations and degrees.

The academic year begins in October, the second semester in March.

For fees, etc., see above; the fee for tuition in the School of Social and Political Science is 50 fr. ($10).

Enquiries may be addressed to the secretary, M. LAVACHERY.

Professors and Lecturers.

ARTS.

LANGUAGES. — CLASSICAL : *Professors* Boisacq, De Moor, Vollgraff, Willems.
  ROMANCE : *Professors* Monseur, Pergameni.
  GERMANIC : *Professors* Monseur, Vollgraff.
SANSCRIT AND COMPARATIVE PHILOLOGY : *Professor* Monseur.
PHILOSOPHY : *Professors* Denis, Leclère, Tiberghien ; *MM.* Berthelot, Dwelshauvers.
POLITICAL SCIENCE : *Professors* Denis, P. Errera, Giron, Goblet D'Alviella, Lameere, Nys, Vauthier ; *MM.* Ansiaux, Cattier, Hymans, Waxweiler, Wodon.
HISTORY : *Professors* Goblet d'Alviella, Leclère, Lonchay, Pergameni, Vanderkindere.
PEDAGOGY : *Professor* Lonchay.

SCIENCE.

MATHEMATICS : *Professors* Anspach, Brand, Charbo, Mineur, Tassel ; *M.* Stroobant.
PHYSICS : *Professors* Reychler, Rousseau.
CHEMISTRY : *Professors* Daimeries, Joly, Reychler, de Wilde.
GEOLOGY : *Professor* Prinz.
BIOLOGY : *Professors* Bommer, Errera, Francotte, Lameere, Massart, Rommelaere, Yseux.
ENGINEERING : *M.* de Keyser.

LAW AND POLITICAL SCIENCE.

Professors Baudour, Behaeghel, Cornil, Dallemagne, Duvivier, Giron, Nys, Olin, Prins, Van der Rest, Thomas, M. Vautier, A. Vauthier ; *MM.* Berthelot, Cattier, de Hoon, Hanssens.

MEDICINE.

Professors Carpentier, Coppez, Crocq, Desmeth, Destrée, Hauben, Héger, Jacques, Kufferath, Laurent, Rommelaere, Sacré, de Smet, Spehl, Stiénon, Thiriar ; *MM.* Gallet, Wilmart.

TECHNICAL SCHOOL.

Professors Anspach, Bergé, Van Drunen, Horta, Huberti ; *M.* Habets.

UNIVERSITÉ NOUVELLE DE BRUXELLES.

21 and 28 rue des Minimes; 28 rue de Ruysbroeck, Brussels, Belgium.

This university, founded in 1894, consists of the four faculties of Arts, Science, Law and Medicine, and has a technical school, a school of brewing and an *Institut des Hautes Études*. It has the right to give diplomas to students whether foreign or native, but these diplomas do not yet confer the same privileges in the way of admission to learned professions in Belgium as those obtained from other Belgian universities.

Women are admitted to all lectures, examinations and degrees.

The fee for registration (*inscription*) in the different faculties is 150 francs ($30); the fee for admission to a single course is 30 francs ($6). In the *Institut* a card costing 40 francs ($8) admits to all the courses for a year. There are three scholarships of 500 francs ($100) each, giving free admission to all the courses of the university and of the *Institut des Hautes Études*. There are also forty scholarships of 150 francs ($30) each. Candidates for these scholarships should apply, in writing, to *M. le Secrétaire Général*, before the first of October.

For further information apply to the Secretary, M. Charles Dejongh, 21, rue des Minimes, à Bruxelles; or in England to Mr. Cobden Sanderson, 49, Frognat, Hampstead, London, W.

Professors and Lecturers.

ARTS.

LANGUAGES. — CLASSICAL: *Professors* Collette, Grossmann, Huysmans, Zanardelli.

ROMANCE: *Professors* Demblon, Eekhoud, Huysmans, Lemonnier, Spaak, Zanardelli.

PHILOSOPHY: *Professors* de Greef, Delvaux, de Roberty, Hennebicq, Meyer, Nordau, Petrucci, Sollier.

POLITICAL SCIENCE: *Professors* Brouez, de Brouckère, de Greef, Delbastée, Feron, Ferri, Fiamingo, Kovalevsky, Lazare, Vandervelde, Van Elewyck, Vinck; *M.* Salkin.

HISTORY: *Professors* De Greef, Furnémont, Gedoelst, Gheude, Huysmans, Joseph, Meysmans, Reclus, Robert, Seeliger.

GEOGRAPHY: *Professor* Reclus.

ART AND ARCHÆOLOGY: *Professors* Bacha, Destrée, Joseph, Petrucci, Picard, Van de Velde, Verhaeren.

EGYPTOLOGY: *M.* Galiment.

ARCHITECTURE: *Professors* Defontaine, Hankar, Vincent.

PEDAGOGY: *Professors* Cocq, Robin.

SCIENCE.

MATHEMATICS: *Professors* Bernard, Girard, Lebègue, Mongenast, L. Moreau, Picard, Roorda; *M.* Bertrand.

PHYSICS: *Professors* Blancoff, De Brouckère; *M.* Conrardy.

CHEMISTRY: *Professors* Courtoy, Delbastée, Depaepe, Dungelhoeff, Gille Schuyten, Vincent; *M.* Bernard.

GEOLOGY: *Professors* Malaise, Vincent.

BIOLOGY: *Professors* Chalon, Coremans, Delbastée, Depaepe, De Rechter, Noel, Nissen, Petrucci; *M.* Cherbanoff.

LAW.

Professors Adan, Bon, Carlier, Dejongh, Des Cressonnières, Duchaine, Dumont, D'Union, Franck, Frick, Gedoelst, Ghysbrecht, Hamande, Hegener, Hennebicq, Heupgen, Houyoux, P. Janson, P. E. Janson, LaFontaine,

Moreau, Octors, Picard, Prayon van Zuylen, Prévinaire, Robert, Royer, Schoenfeld, Treille, Van der Cruyssen, Van Isterbeek, Van Meenen.

MEDICINE.

Professors Bonmariage, Boulengier,

Brasseur, Delbastée, Delcourt, De Nobele, De Rechter, Félix, Gillion, Henrotay, Jacobs, Lambotte, Lépine, Maréchal, Martha, Michaud, Mineur, C. Moreau, Pirsch, Popelin, Riez, Troost, Van den Bergh, Wodon, *MM.* Branquart, Claessens.

GHENT, Belgium.
UNIVERSITÉ DE L' ÉTAT DE GAND.

This university, founded in 1816, consists of the Faculties of Arts, Science, Law and Medicine. The degrees, lectures and examinations are open to women. In 1898-99 two women were attending courses in the university and both were registered in the Medical Faculty.

The first semester begins on the first Tuesday in October, the second semester on the last Monday in February.

For fees, etc., see above.

Professors and Lecturers.

ARTS.

LANGUAGES. — CLASSICAL.: *Professors* de la Vallée Poussin, Thomas; *MM.* Bidez, Preud' Homme.
FLEMISH: *Professors* Fredericq, Vercoullie; *M.* de Vreese.
GERMANIC: *Professor* Bley.
ENGLISH: *Professor* Logeman.
ROMANCE: *Professor* Discailles.
CHINESE: *M.* Steenackers.
RUSSIAN: *M.* Taitsch.
COMPARATIVE PHILOLOGY AND SANSKRIT: *Professor* de la Vallée Poussin.
PHILOSOPHY: *Professors* Van Biervliet, Hoffmann, Hulin.
HISTORY: *Professors* de Ceuleneer, Cumont, Motte, Pirenne; *MM.* Van der Haeghen, Roersch.

SCIENCE.

MATHEMATICS AND ASTRONOMY: *Professors* Dusausoy, Foulon, Haerens, Mansion, Massau, Mister, Van Rysselberghe, Servais; *MM.* Demoulin, Fagnart, Wolters.
PHYSICS: *Professors* Van Aubel, Boulvin, Van der Mensbrugge, Schoentjes.
CHEMISTRY: *Professors* Delacre, Gilson, Nelissen, de la Royère, Swarts.

GEOLOGY AND MINERALOGY: *Professor* Renard.
PHYSICAL GEOGRAPHY: *Professors* MacLeod, Van der Mensbrugge, Renard.
METALLURGY: *M.* Bréda.
BIOLOGY: *Professors* Van Bambeke, Van Ermengem, MacLeod, Plateau.
ENGINEERING: *Professors* Boulvin, Van der Linden, G. Wolters; *MM.* Colard, Flamache.
ARCHITECTURE: *Professor* Cloquet.
TECHNOLOGY: *Professor* de Wilde; *M.* Foulon.
COMMERCIAL GEOGRAPHY: *M.* Merten.

LAW.

Professors De Brabandere, Dubois, Callier, D'Hondt, Montigny, Nossent, Obrie, Pyfferoen, de Ridder, Rolin, Seresia, Van Wetter; *MM.* Claeys, Dauge, Halleux, Nicolai.

MEDICINE.

Professors Van Bambeke, Boddaert, Bouqué, Van Cauwenberghe, de Cock, Deneffe, Van Duyse, Eeman, Van Ermengem, Gilson, Heymans, Van Imschoot, Lahousse, Leboucq, Verstraeten.

LIÉGE, Belgium.

UNIVERSITÉ DE LIÉGE.

This university, founded in 1817, consists of the Faculties of Arts, Science, Law and Medicine. There is also a Technical School. The degrees, lectures and examinations are open to women. In 1898–99 nine women were attending courses in the university.

The first semester begins on the third Thursday in October, the second in the beginning of March.

For fees, etc., see above.

Professors and Lecturers.

ARTS.

LANGUAGES. — ORIENTAL: *Professor* Chauvin.
CLASSICAL: *Professors* Demarteau, Michel, Parmentier, Waltzing.
ENGLISH: *MM.* Orth, Veerdeghem.
FLEMISH: *MM.* de Block, Veerdeghem.
GERMANIC: *MM.* Bischoff, Orth.
ROMANCE: *Professors* Doutrepont, Wilmotte.
HISTORY OF LITERATURE: *Professors* Francotte, Kurth.
PHILOSOPHY: *Professors* Grafé, Merten.
POLITICAL SCIENCE: *Professors* Dejace, Francotte; *MM.* De Craene, Delescluse.
HISTORY: *Professors* Hubert, Kurth, Lequarré.
PALÆOGRAPHY: *Professor* Bormans.
ART AND ARCHÆOLOGY: *Professor* Demarteau; *M.* Renard.

SCIENCE.

MATHEMATICS: *Professors* Lepaige, Neuberg, de Locht, J. de Ruyts; *MM.* Hubert, F. de Ruyts.
PHYSICS: *Professors* de Heen, Ronkar.
CHEMISTRY: *Professors* Spring, de Koninck.
GEOLOGY AND MINERALOGY: *Professors* Cesaro, Dewalque, Lohest; *M.* Firket.
BIOLOGY: *Professors* Van Beneden, Fraipont, Gravis.
HYGIENE: *M.* Kuborn.

LAW.

Professors Dejace, Galopin, Lemaire, Mahaim, Orban, De Senarclens, Van der Smissen, Thiry; *MM.* Bellefroid, Crahay, Prost, Schneider, Willems.

MEDICINE.

Professors Firket, Francotte, Fraipont, Frédericq, Gilkinet, Jorrisen, Julin, Masius, Nuel, Putzeys, Scheffers, Swaen, v. Winiwarter; *MM.* Chandelon, Henrijean, Jorissen, Malvoz, Troisfontaines.

TECHNICAL SCHOOL.

Professors Bréda, Dechamps, Duguet, v. Dwelshauvers de Ry, Gérard, Gillon Habets, Holzer, Krutwig, Stévart.

CANADA.

There are in Canada the following universities: the University of New Brunswick, Fredericton, New Brunswick; Dalhousie College and University, Halifax, Nova Scotia; Queens College and University, Kingston, Ontario; the University of Bishop's College, Lennoxville, Quebec; McGill University, Montreal; the University of Toronto, University College, Victoria University and Trinity University, Toronto; the University of Manitoba, Winnipeg, Manitoba.

The courses and degrees of these universities are in general open to women. In some cases there are special Medical Schools for Women connected with the university and giving preparation for the university degrees.

The colleges have as a rule no halls of residence; the students reside in boarding houses, which must be approved by the college authorities.

FREDERICTON, New Brunswick.

UNIVERSITY OF NEW BRUNSWICK.

The University of New Brunswick, founded in 1800, gives instruction and confers degrees in Arts, Science and Law.

Four classes of students are recognised: undergraduates, students in special undergraduate courses, partial students (those who attend two or more courses of lectures and are matriculated), and occasional students (those admitted by the Faculty to a particular course of lectures.)

Women are admitted to the university on the same terms as men, that is, unless they are merely occasional students, they have to pass the ordinary entrance examinations.

The academic year consists of two terms, the Michaelmas term, beginning on September 28th and ending on December 20th, the Easter term, beginning on January 5th and ending on May 31st.

The matriculation fee is $2 and the tuition fee $30 annually. In addition every student upon matriculating must give to the registrar a bond to the amount of $40 to pay all charges accruing under the regulations of the university.

The average cost of board and lodging in Fredericton is $3 a week.

Six scholarships are offered at the University of New Brunswick, but women are excluded from three of these.

For further information address PROF. STOCKLEY, Fredericton, New Brunswick.

Professors and Lecturers.

ARTS.

LANGUAGES. — CLASSICAL: *Professor* Raymond.
ENGLISH AND FRENCH: *Professor* Stockley.
PHILOSOPHY AND POLITICAL ECONOMY: *Professor* John Davidson.
HISTORY: *Professor* Raymond.

SCIENCE.

MATHEMATICS: *Professor* Harrison.
PHYSICS: *Professor* Downing.
CHEMISTRY AND NATURAL SCIENCE: *Professor* Bailey.
ENGINEERING: *Professors* Dixon, Downing.

HALIFAX, Nova Scotia.

DALHOUSIE COLLEGE AND UNIVERSITY.

Dalhousie College was founded in 1821, and by an act passed in 1841 university powers were granted to the college.

Courses are given and degrees conferred in Arts, Science, Law and Medicine.

Persons of either sex may become students at the college by furnishing satisfactory references, entering their names in the register and paying the annual registration fee. Registered students may, after paying the proper fee, enter any of the ordinary classes of the college. The advanced classes are open to students who have sufficient knowledge of the subjects taught in them.

The college has no hall of residence, but women undergraduates are admitted, under special conditions, as boarders at the Halifax Ladies' College.

The academic year consists of one session. The session in Arts and Science begins about the middle of September, the School of

Law begins about September 1st, and that of Medicine about October 1st. All the sessions close at the end of April.

The registration fee is $4 to be paid annually. $6 is paid for attendance in each class which is not practical; for the practical classes the fees vary from $6 to $14 per class. The average amount of fees per session is $34.

Seven scholarships are awarded at Dalhousie College. Five of these are of the value of $40 each, while the others entitle the holders to exemption from fees during the entire course.

For further information apply to the secretary, Dalhousie College, Halifax, Nova Scotia.

Professors and Lecturers.

ARTS.

LANGUAGES. — CLASSICAL : *Professors* Johnson (Emeritus), Murray; *Mr.* J. W. Logan.
ENGLISH : *Professor* MacMechan.
MODERN : *Professor* Liechti.
PHILOSOPHY : *Professor* W. C. Murray.
POLITICAL SCIENCE AND HISTORY : *Professor* Forrest.
PEDAGOGY : *Professor* W. C. Murray; *Messrs.* Kennedy, McKay, Miller.

SCIENCE.

MATHEMATICS : *Professor* Macdonald; *Mr.* Morton.
PHYSICS : *Professor* MacGregor.
CHEMISTRY AND MINERALOGY : *Professor* Mackay.
BIOLOGY : *Mr.* Halliday.
ENGINEERING : *Drs.* Gilpin, Murphy; *Messrs.* Archibald, Dick, Doane, Dodwell, Johnston, E. Gilpin, Jr., McColl.

LAW.

Professors Russell, Weldon; *Messrs.* Cahan, Harrington, McInnes, Ritchie.

MEDICINE.

Examiners Anderson, Black, Campbell, Cowie, Curry, Farrell, Goodwin, Henry, Lindsay, McLaren, Muir, Page, Parker, Reid, Silver, Sinclair, Stewart, Tobin.

KINGSTON, Ontario.

QUEEN'S COLLEGE AND UNIVERSITY.

This university, which has been open to women on the same conditions as to men since its foundation in 1830, and has had women students attending its courses since 1876, gives instruction and confers degrees in Arts, Science, Law, Medicine and Theology.

The classes and pass examinations are open to unmatriculated students, but candidates for a degree must pass the matriculation examination. Certain equivalent examinations are accepted.

Students, when registering, must produce a certificate of character and pay the required fees.

Classes in Arts, Applied Science and Medicine begin about October 1st and end about April 10th. Classes in Theology begin on November 1st and end on April 14th.

There is a short summer session in Medicine, beginning on April 27th and ending on June 24th, and a summer session in Science, beginning on July 5th and lasting four weeks.

Class fees in the Faculty of Arts are $25 per session; in the Faculty of Science about $40; in the Faculty of Medicine $75. Fees for single classes are $8 per session. Fees for registration, etc., are $10.

There are numerous prizes and scholarships.

For further information apply to the registrar, MR. GEORGE Y. CHOWN.

Professors and Lecturers.

ARTS.

LANGUAGES. — CLASSICAL: *Professors* Glover, Macnaughton, Nicholson; *Messrs.* Black, Misner, Wallace.

ENGLISH: *Professor* Cappon.

GERMANIC: *Professor* Macgillivray; *Mr.* Day.

ROMANCE: *Professor* Macgillivray; *Mr.* McIntosh.

COMPARATIVE PHILOLOGY: *Professor* Nicholson.

PHILOSOPHY: *Professors* Dyde, Watson; *Messrs.* Burton, Hall.

POLITICAL SCIENCE: *Professor* Shortt; *Mr.* Cannon.

HISTORY: *Professor* Ferguson; *Mr.* Carmichael.

SCIENCE.

MATHEMATICS: *Professor* Dupuis; *Mr.* Metzler.

PHYSICS: *Professor* Marshall; *Mr.* Baker.

CHEMISTRY: *Professor* Goodwin; *Mr.* Wood.

MINERALOGY: *Professor* Nicol.

GEOLOGY: Mr. Miller.

BIOLOGY: *Professors* Fowler, Knight; *Messrs.* Watson, Williamson.

LAW.

Lecturers Britton, Macdonnell, Machar, McIntyre, Rogers, Walkem.

MEDICINE.

Professors Anglin, Campbell, Fowler, Garrett, Herald, Mundell, Ryan, Sullivan, Wood; *Drs.* Clarke, J. C. Connell, W. T. Connell.

THEOLOGY.

Professors Grant, Mowat, Ross; *Dr.* Thompson.

LENNOXVILLE, Quebec.

UNIVERSITY OF BISHOP'S COLLEGE.

Bishop's College, founded in 1843, is a small college giving an academic course in Arts and Divinity, and conferring degrees in Arts, Medicine, Theology and Music, in connection with the Faculty of Medicine in Montreal and the Dominion College of Music. Almost all the students reside in the college buildings, and chiefly on this account the college is not open to women, though women have attended the courses in medicine.

The fees for board, lodging and tuition for the year are $190.

Further information may be obtained from the registrar, Mr. F. W. FRITH, Lennoxville, Quebec.

MONTREAL, Canada.
McGILL COLLEGE AND UNIVERSITY.

McGill College and University, founded in 1821, comprises the Faculties of Arts, Applied Science, Law, Medicine and Comparative Medicine and Veterinary Science; it gives instruction and confers degrees in these subjects. The educational work of the University is carried on in McGill College and the Royal Victoria College for women, and in the following affiliated colleges: Morrin College, Quebec; St. Francis College, Richmond, P. Q.; Vancouver, College, Vancouver, B. C., and five Theological Colleges.

Students in the Faculty of Arts are classified as undergraduates and partial students. Undergraduates alone can proceed to the degree of B.A., and must pass the required entrance examinations. Candidates for admission as partial students must satisfy the professors of the several subjects they select of their fitness to attend the lectures or be examined in these subjects. Students of other universities may be admitted to a like standing in this University on production of certificates and after examination by the Faculty.

The classes in Arts and Science (except Engineering) are open to women on the same conditions as to men, and in these subjects women take the same examinations as men, under the same regulations, and may obtain the same degrees. Separate classes are held for women in McGill College and the Royal Victoria College, but women attend the honours classes, advanced sections, and the laboratories with the men students.

The session begins on September 15th and ends on April 30th.

Undergraduates pay $60 per session, including gymnasium, matriculation and graduation fees. Partial students pay $16 per session for one course of lectures in the first or second year, including the use of the library, and $12 for each additional course; in the third or fourth year, $25 for one course, and $20 for each additional course, including laboratories and laboratory materials.

About thirty exhibitions and scholarships, tenable for one or two years, are offered annually. Women have the same privileges as men with reference to exhibitions, scholarships, honours, prizes and medals.

The Royal Victoria College, which is situated within the precincts of McGill University, is open to women only. It consists of one large hall of residence, providing accommodation for the mistress, resident tutors, and about one hundred students, and comprises several lecture halls, theatre and gymnasium. The charge for board, lodging and tuition is from $300 to $450 per session, and this covers all university and college charges. Each student has a bedroom and sitting room or one large sitting room divided.

For further information apply to Mr. W. VAUGHAN, Registrar, McGill University, Montreal.

Professors and Lecturers.

ARTS.

LANGUAGES. — ORIENTAL: *Professor* Coussirat.
CLASSICAL: *Professors* Carter, Eaton, Peterson; *Messrs.* Sanders, Slack.
ENGLISH: *Professor* Moyse; *Messrs.* Archibald, P. T. Lafleur; *Miss* Mitchell.
GERMANIC: *Messrs.* Gregor, Lambert.
ROMANCE: *Messrs.* Ingres, Lambert, Morin.
PHILOSOPHY: *Professor* Murray; *Mr.* Lafleur.
HISTORY: *Professor* Colby.
ELOCUTION: *Mr.* Stephen.

SCIENCE.

MATHEMATICS: *Professors* Chandler, Johnson; *Messrs.* Lea, Tory.
PHYSICS: *Professors* Cox, Rutherford; *Messrs.* Barnes, King, Pitcher.
CHEMISTRY: *Professors* Girdwood, Harrington, Ruttan, Walker; *Messrs.* Brodie, Evans, Saunders, Wolf.
MINERALOGY: *Professor* Harrington.
GEOLOGY: *Professor* Adams; *Mr.* Leroy.

BIOLOGY: *Professors* MacBride, Mills, Penhallow; *Drs.* J. D. Cameron, Elder, Henderson, McCarthy, Morrow, Robertson, Ross, Scane, Springle; *Mr.* Jackson; *Miss* Derick.
ENGINEERING: *Professors* Bovey, McLeod, Nicolson, Owens, Porter; *Messrs.* Armstrong, Bell, Durley, Herdt, Jaquays, Kerry, Lea.
ARCHITECTURE: *Professor* Capper.

LAW.

Professors Davidson, Doherty, Fortin, Geoffrion, E. Lafleur, Macmaster, Marler, McGoun, Walton; *Messrs.* Geoffrion, Macdougall, Ryan.

MEDICINE.

Professors Adami, Armstrong, Baker, Bell, Birkett, Blackader, Buller, J. C. Cameron, Craik, Finley, Gardner, Johnston, H. A. Lafleur, C. McEachran, D. McEachran, Roddick, Shepherd, Stewart, Wilkins; *Drs.* Anderson, Bradley, Burgess, K. Cameron, G. G. Campbell, Evans, Gardner, Garrow, Gunn, Hamilton, Hutchison, Kerry, Lockhart, Martin, McKenzie, McTaggart, Nicolls, Orr, Semple, Shaw, Webster.

TORONTO, Canada.

UNIVERSITY OF TORONTO AND UNIVERSITY COLLEGE.

The University of Toronto, founded in 1827, has connected with it University College and Victoria University.

Instruction is given in different subjects of the Arts course by the Arts Faculties of the University of Toronto, Victoria University and University College; Latin, Greek, Ancient History, English, French, German, Oriental Literature and Ethics are taught by the latter two Faculties and the remaining subjects by the University of Toronto. Knox College, Wycliffe College and St. Michael's College give instruction in Theology and allied subjects.

All courses, examinations and degrees are open to women on exactly the same conditions as to men.

No conditions are imposed in regard to residence; women students are under the supervision of a lady superintendent whose directions as to conduct are to be observed. Comfortable board and lodging may be had from $3 a week.

There are two terms in the year: the Michaelmas term, beginning October 1st and ending December 22nd; the Easter term, beginning January 9th and ending April 21st.

The annual fee for each course of not more than fifteen hours of lectures is $2. The fees for matriculation are $5 and $15.

There are numerous scholarships and fellowships varying in value from $50 to $500, full particulars concerning which can be obtained from the calendar, or from the registrar.

VICTORIA UNIVERSITY.

This university, founded in 1830, has the affiliated Colleges, Albert College, Belleville; the Wesleyan Ladies' College, Hamilton; the Ontario Ladies' College, Whitby; Alma College, St. Thomas; and Columbian Methodist College, New Westminster, B. C.

The Faculty of Arts in Victoria University provides instruction in all subjects assigned to it by the Federation Act of University College (see above). In other subjects the students of Victoria

University attend the lectures and use the laboratories of the University of Toronto.

The general fees are the same as for Toronto University, but there are additional college fees of from $25 to $30 a year.

Professors and Lecturers.

ARTS.

LANGUAGES. — ORIENTAL: *Professors* McCurdy, McLaughlin; *Mr.* Murison.

CLASSICAL: *Professors* Bell, Fletcher, Hutton, Wallace; *Dr.* Johnston; *Messrs.* Carruthers, Langford, Milner, J. C. Robertson.

ENGLISH: *Professors* Alexander, Horning, Reynar; *Mr.* Keys.

GERMAN: *Professors* Horning, Van der Smissen; *Drs.* Needler, Toews; *Mr.* Lang.

ROMANCE: *Professors* W. H. Fraser, Petch, Squair; *Drs.* Edgar, Toews; *Messrs.* Cameron, de Champ, Masson, Sacco.

COMPARATIVE PHILOLOGY: *Professor* Hutton.

PHILOSOPHY: *Professors* Badgley, Hume; *Drs.* Kirschmann, F. Tracy.

POLITICAL SCIENCE: *Professors* Burwash, Mavor, Hon. David Mills, the Hon. Justice Proudfoot; *Mr* Moore.

HISTORY: *Professors* Bain, Wrong.

SCIENCE.

MATHEMATICS: *Professor* A. Baker; *Messrs.* de Lury, Rusk.

PHYSICS: *Professor* James Loudon; *Messrs.* Chant, W. J. Loudon, McLennan.

CHEMISTRY: *Professor* Pike; *Drs.* Ellis, W. L. Miller, Smale; *Mr.* F. B. Allan.

MINERALOGY AND GEOLOGY: *Professor* Coleman; *Mr.* W. A. Parks.

BIOLOGY: *Professors* A. B. Macallum R. Ramsay Wright; *Messrs.* B. A. Bensley, R. R. Bensley, E. C. Jeffrey.

HYGIENE: *Professor* Oldright.

LAW.

Professors the Hon. David Mills, Hon. Justice Proudfoot.

MEDICINE.

Professors H. W. Aikins, Bruce, Burnham, Cameron, J. Caven, W. P. Caven, Daniel Clark, Ellis, Graham, Heebner, A. B. MacCallum, J. M. MacCallum, McDonagh, McPhedran, Ogden, Peters, Primrose, Reeve, Ross, Spencer, Sweetnam, A. H. Wright; *Drs.* Kendrick, Machell, Spencer, Thistle, Winnett; *Messrs.* Amyot, Bensley, Boyd, Dwyer, Goldie, Gordon, Hon. David Mills, McCollum, McIlwraith, MacKenzie, Rudolf, Small, Starr, Stenhouse.

THEOLOGY.

Professors Badgley, J. Burwash, N. Burwash, McLaughlin, Reynar, Wallace.

TRINITY UNIVERSITY.

This university, founded by a Royal Charter in 1852, gives instruction and confers degrees in Arts, Science, Law, Medicine and Theology (Church of England). All candidates for a degree must pass the matriculation examination.

Women are admitted to the arts course on the same conditions as men; women studying medicine attend the Woman's Medical College.

The year is divided into three terms, the Michaelmas term beginning on October 3rd and ending on December 6th; the Lent term beginning on January 12th and ending on March 26th; the Easter term beginning on April 18th and ending on June 25th. The tuition fee for each term is $21.66, and is paid to the Bursar.

Residence in the college buildings is not compulsory, but is strongly recommended. The hall of residence for women is St. Hilda's College. The fees for board are $70 per term, with an entrance fee of $12. Occasional students are admitted at the discretion of the Lady Principal to take partial courses in one or more subjects. For further information apply to MRS. RIGBY, 337 Shaw Street, Toronto.

Professors and Lecturers.

ARTS.

LANGUAGES. — CLASSICAL : *Professor* Huntingford; *Mr.* W. H. White.
MODERN : *Mr.* A. H. Young.
PHILOLOGY : *Mr.* A. H. Young.
PHILOSOPHY : *Professor* W. Clark.
HISTORY : *Professor* Rigby.
ELOCUTION : *Mr.* H. N. Shaw.

SCIENCE.

MATHEMATICS : *Professor* M. A. MacKenzie.
SCIENCE : *Messrs.* Montgomery, Simpson.

THEOLOGY.

Professors Cayley, Welch; *Mr.* Bedford-Jones.

WOMAN'S MEDICAL COLLEGE.

This college, founded in 1883, was affiliated with the University of Toronto in 1890.

It gives instruction in all the subjects required by the College of Physicians and Surgeons of Ontario for admission to a license to practice, and also in all the subjects required for examination by the faculty of Medicine of the University of Toronto.

The recently erected building is situated in Sumach Street, Toronto.

St. Hilda's College is a hall of residence for women students; see above.

For full particulars see the annual announcement of the college, to be obtained from the dean, DR. R. B. NEVITT.

Professors and Lecturers.

MEDICINE.

Professors Susanna Boyle, Chambers, Cleland, Duncan, Eadie, Gullen, J. MacCallum, Machell, McMahon, Nevitt, Powell, Pyne, J. F. W. Ross, G. B. Smith, Sweetnam, Thistle, Tyrell, Wishart; *Lecturers*, *Drs.* Bryans, Creasor, J. Gray, McKenzie, Parsons; *Misses* Curzon, L. A. Davis, Lynd; *Messrs.* Cane, Cleland, Dwyer, C. B. Shuttleworth, E. B. Shuttleworth, Stenhouse.

WINNIPEG, Manitoba.

THE UNIVERSITY OF MANITOBA.

This university, founded in 1877, is the only body having power to confer degrees in Arts, Law and Medicine in the Province of Manitoba. It is an examining body, the educational work being carried on in the affiliated colleges, St. Boniface College, St. John's College, Manitoba College, Wesley College and the Manitoba Medical College. All the courses are open to women on the same conditions as to men.

Further particulars may be obtained from the registrar, Mr. I. PITBLADO, Winnipeg, Manitoba.

FINLAND.

HELSINGFORS, Finland.

KEJSERLIGA ALEXANDERS-UNIVERSITETET I FINLAND.

This university, founded in 1640, resembles the Swedish universities in constitution and consists of the four faculties of Philosophy (Arts and Science) Law, Medicine and Theology.

Men students, in order to be admitted, must have obtained the *Abgangszeugniss* of a gymnasium or a lyceum, but although the gymnasia are attended by both sexes, women who wish to enter the university in any faculty except that of medicine must obtain special permission from the Chancellor. At present, over 200 women are studying in the university. The recent action of Russia in regard to Finland may to some extent affect the position of women in the university.

In the Philosophical Faculty the four degrees of Candidate, Master, Licentiate and Doctor are conferred; in the other faculties only three, the Candidate, Licentiate and Doctor. Before entering for degrees in Law, Medicine or Theology the student must have passed the examination for the degree of Candidate in Philosophy. For the degree of Licentiate in Law, Medicine or Theology, two years' practice is required. The degree of M.A. was conferred on a woman for the first time in 1882.

The academic year begins in the middle of September. Many of the lectures are free, for others a fee of 12 francs ($2.40) is charged. The fees for examinations vary from 12 francs ($2.40) to 200 francs ($40).

For further information see the *Programme*, *Kataloge*, *Finlands Statskalender*, *Handbuch des Finnländischen Frauenvereins*; also statistics concerning the higher education and public position of women in Finland published by Professor Dr. Seiling, of the Polytechnic Institute (*Polytekniska Institutet*), Helsingfors.

Professors and Lecturers.

ARTS.
LANGUAGES. — ORIENTAL: *Professor* ———
———; *Docent* Tallqvist.

CLASSICAL: *Professor* Heikel.
ENGLISH: *Reader* Florell.
FINNISH, SWEDISH: *Professors* Freu-

denthal, Genetz, Setälä; *Docents* Krohn, Paasonen, Vendell, Wichmann; *Readers* Bergroth, Cajander.

RUSSIAN, SLAVONIC: *Professors* Mandelstam; *Docent* Mikkola; *Readers* Almberg, Brotherus.

GERMANIC: *Docents* Karsten, Lindelöf; *Readers* Godenhjelm, Öhqvist.

ROMANCE: *Professors* Gustafsson, Söderhjelm; *Docent* Wallensköld; *Reader* Kalm.

SANSCRIT AND COMPARATIVE PHILOLOGY: *Professor* Donner; *Docent* Reuter.

PHONETICS: *Docent* Pipping.

PHILOSOPHY: *Professors* Rein, Tudeer; *Docent* A. Grotenfelt.

HISTORY: *Professors* Danielson, Palmén, Schybergson; *Docents* v. Bonsdorff, Crohns, K. Grotenfelt, Snellman.

POLITICAL SCIENCE: *Docents* Tallqvist, Westermarck.

MODERN LITERATURE AND ÆSTHETICS: *Professors* Aspelin, Estlander, Tikkanen; *Docents* Donner, Hirn.

ARCHÆOLOGY: *Docent* Nordström.

PEDAGOGY: *Professor* Ruin; *Docent* Johnsson.

SCIENCE.

MATHEMATICS AND ASTRONOMY: *Professors* Donner, Neovius; *Docents* Levänen, Lindelöf, Stenberg, Tallqvist.

PHYSICS: *Professors* Lemström, Sundell; *Docents* Homén, Melander.

CHEMISTRY: *Professors* Aschan, Hjelt; *Docents* Komppa, af Schultén.

MINERALOGY AND GEOLOGY: *Professor* ———; *Docent* Ramsay.

ZOOLOGY: *Professors* Palmén, Reuter, Sahlberg; *Docents* Levander, E. F. Reuter.

BOTANY: *Professors* Elfving, Kihlman, Norrlin; *Docent* Wainio.

GEOGRAPHY: *Docent* Hult.

LAW.

Professors Chydenius, Forsman, Hermanson, Lang, Ståhlberg, Wrede; *Docent* Charpentier; *Reader* Favén.

MEDICINE.

Professors Asp, Engström, Hällstén, Heinricius, Holsti, Homen, Pipping, Runeberg, v. Schultén, Sundvik, Wahlfors; *Docents* v. Bonsdorff, Clopatt, af Forselles, Gröwroos, Hagelstam, Hougberg, Kolster, Krogius, Lundström, Möller, Nordman, Schauman, Sibellius, Sievers, Törngren.

THEOLOGY.

Professors Appelberg, Johansson, Rosenqvist, Stenij, Tötterman.

DENMARK.

COPENHAGEN, Denmark.

KJOBENHAVNS UNIVERSITET.

There is one university in Denmark, that of Copenhagen, Kjobenhavns Universitet, founded in 1478. It comprises the five Faculties of Arts, Science, Law, Medicine and Theology; the Faculty of Theology confers the degrees of Doctor and Licentiate, the other Faculties that of Doctor only.

Women have been admitted on the same conditions as men since 1875, and may take examinations and degrees in all the Faculties except that of Theology, in which there is a special examination for women.

The conditions for entrance are that the candidate must have passed the matriculation examination of a lyceum, or of a private school having the same privileges; certain other examinations qualify for entrance provided that a supplementary examination be taken. Before taking the special examinations of any Faculty the student must have attended a preparatory course in philosophy for two semesters.

There are two semesters, the first beginning February 1st and ending June 9th; the second beginning September 1st and ending December 22nd.

There are no fees for lectures; the matriculation fee is 22 Kr. ($5.94); the fee for the Doctor's degree is 160 Kr. ($43.20). Scholarships founded before 1875 are not open to women.

Further information may be found in the *Aperçu sur l'Organisation de l'Université de Copenhague*, or obtained on application to the rector.

Professors and Lecturers.

ARTS.

LANGUAGES.—SEMITIC : *Professor* Buhl; *Docent* Östrup.
INDO-IRANIAN : *Professor* Fausboll.
CLASSICAL : *Professors* Gertz, Heiberg; *Docents* Drachmann, Siesbye.
ENGLISH : *Professor* Jespersen; *Docent* Hansen.
GERMANIC (Norse, Slavonic): *Professors* Gudmundsson, Johnsson, Moller, Paludan, Verner, Wimmer; *Docent* Olrik.

ROMANCE: *Professor* Nyrop.
COMPARATIVE PHILOLOGY: *Professor* Thomsen.
PHILOSOPHY AND PSYCHOLOGY: *Professors* Höffding, Kroman, Wilkens; *Docent* Lehmann.
HISTORY: *Professors* Erslev, Holm, Steenstrup; *Docent* Gudmundsson.
ART AND ARCHÆOLOGY: *Professors* Lange, Paludan, Schmidt, J. L. Ussing.
HISTORY OF LITERATURE: *Dr.* Vedl.

SCIENCE.

MATHEMATICS AND ASTRONOMY: *Professors* Petersen, Thiele, Zeuthen.
PHYSICS: *Professor* Christiansen.
CHEMISTRY: *Professor* Jorgensen, Thomsen; *Docent* E. Petersen.
MINERALOGY: *Professor* N. V. Ussing.
BIOLOGY: *Professor* Lütken; *Docents* Bergh, Jungersen, Levinson, Meinert.
BOTANY: *Professors* Pedersen, Warming; *Docent* Rosenvinge.
GEOGRAPHY: *Professor* Löffler.

LAW AND POLITICAL SCIENCE.

Professors Bentzon, Deuntzer, Hansen, Lassen, Matzen, Scharling, Torp, Westergaard.

MEDICINE.

Professors Bjerrum, Bloch, Bohr, Chievitz, Faber, Gaedeken, Gram, Grut, Haslund, Hirschsprung, Lange, Meyer, J. J. Petersen, Plum, Pontoppidan, Reisz, Salomonsen, Saxtorph, Sörensen, Stadfeldt, Studsgaard, With; *Docents* Brünniche, Flöystrup, Friedenreich, Holm, Mygge, Nielsen, Rosenthal, Tscherning, Wanscher.

THEOLOGY.

Professors Jacobsen, Madsen, Nielsen, Petersen, Scharling; *Instructors* Paulli, Schepelern.

MUSIC.

Instructors Bielefeldt, Hammerich.

FRANCE.

Higher education in France is almost entirely under the control of the State. All that remained, up to 1896, of the old universities was certain distinct Faculties, Faculties of Arts (*Lettres*), Science, Law, Medicine and Protestant Theology, both teaching and examining bodies; these were united into the University of France.

By a law passed in 1896 these *corps de Facultés* were reconstituted into smaller universities under the control of separate councils, the *conseils de l'université*, formed of professors chosen from each Faculty constituting the University, and in 1898 they were allowed to use for their own maintenance a portion of the fees paid them.

There are Faculties of Arts and Science at Besançon, Bordeaux, Caen, Clermont, Dijon, Grenoble, Lille, Lyons, Montpellier, Nancy, Paris, Poitiers, Rennes and Toulouse; a Faculty of Arts at Aix and a Faculty of Science at Marseilles; Faculties of Law at Aix, Bordeaux, Caen, Dijon, Grenoble, Lille, Lyons, Montpellier, Nancy, Paris, Poitiers, Rennes and Toulouse; Faculties of Medicine at Bordeaux, Lille, Lyons, Montpellier, Nancy, Paris and Toulouse; and Faculties of Theology (Protestant) at Montauban and Paris.

In addition to these there are certain *écoles supérieures*, corresponding in some respects to American or English colleges the most important of which are mentioned below (pp. 38–45). These are all controlled by the *Ministre de l'Instruction publique*. The *facultés libres* at Angers, Lille, Lyons, Marseilles, Paris, and Toulouse and the *écoles libres* at Lille, Nantes and Paris are more independent institutions.

All the courses in all these Faculties and schools, with the exception of the *cours fermés*, the *conférences* and the practical work are public, and open free of charge to persons of either sex as hearers (*auditeurs*).

Permission to attend the *cours fermés*, the *conférences* and the practical work is now granted to matriculated students only, and in order to matriculate, candidates, whether men or women, must present a *diplôme de l'enseignement secondaire*, or, if foreigners, an equivalent diploma, and must pay a matriculation fee of 20 frs. ($4) and a library fee of 10 frs. ($2).

Women may become registered students (*inscrites*), *i. e.*, candidates for degrees, on the same conditions as men, that is, they must be *bacheliers* * *de l'enseignement secondaire*, either *classique* or *moderne*, depending on the Faculty in which they wish to graduate; in the Faculties of Arts, Science (see p. 34), and Medicine the bachelor's degree of a foreign university in general qualifies for registration. The Faculty in which the student wishes to register enquires into the degree held by the student, and if the degree is accepted as equivalent, the student is allowed to register on payment of a sum equal to the amount that would have been paid in fees, if the student had obtained the degree from the French Faculty. The application for a dispensation from the French baccalaureat must be addressed to the *Ministre de l'Instruction publique* and must be accompanied by the original diplomas and certificate of birth of the applicant, together with their translations into French made by an official translator. The dispensation, if obtained, costs 120 frs. ($24). All registered students must pay a fee of 30 frs. ($6) quarterly; if at Paris, to the *recéveur des droits universitaires*, quai des Grands-Augustins, 25; if in the provinces, to a receiver appointed by the Faculty. They must at the same time present to this official a *bulletin de versement* obtained from the secretary of the Faculty or School they attend.

---

* The *baccalauréat de l'enseignement classique* is a preliminary diploma given on the result of an examination, partly oral and partly written, in Latin, Greek, French, either English or German, history, physics, chemistry and biology, geography and elementary mathematics, and a further examination in *either* philosophy *or* elementary mathematics. The *baccalauréat de l'enseignement moderne* is given on a similar examination in which modern languages are substituted for Greek and Latin. The examinations are preliminary to the work in the Faculty and are held by the professors of the Faculties of Arts and Science for candidates leaving the secondary schools. These two diplomas have been recently established and take the place of the *baccalauréat ès lettres* and the *baccalauréat ès sciences*.

Each state Faculty confers, in its own subject, the state degrees of *licencié* and *docteur*. These degrees give certain privileges in the way of practising professions and are awarded to candidates who have studied for a prescribed time and passed a series of examinations. They are seldom obtained by foreigners who are usually unwilling to spend the time necessary to obtain them. The *facultés libres* and *écoles libres* give instruction but have no power to confer degrees. The regulations for degrees differ greatly in the different Faculties. In Arts and Science the *licence* is given one year after the *baccalauréat* and the *doctorat* as soon after the *licence* as the candidate has written and is prepared to sustain two theses.

Attestations d'études supérieures or *certificats d'études* are given by certain of the Faculties of Arts and Science to hearers who have attended the courses regularly. In the provinces no requirement is made as to age, sex, nationality, etc., but in Paris the hearer, in order to be eligible for this certificate, must hold the degree of *bachelier ès lettres* or an equivalent degree.

The *diplôme d'études supérieures d'histoire et de géographie* of the Faculty of Arts of the Normal School is open without any restrictions as to age, sex, degree, or nationality.

The new law passed in 1897 gave the *conseils de l'université* power to grant *titres d'ordre exclusivement scientifique*. These are distinguished from degrees in being merely titles granting no rights or privileges to the holders. The first of these to be organised is the *doctorat de l'Université de Paris*, instituted in 1897–98. In the Faculty of Letters candidates for this degree must hold, if Frenchmen, the degree of *licencié ès lettres* or, if foreigners, certificates showing an equal amount of preparation; they must study at least four semesters, either in a French or a foreign university, or in one of the scientific institutions in Paris; they must pass an examination on subjects agreed upon by the Faculty and defend a thesis written in French or Latin. In the Faculty of Science applicants must produce certificates of advanced work in two out of seventeen scientific subjects, must study for one year and must pass an examination and defend a thesis. In the Faculty of Medicine the degree is conferred on foreign students who have been allowed to study and to take the ordinary examinations without having first obtained the degree of *bachelier*. The degree is also given in Pharmacy.

The examinations in the Faculty of Science have recently been reorganised in such a way as to give greater facilities to foreign students. In addition to being free to offer an equivalent for the French baccalaureat degree, the student is now allowed to select the subjects in which he desires to be examined. He may take his examinations either simultaneously or in succession, and obtain for each a *certificat d' étude*. Three such certificates may be exchanged for the *diplôme de licencié*. This gives the student liberty to travel from one university to another and present himself for examination when he wishes.

Though not quite all the medical courses are open to women it is not difficult for women doctors of medicine to obtain admittance to the different hospitals, of which there are 24 in Paris alone with accommodation for upwards of 17,000 patients.

University libraries are open to students on presentation of their student's card and to all persons authorised by the rector. The reading room of the Bibliothèque Nationale, Paris, is open to all persons over 16 years of age. To obtain admission to the *salle de travail* for the study of manuscripts, a special card of admittance from the administrator general is required. Foreigners applying for this card should present a recommendation from their ambassador.

All courses open in the beginning of November and continue nominally for eight or nine months, in general actually for only six or seven.

Hearers pay no fees, registered students pay 30 frs. ($6) quarterly. The library fee is 10 frs. ($2) yearly.

Scholarships (*bourses*) are as a rule not open to foreigners. The *Comité de Patronage des Étudiants Étrangers de Paris* has, however, some scholarships of 200 frs. ($40), and 350 frs. ($70), to offer to specially recommended students, the whole sum to be devoted to the payment of fees.

NOTE.—English-speaking women who wish to reduce their expenses while studying in France may apply to be admitted as assistant teachers of foreign languages in one of the numerous training colleges for primary teachers. These teachers are required to give to the students (girls of from fifteen to twenty years of age), and to any of the teachers who may desire it, practical instruction in English and practice in English conversation for an hour and a half or two hours daily. For the rest of the time they are free to study privately, to attend lectures or employ themselves as they think fit. They pay into [the college funds the sum of 400 francs, ($80) and for this have a room, light, firing and board in the College for the college year, October 1st to July 31st, holidays included. Candidates for these posts should fill out a form of application, to be obtained from M. le Ministre de l' Instruction publique, Direction de l' Enseignement primaire, 6e bureau, Paris, and return it to him filled up, together with copies of certificates, etc. It is advisable to have these testified to by one of the American members of the *Comité Franco-Americain*.

    President J B. ANGELL, University of Michigan, Ann Arbor.
    President TIMOTHY DWIGHT, Yale University, New Haven.
    President CHARLES W. ELIOT, Harvard University, Cambridge.
    President D. C. GILMAN, Johns Hopkins University, Baltimore.
    Mr. G. BROWN GOODE, Assistant Secretary U. S. National Museum, Washington (Secretary).
    Professor E. R. L. GOULD, Secretary, International Statistical Institute, Chicago.
    President G. STANLEY HALL, Clark University, Worcester.
    Mr. W. T. HARRIS, U. S. Commissioner of Education, Washington.
    Mr. S. P. LANGLEY, Secretary, Smithsonian Institution, Washington.
    President SETH LOW, Columbia College, New York.
    Professor SIMON NEWCOMB, U. S. N., Superintendent Nautical Almanac, Washington (President).
    President J. C. SCHURMAN, Cornell University, Ithaca, N. Y.
    Hon. ANDREW D. WHITE, former U. S. Minister to Germany, Ithaca, N. Y.
    President B. L. WHITMAN, Columbian University, Washington.
    Mr. CARROLL D. WRIGHT, Commissioner of Labor, Washington.

    Students from American universities or colleges going to study in France are allowed a reduction of 30 per cent. on the rates of the steamers of the Compagnie générale Transatlantique. This reduction is not allowed to first class passengers, and can be obtained only by application to M. Paul Melon Secretary of the *Comité de Patronage des Étudiants Étrangers* at the Sorbonne.

Further information is to be found in the *Annuaire de la Jeunesse* by H. Vuibert (Nony et Cie, rue des Écoles, 17, Paris), price 4 frs. ($.80); in the *Annuaire de l'Instruction Publique* (Delalain frères, rue des Écoles, 56, Paris) price 5 frs. ($1), and in *Le Livret de l'Étudiant de Paris* (published by Delalain frères), price 11 frs. ($2.20).

An amount of interesting and valuable information is given in *L'Enseignement supérieur et l'Enseignement technique en France*, by M. Paul Melon (Librairie Classique Armand Colin et Cie, Paris, 1893).

Enquiries may be addressed to the *Comité de Patronage des Étudiants Étrangers*, Bureaux à la Sorbonne, rue de la Sorbonne, 15, Paris. This association, which has branches at Aix, Bordeaux, Lyons, Montpellier, Nancy and Toulouse, in addition to giving advice and help to individual students, devotes itself to furthering the interests of foreign students as a body. In Paris, Aix and one or two other places it has been instrumental in establishing courses in the French language especially for foreigners. Some of these are summer courses.

PARIS, France.

UNIVERSITÉ DE PARIS.

The old University of Paris, founded in the Middle Ages, survived till 1896, in the form of the separate Faculties of Arts, Science, Law, Medicine and Protestant Theology, and these have now been reconstituted into the University of Paris. All particulars in regard to these have been given above (pp. 31–36).

FACULTÉ DES LETTRES.

The Sorbonne, Paris.

Professors and Lecturers.

LANGUAGES. — CLASSICAL: *Professors* Aug. Cartault, Chatelain, Croiset, Decharme, Goelzer, J. Martha; *MM.* Em. Chatelain, Edet, Hauvette, Lafaye, Puech.
ENGLISH: *MM.* Baret, Al. Beljame.

FRANCE.

GERMANIC : *Professor* Lichtenberger ; *M.* Lange.
ROMANCE: *Professors* Crouslé, Gebhart, Lenient, Mézières, Petit de Julleville ; *MM.* Dejob, Faguet, Gazier, Larroumet, Lichtenberger, Thomas.
COMPARATIVE PHILOLOGY : *Professor* Henry ; *MM.* Brunot, Havet.
PHILOSOPHY : *Professors* Boutroux, Brochard, P. Janet ; *MM.* Egger, Séailles-Ransan.
SOCIOLOGY : *Professors* Espinas, Michel.
HISTORY : *Professors* Aulard, Bouché-Leclercq, Lavisse, Luchaire, Rambaud ; *MM.* Denis, Grébaut, Guiraud, Langlois, Seignobos, Zeller.
ART AND ARCHÆOLOGY : *Professor* Perrot ; *MM.* Collignon, Lemonnier.
GEOGRAPHY : *Professors* Dubois, Himly, Marcel ; *M.* Gallois.
PEDAGOGY : *Professor* Buisson.

FACULTÉ DES SCIENCES.

The Sorbonne, Paris.

Professors and Lecturers.

MATHEMATICS AND ASTRONOMY : *Professors* Darboux, Goursat, Hadamard, Hermite, Picard, H. Poincaré, Wolf ; *MM.* Andoyer, Blutel, Koenigs, Puiseux, Raffy.
PHYSICS : *Professors* Appell, Béhal, Boussinesq, Bouty ; *MM.* Alph. Combes, Paul Janet, Jannettaz, Joly, Krouchkoll, Leduc, Matignon, Pellat, L. Perrin, Poincaré, Puiseux, Riban, Robin.
CHEMISTRY : *Professors* Auger, Ditte, Friedel, Troost : *MM.* Chabrie, Etaix, Freundler, Joannis, Péchard, Riban.
MINERALOGY : *Professors* Hautefeuille, Jannetaz.
GEOLOGY AND GEOGRAPHY : *Professor* Munier-Chalmas ; *MM.* Bertrand, Kaug, Velain.
BIOLOGY : *Professors* Bonnier, Dastre, Delage, Duclaux, Giard, de Lacaze-Duthiers ; *MM.* Chatin, Chauveaud, Daguillon, Fischer, Matruchot, Perrier, Vélain.

FACULTÉ DE DROIT.

Place du Panthéon, Paris.

Professors and Lecturers.

LAW.

Professors Alglave, Beauregard, Berthélemy, Boistel, Cauwès, Chavegrin, Colmet de Santerre, Cuq, Deschamps, Ducrocq, Esmein, Estoublon, Faure, Garsonnet, Gérardin, Girard, Glasson, Jobbé-Duval, Lainé, Larnaude, Lefebvre, Le Poittevin, Lyon-Caen, Massigli, Léon Michel, Planiol, Renault, Saleilles, Thaller, Weiss ; *MM.* Chénon, Jay, Leseur.

FACULTÉ DE MÉDECINE.

Place de l'École-de-Médecine, Paris.

Professors and Lecturers.

MEDICINE.

Professors P. Berger, Blanchard, Bouchard, Brouardel, Chantemesse, Cornil, Debove, Dieulafoy, Duplay, Mathias Duval, Farabeuf, Alf. Fournier, Gariel, Armand Gautier, Grancher, Guyon, Hayem, Hutinel, Jaccoud, Joffroy, Laboulbène, Landouzy, Lannelongue, Le Dentu, Pajot, Panas, Pinard, Potain, Pouchet, Proust, Raymond, Richet, Sappey, Terrier, Tillaux ; *MM.* Achard, Albarran, André, Auvray, Bar,

Baraduc, Bellan, Benoit, Bernard, Bonnaire, Bouglé, Bourges, Bousquet, Brault, Brin, Broca, Camus, Castex, Charrin, Chassevant, Chatellier, Courtillier, Critzman, Cunéo, Delahousse, Delbet, Paul Delbet, Deschamps, Dujarier, Fredet, Gaucher, Gilbert, Gilles de la Tourette, Glantenay, Gley, Gosset, Guiart, Guibé, Hanriot, Hartmann, Hébert, Herbet, Junien-Lavillauroy, Laborde, Launois, Leclerc, LeFur, Legry, Leh, Lejars, Letulle, Luys, Malbec, Marfan, **Marie,** Marion, Martin Dürr, Mauclaire, **Maugery, Mene**trier, Mergier, Morau, Morin, **Mulon,** Nélaton, Netter, Ombrédanne, Pasteau, Perret, Poirier, Potier, Proust, Rabaut, Remy, Retterer, Reynaud, Ricard, Riche, Roger, Sandoz, Savariaud, Sebileau, Thérèse, Thiéry, Thoinot, Tuffier, Varnier, Veau, Vincent, Walther, Weber, Weil, Weiss, Widal, Wurtz.

FACULTÉ DE THÉOLOGIE PROTESTANTE.
Boulevard Arago, 83, Paris.
Professors and Lecturers.

THEOLOGY.
Professors Allier, Bonet-Maury, Ehrhardt, Lods, Massebieau, Ménégoz, J. Réville, Sabatier, Stapfer, Vaucher; *M.* Berger.

FACULTÉS LIBRES DE PARIS.
Rue de Vaugirard, 74, Paris.

These are Catholic institutions giving instruction similar to that given by the state Faculties, but without the power to confer degrees. Students who obtain their instruction from the *Facultés libres* are examined by and obtain degrees from the state Faculties. The general regulations, fees, etc., are the same as for the state Faculties. (See pp. 31-36.) Women, however, are not admitted to the courses, but special courses for women have lately been arranged in connection with the *Facultés libres.*

The secretary is M. JOSEPH CHOBERT, rue de Vaugirard, 74, Paris.

Professors and Lecturers.

THEOLOGY.
SEMITIC LANGUAGES: *Professor* Graffin.
PHILOSOPHY: *Professors* Bulliot Peillaube.
THEOLOGY: *Professors* Auriault, de la Barre, Baudrillart, Boudinhon, Clerval, Fillion, Gasparri, Gaudeau, Largent, Pisani, Vigouroux.

LAW AND POLITICAL SCIENCE.
Professors G. Alix, Bureau, Cauvière, Ch. Chobert, Clotet, Corret, Guyot, Jamet, de Lamarzelle, Larcher, Laurent, Lescoeur, Merveilleux du Vignaux, Taudière, Terrat.

ÉCOLE LIBRE DE HAUTES ÉTUDES LITTÉRAIRES ET SCIENTIFIQUES.
Professors and Lecturers.

ARTS.
LANGUAGES.—CHINESE: *Professor* Paul Antonini.

SEMITIC: *Professor* le baron Carra de Vaux.
CLASSICAL: *Professors* Bertrin, Beur-

lier, Boxler, Bousquet, Le Chatellier, Lejay, Ragon.
ROMANCE: *Professors* Bertrin, Le Bidois, Jacquet, Klein, Rousselot.
PHILOSOPHY: *Professor* Piat.
HISTORY: *Professors* Baudrillart, Digard.

SCIENCE.

MATHEMATICS AND ASTRONOMY: *Professors* D'Esclaibes, Nau; *MM.* Chailan, Fouet.
PHYSICS: *Professor* Branly.
CHEMISTRY: *Professor* Hamonet.
MINERALOGY AND GEOLOGY: *Professor* de Lapparent.
GEOGRAPHY: *Professors* de Lapparent, Pisani.

ALLIANCE FRANÇAISE.

Siége Social, rue de Grenelle, 45, Paris.

The Alliance Française, a national association for the propagation of the French language in the colonies and abroad, decided in 1893 to organise summer courses to be held at Paris in the months of July and August for the purpose of assisting foreigners to obtain a knowledge of the French language. Diplomas are granted to the successful students; the advanced diploma certifies that the student is able to teach French. The courses are open without any distinction of age, sex or nationality.

The lectures are divided into two series, one lasting from July 1st to August 1st, the second from August 1st to September 1st.

Admission to the lectures is 1 franc (20 cents) each lecture; admission to the conferences, held in the evening, is 50 centimes (10 cents). A ticket admitting to the complete course of about 160 lectures and 24 conferences is 150 francs ($30).

The courses are held in the École Coloniale, Avenue de l'Observatoire, près le Petit-Luxembourg, and at the Collège de France.

Professors for 1898.

FRENCH LANGUAGE AND LITERATURE: *Professors* Berr, Brunot, Carl, Cirot, Clément, Debidour, Doumic, Huguet, Jacquinet, Raguet, Rousselot, Roy, Texte, Thalamas, Zund-Burguet.

CONFERENCES: *Professors* Blin. Gobron, Guy, Huguet, Martin, Minel, Peyraffite, Tridon, Turman Vermeulen, *Mlle.* Dequin and others.

COLLÈGE DE FRANCE.

Place du Collège de France, 1, Paris.

This college, open to women since its foundation in 1518–45, gives instruction in Arts, Science and Medicine, but confers no degrees. Students desiring certificates of attendance should register their courses.

The first semester begins on the first Monday in December; the second semester begins in the week after Easter and ends between the 20th and 30th of July.

All the courses are free.

The secretary is M. ABEL LEFRANC.

Professors and Lecturers.

ARTS.

LANGUAGES.—CHINESE AND TARTAR: *Professors* Chavannes, Courant.

SEMITIC: *Professors* Barbier de Meynard, Berger, Duval, Houdas, Maspero, Oppert.

INDO-IRANIAN: *Professors* Foucher, Lévi.

CLASSICAL: *Professors* Boissier, Croiset, Havet.

GERMANIC: *Professor* Chuquet.

SLAVONIC: *Professor* Léger.

ROMANCE: *Professors* d'Arbois de Jubainville, Deschanel, Meyer, Gaston Paris; *M.* Morel-Fatio.

COMPARATIVE PHILOLOGY: *Professor* Bréal.

PHILOSOPHY: *Professors* Lévêque, Nourisson, Ribot, Tannery, Thamin; *M.* Bergson.

HISTORY OF RELIGIONS: *Professor* Réville.

POLITICAL SCIENCE: *Professors* Flach, Leroy-Beaulieu, Izoulet, Levasseur, Longnon.

ART AND ARCHÆOLOGY: *Professors* Cagnat, Clermont-Ganneau, Foucart, Guillaume, Maspero, Oppert; *M.* Lafenestre.

SCIENCE.

MATHEMATICS AND ASTRONOMY: *Professors* Jordan, Lévy; *MM.* Hadamard, Koenigs.

PHYSICS: *Professors* Angot, Bertrand, Brillouin, Mascart; *M.* Deprez.

CHEMISTRY: *Professors* André, Berthelot, Le Chatelier, Schützenberger.

GEOLOGY AND GEOGRAPHY: *Professors* Fouqué, Longnon.

BIOLOGY: *Professors* Balbiani, Henneguy, Marey; *M.* Franck.

GENERAL HISTORY OF THE SCIENCES: *Professor* Lafitte.

MEDICINE.

Professors d'Arsonval, Ranvier; *M.* Charrin.

COLLÈGE LIBRE DES SCIENCES SOCIALES.

Rue de Tournon, 8, Paris.

The object of this college, founded in 1896, is to provide instruction in Economic and Social Science. Anyone is admitted on paying the registration fee of 30 fr. ($6). The courses begin in November, and the lectures are held in the afternoon and evening.

A *certificat d'études sociales* is given by the director to any student who writes a thesis and obtains certificates from three professors. The professors are well-known men and each is responsible for his own subject.

For further information apply to the Secretary, rue de Tournon, 8, Paris.

Professors and Lecturers.

POLITICAL SCIENCE.

MM. Andler, Barrat, Bertillon, Brunhes, Dalle, Dauriac, Delaire, Delbet, Dufourmantelle, Fontaine, Kellès-Krauz, Kovalevsky, Lichtenberger, Marin, du Maroussem, du Mesnil, Métin, de Pascal, Paulalion, Révelin, Saleilles, Seignobos, Strauss, Tarbouriech, Tarde, Turmann, Wahl, Weber.

ÉCOLE DU LOUVRE.

The Louvre, Cour Lefuel (ancienne Cour Coulaincourt), Paris.

The object of this school is to give instruction in regard to the collections in the Louvre and to educate librarians and custodians in the history of art and archæology. The instruction is given in the form of *conférences*.

Regular students and hearers are admitted on application to the secretary of the school (*pavillon de la Horloge au Louvre*), from whom cards of admission can be obtained.

The full course lasts three years, the lectures in each year beginning in the first week of December and ending about the 15th of June.

All the lectures are free.

Professors and Lecturers.

ARCHÆOLOGY: *Professors* Bertrand, Heuzey, Pierret, Pottier, Reinach.

HISTORY OF ART: *Professors* Lafenestre, Michel, Molinier.

INSCRIPTIONS: MM. Ledrain, Revillout.

ÉCOLE LIBRE DES SCIENCES POLITIQUES.

Rue Saint Guillaume, 27, Paris.

This school is established for the training of diplomatists, consuls, ambassadors, etc., in administration, finance and kindred subjects.

Students and hearers are admitted without a degree and without undergoing any examination. The number of men students is so great that it has been found impossible to admit women to the lectures or even to the libraries and reading rooms of the school.

The academic year begins in the second week of November and ends on June 8th.

The general secretary is M. CH. DUPUIS, rue Saint Guillaume, 27, Paris

Professors and Lecturers.

ADMINISTRATION: *Professors* Alix, le Vavasseur de Précourt, Romieu.
FINANCE: *Professors* Arnauné, Boulanger, de Colonjon, Courtin, Des Essarts, Lévy, Plaffain, René Stourm.
COMMERCIAL AND STATISTIC GEOGRAPHY: *Professors* de Foville, Levasseur, Viallate, Zolla.
POLITICAL AND SOCIAL ECONOMY: *Professors* Cheysson, Dunoyer.
LEGISLATION: *Professors* Lyon-Caen, Dietz, Flach, Paulet, Romieu.
GEOGRAPHY AND ETHNOGRAPHY: *Professors* Gaidoz, Pelet.
GEOGRAPHY AND MILITARY ORGANISATION: *MM.* le Commandant Leblond, Malleterre.
INTERNATIONAL LAW: *Professors* Dupuis, Renault.
HISTORY OF DIPLOMATICS AND OF PUBLIC OPINION: *Professors* Bourgeois, Funck-Brentano, Levy-Brühl, Koechlin, Christian Schefer, Sorel, Vandal.
CONSTITUTIONAL HISTORY: *Professors* Benoist, Dietz, André Lebon.
MODERN EUROPE: *Professors* Bourgeois, Halévy, Leroy-Beaulieu.
COLONIAL QUESTIONS: *Professors* Chailley-Bert, Cordier, Houdas, Pelet, Schefer, Silvestre, Vandal, Wilhelm.
MODERN LANGUAGES: *Professors* Cart, Houdas, Leger, Morel.
HYGIENE: *Professor* Fleury.
LAW: *Professor* Tarde.

ÉCOLE NATIONALE DES CHARTES.
Rue de la Sorbonne, 17, Paris.

The object of this school is to prepare students for the position of public librarians and keepers of archives. French students are admitted on the results of a competitive examination; foreigners are admitted on presenting a diploma equivalent to that of the *bachelier ès lettres*. The number of French students is limited to 20.

Students who have taken the three years' course and passed each of the two examinations in each year, and presented a satisfactory thesis, obtain a diploma (*diplôme d' archiviste paléographe*). Women are admitted to the school as hearers (*auditrices libres*) on registering their names at the secretary's office. The use of the library is a privilege reserved for regular students.

The academic year begins in the first week of November and lasts till the first of July.

All the courses are public and free.

For information apply to the secretary, École des Chartes, rue de la Sorbonne, 17, Paris.

Professors and Lecturers.

ROMANCE PHILOLOGY: *Professor* Paul Meyer.
BIBLIOGRAPHY: *M.* Mortet.
DIPLOMATICS: *Professor* Giry.
POLITICAL INSTITUTIONS: *Professor* Roy.
HISTORY: *Professors* Molinier, Viollet.
ARCHÆOLOGY: *Professor* de Lasteyrie; *M.* Enlart.
PALEOGRAPHY: *Professor* Berger.
ARCHIVES: *M.* Desjardins.

ÉCQLE PRATIQUE DES HAUTES ÉTUDES.

The object of this institution, which was founded in 1868, is to provide opportunities for practical work in connection with the lectures given at the Collège de France, the Sorbonne, the Muséum d'histoire naturelle, the Faculty of Medicine, etc. The courses of the school are held at these various institutions, and the laboratories for the purposes of instruction and research are situated in various parts of Paris and at different places on the coast (Villefranche, Wimereux, Marseilles, Cette, Roscoff, Banyuls-sur-Mer).

The courses are open free without any restrictions as to age, degree, or nationality; but a year's probation is necessary before the title of *élève titulaire* is conferred. Certain professors reserve the right of refusing to admit women to their classes, but with the exception of a few hospital courses, practically all are open to women.

There are five independently organised sections, the second and third of which (those of Physics, Chemistry and Natural Science), consist entirely of laboratory courses.

It is intended that students should attend the courses for three years. The academic year begins on the 1st of November and ends on the 30th of June.

Enquiries should be addressed to the *Secrétariat de la Faculté des Sciences, à la Sorbonne.*

Professors and Lecturers.

FIRST SECTION: MATHEMATICAL SCIENCES.
Professors Hermite, Koenigs, Puiseux, Raffy.

SECOND SECTION: PHYSICO-CHEMICAL SCIENCES.
(The courses in this and the following section are all laboratory courses.)
PHYSICAL LABORATORIES: *Directors MM.* Bouty, Brillouin, Lippmann, Maneuvrier, Violle; *Assistants MM.* Abraham, Guillard, Guillet.
CHEMICAL LABORATORIES: *Directors MM.* Berthelot, Didier, Duclaux, Friedel, Gernez, Moissan, Péchard, Troost; *Assistants MM.* Brion, Burais, Chamberland, Charon, Job, Martin, Mesnil, Mourlot, Pottevin, Roux, Valeur.

MINERALOGICAL LABORATORIES: *Directors MM.* Hautefeuille, Lacroix, Perrey.

THIRD SECTION: NATURAL SCIENCES.
BOTANICAL LABORATORIES: *Directors MM.* Bonnier (Paris and Fountainebleau), Bureau, Chauveaud, Dufour, Van-Tieghem; *Assistants MM.* Francet, Hua, Jolly, Poisson.
LABORATORY OF BIOLOGICAL PHYSICS: *Directors MM.* d'Arsonval, Hénocque; *Assistants MM.* Guyon, Roussy.
ANATOMICAL LABORATORY: *Directors MM.* Beauregard, Filhol; *Assistant M.* Saint-Loup.
PHYSIOLOGICAL LABORATORIES: *Directors MM.* Dastre, François-Franck,

Gréhant, Marey; *Assistants MM.* Arthaud, Hallion, Lamy.

ZOOLOGICAL LABORATORIES: *Directors MM.* d'Arsonval (Concarneau), Barrois (Villefranche), Delage, Girard (Wimereux), Lacaze-Duthiers (Paris, Roscoff and Banyuls-Sur-Mer), Marion (Marseilles), Milne-Edwards, Oustalet, Perrier, Sabatier (Cette); *Assistants MM.* Bernard, Bordas, Brumpt, Lépine, Roché.

MEDICAL LABORATORIES: *Directors MM.* Charrin, de la Chavanne, Javal, Laborde, Tscherning; *Assistants MM.* Manouvrier, Papillant.

HISTOLOGICAL LABORATORY: *Directors MM.* Malassez, Ranvier; *Assistant M.* Jolly.

PSYCHOLOGICAL LABORATORY: *Directors MM.* Binet, Henry; *Assistants MM.* Courtier, Philippe.

GEOLOGICAL LABORATORIES: *Directors MM.* Fouqué, Gosselet (Lille), Munier-Chalmas, Rivière; *Assistant M.* Glangeaud.

FOURTH SECTION: HISTORICAL AND PHILOLOGICAL SCIENCES.

(Office and Lecture Room at the University Library, The Sorbonne.)

LANGUAGES.—ETHIOPIAN AND HIMYARITE: *M.* Halévy.

ARABIC: *M.* Derenbourg.
SEMITIC: *M.* Carriére.
SANSKRIT, ZEND: *MM.* Blochet, Finot, S. Lèvi, Meillet, Specht.
MODERN GREEK: *M.* Psichari.
ROMANCE: *MM.* Gardoz, Gilliéron, Morel-Fatio, Thomas, Paris.
COMPARATIVE PHILOLOGY: *MM.* Duvau, Meillet.
CLASSICAL PHILOLOGY AND ARCHÆOLOGY: *MM.* Chatelain, Desrousseaux, Haussoulier, Jacob, Lebégue, de Nolhac, de Villefosse.
ASSYRIAN, EGYPTIAN AND ORIENTAL PHILOLOGY AND ARCHÆOLOGY: *MM.* Clermont-Ganneau, Guieysse, Maspero, Scheil.
PHILOSOPHY: *M.* Soury.
HISTORY: *MM.* Bémont, Giry, Monod, Reuss, Roy.

FIFTH SECTION: RELIGIOUS SCIENCES.

(Office and Lecture Room at the University Library, The Sorbonne.)

THEOLOGY: *MM.* Amélineau, Berthelot, Deramey, Derenbourg, Esmein, de Faye, Foucher, I. Lévi, Marillier, Picavet, A. Quentin, G. Raynaud, Albert Réville, Jean Réville, de Rosny, Sabatier, Vernes.

ÉCOLE SPÉCIALE DES LANGUES ORIENTALES VIVANTES.

Rue de Lille, 2, Paris.

The object of this school, founded in 1795, is to give instruction in modern oriental languages for political and commercial purposes.

Regular students must be *bacheliers ès sciences* or *ès lettres*, between 16 and 24 years of age, and of French nationality. Exceptions are sometimes made in respect to age and nationality.

The courses and diploma (*diplôme d' élève breveté*) are open to women.

The lectures begin early in November and the course lasts three years.

All the lectures are public; the fees are 50 fr. ($10) a semester.

For further information apply to the secretary, rue de Lille, 2, Paris.

Professors and Lecturers.

ORIENTAL LANGUAGES: *Professors* Bonet, Boyer, Carrière, Cordier, Derenbourg, Devéria, Houdas, Huart, Legrand, Barbier de Meynard, Picot, León de Rosny, Vinson; *MM.* Durnid, Kalpakdjian, Lorgeou, Marre Mondon-Vidailhet, Aboul Nasr, Oda, Pernot, Ramisiray, Ravaisse, Lien Young.

MUSÉUM D' HISTOIRE NATURELLE.

Jardin des Plantes, rue Cuvier, 57, Paris.

The *Muséum d' histoire naturelle* was founded in 1626 for the purpose of making scientific collections and for research. Each department is in the charge of a professor, and each professor is obliged to give forty public lectures yearly on the subject with which his department deals.

The courses are unconditionally open to the public. Regular hearers, by producing certificates of attendance from the professors, may obtain cards which give them access for a year to the galleries and collections. For the conferences and practical work, registration is required, but diplomas are not necessary. Botanical and entomological excursions into the country are arranged weekly during the summer months. Lectures begin on April 27th.

Secretary, M. H. CHÂTELAIN, Muséum d' Histoire Naturelle, Jardin des Plantes, rue Cuvier, 57, Paris.

Professors and Assistants.

PHYSICS: *Professor* Becquerel; *M.* Berthelot.
CHEMISTRY: *Professor* Arnaud; *M.* Bourgeois.
MINERALOGY: *Professor* Lacroix; *M.* Jannettaz.
GEOLOGY AND GEOGRAPHY: *Professors* Gaudry, Meunier; *MM.* Boule, Ramond.
BIOLOGY: *Professors* Bouvier, Bureau, Dehérain, Filhol, Grehant, Hamy, Maquenne, Milne-Edwards, Perrier, Vaillant, Van-Tieghem; *MM.* Bernard, Beauregard, Brongniart, Gervais, Gley, Künckel d'Herculais, Mocquard, Morot, Oustalet, Poisson, Renault, Roux, Sauvinet, Trémeau de Rochebrune, Verneau.
AGRICULTURE: *Professor* Cornu; *M.* Bois.
PATHOLOGY: *Professor* Chauveau; *M.* Phisalix.
DRAWING: *M.* Fremiet, *Mme.* Lemaire.

THE FRENCH PROVINCES.

The following is a list of the professors in the different *Facultés* of the French provinces. The organisation of these *Facultés* is exactly the same as at Paris, and is described on pp. 31–36.

AIX, France.

UNIVERSITÉ D'AIX-MARSEILLE.

This university, dating from the 13th century, comprises the Faculties of Arts and Law, situated at Aix, and the Faculties of Science, Law and Medicine at Marseilles.

There is a branch of the *Comité de Patronage des Étudiants Étrangers* at Aix, and by its means courses in French language and literature especially for foreigners have been arranged.

FACULTÉ DES LETTRES D'AIX.

Professors and Lecturers.

ARTS.

LANGUAGES.—SEMITIC : *M.* Duranti de La Calade.
CLASSICAL : *Professor* Constans ; *MM.* Brenous, de Ridder.
ROMANCE : *Professors* Constans, Ducros ; *M.* Bonafous.
LITERATURE : *Professor* Joret.
PHILOSOPHY : *Professor* Blondel.
POLITICAL ECONOMY : *MM.* Masson, C. Perreau.
HISTORY : *Professors* Clerc, Guibal.
ARCHÆOLOGY : *M.* de Ridder.
GEOGRAPHY : *M.* Girbal.

FACULTÉ DE DROIT D'AIX.

Professors and Lecturers.

POLITICAL SCIENCE : *Professor* Jourdan ; *M.* C. Perreau.

LAW.

Professors Audinet, Bouvier-Bangillon, Bry, Jourdan, Lacoste, Moreau, Pison, Vermond ; *MM.* César-Bru, C. Perreau, E. Perreau, de Pitti-Ferrandi, Thélohan.

FACULTÉ DES SCIENCES DE MARSEILLE.

Connected with this Faculty is the Marine Zoological Laboratory at Endoume and a large astronomical observatory. Supplementary courses are given by the professors of the *Faculté des Lettres d'Aix.*

Professors and Lecturers.

SCIENCE.

MATHEMATICS AND ASTRONOMY : *Professors* Charve, Sauvage, Stephan ; *M.* Jamet.
PHYSICS : *Professors* Macé de Lépinay, Pérot ; *MM.* Fabry, Répelin, Vayssière.
CHEMISTRY : *Professors* Duvillier, Reboul ; *MM.* Berg, Perdrix.
MINERALOGY : *Professor* Vasseur.
GEOLOGY : *Professor* Vasseur.
BIOLOGY : *Professors* Heckel, Marion ; *MM.* Gourret, Jourdan, Jumelle, Léger, Vayssière.
AGRICULTURE : *Professor* Pauchon.

LAW.

Professors Bouvier-Bangillon, de Pitti-Ferrandi.

ÉCOLE DE MÉDECINE ET DE PHARMACIE DE PLEIN EXERCICE DE MARSEILLE.

Professors and Lecturers.

MEDICINE.

Professors Arnaud, Boinet, Bouisson, Caillol de Poncy, Chapplain, Combalat, Domergue, Fallot, Gourret, Heckel, Jourdan, Laget, Livon, Magon, Nepveu, Queirel, Rietsch, Vigneron, Villard, Villeneuve; *MM.* Alezais, Berg, Carrière, Delanglade, Gerber, Laplane, Roux fils.

FACULTÉ MARSEILLAISE LIBRE DE DROIT.

This Faculty was founded in 1881.

Professors and Lecturers.

POLITICAL SCIENCE: *Professor* Peyron; M. Henrion.

LAW.

Professors Aicard, Alphandéry, Autran, Bally, Barrême, Bédarride, Bérenger, de Bévotte, Berlier de Vauplane, David, Enile Fabre, Eugène Fabre, Martin, Peyron, P. Rolland, Rolland-Chevillon, Tassy, Thumin, Vial; *MM.* Charlois, Gravier.

BESANÇON, France.

UNIVERSITÉ DE BESANÇON.

This is a small university, founded in 1422, comprising Faculties of Arts and Science and a Preparatory School of Medicine. Total number of students, 197.

FACULTÉ DES LETTRES DE BESANÇON.

Professors and Lecturers.

ARTS.
LANGUAGES:—CLASSICAL: *Professor* Nageotte; *MM.* Charrot, Vernier.
GERMANIC: *M.* Kontz.
ROMANCE: *Professor* Droz.

LITERATURE: *Professors* Boucher, Nageotte.
PHILOSOPHY: *Professor* Colsenet.
HISTORY AND GEOGRAPHY: *Professors* Guiraud, Pingaud.

FACULTÉ DES SCIENCES DE BESANÇON.

Professors and Lecturers.

SCIENCE.
MATHEMATICS AND ASTRONOMY: *Professors* Gruey, Saint-Loup, Stouff.
PHYSICS: *Professor* Joubin.
CHEMISTRY: *Professor* Boutroux; *M.* Genvresse.

MINERALOGY AND GEOLOGY: *Professor* Fournier.
BIOLOGY: *Professors* Charbonnel-Salle, Magnin.

ÉCOLE PRÉPARATOIRE DE MÉDECINE ET DE PHARMACIE DE BESANÇON.

Professors and Lecturers.

MEDICINE.
Professors Boisson, Bolot, Chapoy, Gauderon, Heitz, Magnin, Mandereau, Prieur, Roland, Saillard, Thouvenin; *MM.* Bruchon, Colléatte, Morin.

BORDEAUX, France.

UNIVERSITÉ DE BORDEAUX.

This university, founded in 1441, comprises Faculties of Arts, Science, Law, Medicine and Pharmacy. In addition to the usual laboratories and museums, there is a School of Chemistry Applied to Manufacturers and Agriculture, a School of Industrial Electricity, an Astronomical and Meteorological Observatory at Florac, and a Zoological Laboratory at Arcachon.

There is a branch of the *Comité de Patronage des Étudiants Étrangers* in Bordeaux, secretary, PROFESSOR DUGUIT.

FACULTÉ DES LETTRES DE BORDEAUX.

Professors and Lecturers.

ARTS.
LANGUAGES. — CLASSICAL : *Professors* Ouvré, Waltz; *MM.* Cirot, de la Ville de Mirmont, Masqueray, Zyromski.
ENGLISH : *M.* Biard.
GERMANIC : *M.* Rouge.
ROMANCE : *Professors* Bourcier, Stapfer ; *M.* Le Breton.
LITERATURE : *Professor* de Tréverret.
COMPARATIVE PHILOLOGY : *M.* Masqueray.

PHILOSOPHY : *Professor* Espinas ; *MM.* Hamelin, Rodier.
SOCIOLOGY : *Professor* Durkheim.
HISTORY : *Professors* Denis, Imbart de la Tour, Jullian, Radet ; *MM.* Bouvy, Marion.
ART AND ARCHÆOLOGY : *Professor* Paris ; *M.* Bouvy.
GEOGRAPHY : *Professor* Gebelin ; *M.* Lorin.
PEDAGOGY : *M.* Durkheim.

FACULTÉ DES SCIENCES DE BORDEAUX.

Professors and Lecturers.

SCIENCE.
MATHEMATICS AND ASTRONOMY : *Professors* Brunel, Rayet ; *MM.* Brunel, Giraud, Picart, de Tannenberg.
PHYSICS : *Professors* Duhem, Morisot ; *MM.* Gossart, Marchis.
CHEMISTRY : *Professors* Gayon, Joannis ; *MM.* Dubourg, Gruvel, Vèzes, Vigouroux.
MINERALOGY : *Professor* Fallot ; *M.* Goguel.
GEOLOGY : *Professor* Fallot.
BIOLOGY : *Professors* Millardet, Pérez ; *MM.* Devaux, Kunstler.

FACULTÉ DE DROIT DE BORDEAUX.
Professors and Lecturers.

POLITICAL SCIENCE: *MM.* Benzacar, Sauvaire-Jourdan.
LAW: *Professors* Barckhausen, Baudry-Lacantinerie, de Boeck, Despagnet, Didier, Duguit, Le Coq, Levillain, de Loynes, Marandout, Monnier, Saignat, Vigneaux.

FACULTÉ MIXTE DE MÉDECINE ET DE PHARMACIE DE BORDEAUX.
Professors and Lecturers.

MEDICINE.
Professors Arnozan, Badal, Bergonié, Blarez, Boursier, Bouchard, Coyne, Demons, Ferré, Figuier, Guillaud, Jolyet, Lanelongue, Layet, Masse, Morache, Moussous père, de Nabias, Picot, Piéchaud, Pitres, Vergely, Viault; *MM.* Denigès, Denucé, Dubreuilh, Moure, Moussous fils, Pousson, Régis, Rivière.

CAEN, France.
UNIVERSITÉ DE CAEN.

This university, founded in 1437, comprises Faculties of Arts, Science, Law, and a Preparatory School of Medicine and Pharmacy. There is a Marine Laboratory at Luc-sur-Mer, open all the year.

FACULTÉ DES LETTRES DE CAEN.
Professors and Lecturers.

ARTS.
LANGUAGES.—CLASSICAL: *Professors* Lehanneur, Lemercier; *M.* Renel.
ENGLISH: *M.* Barbeau.
ROMANCE: *Professor* Gasté; *M.* Souriau.
COMPARATIVE PHILOLOGY: *M.* Huguet.
PHILOSOPHY: *Professor* Mabilleau; *M.* Couturat.
HISTORY: *Professor* Tessier; *M.* Toutain.
ART: *Professor* Gasté.
SCIENCE AND GEOGRAPHY: *M.* Camena d'Almeida.

FACULTÉ DES SCIENCES DE CAEN.
Professors and Lecturers.

SCIENCE.
MATHEMATICS AND ASTRONOMY: *Professors* Riquier, de Saint-Germain; *M.* Lelieuvre.
PHYSICS: *Professor* Neyreneuf; *M.* Guinchant.
CHEMISTRY: *Professor* Louise; *M.* Besson.
GEOLOGY: *Professor* Bigot.
BIOLOGY: *Professors* Joyeux-Laffuie, Lignier; *MM.* Huet, Léger.

FACULTÉ DE DROIT DE CAEN.
Professors and Lecturers.

POLITICAL SCIENCE: *Professor* Villey; *M.* René Worms.

LAW.
Professors Biville, Bouvier, Cabouat, Carel, Colin, Danjon, Debray, Gauckler, Guillouard, Laisné-Deshayes, Lebret, Le Fur, Marie, Toutain, Villey; *M.* Ambroise Colin.

ÉCOLE PRÉPARATOIRE DE MÉDECINE ET DE PHARMACIE DE CAEN.
Professors and Lecturers.

MEDICINE.
Professors Auvray, Barette, Catois, Charbonnier, Demerliac, Fayel-Deslongrais, Gidon, Guillet, Louïse, Moutier, Noury, Pihier; *MM.* Besson, Chevrel, Gosselin, Osmont, Vigot.

CLERMONT-FERRAND, France.
UNIVERSITÉ DE CLERMONT.

This is a small university, founded in 1808, comprising Faculties of Arts and Science, and a Preparatory School of Medicine and Pharmacy. Total number of students, 179.

FACULTÉ DES LETTRES DE CLERMONT.
Professors and Lecturers.

ARTS.
LANGUAGES. — CLASSICAL: *Professor* Baron; *M.* Audollent.
ENGLISH: *M.* Mahieu.
ROMANCE: *Professor* des Essarts; *M.* Leclerc.
LITERATURE: *Professor* Ehrhard.
COMPARATIVE PHILOLOGY: *M.* Colardeau.
PHILOSOPHY: *Professor* Joyau.
HISTORY: *Professors* Desdevises du Dézert, Hauser; *M.* Rouchon.
PALEOGRAPHY: *M.* Rouchon.
GEOGRAPHY: *Professor* Desdevises du Dézert.

FACULTÉ DES SCIENCES DE CLERMONT.
Professors and Lecturers.

SCIENCE.
MATHEMATICS AND ASTRONOMY: *Professor* Pellet; *M.* Le Cordier.
PHYSICS: *Professors* Guichard, Hurian; *M.* Lugol.
CHEMISTRY: *Professor* Parmentier; *M.* Duboin.
MINERALOGY AND GEOLOGY: *Professor* Julien.
BIOLOGY: *Professors* Girod, Poirier.

ÉCOLE PRÉPARATOIRE DE MÉDECINE ET DE PHARMACIE DE CLERMONT.
Professors and Lecturers.

MEDICINE.
Professors Bardier, Bousquet, Dourif, Fouriaux, Gagnon, Girod, Huguet, Lepetit, Planchard, Rocher, Tixier, Truchot; *MM.* Bide, Bruyant, Gros, Lafont, Maurin, Mosnier.

DIJON, France.
UNIVERSITÉ DE DIJON.

This university, founded in 1722, comprises Faculties of Arts, Science and Law, and a Preparatory School of Medicine and Pharmacy. Total number of students, 594.

FACULTÉ DES LETTRES DE DIJON.
Professors and Lecturers.

ARTS.
LANGUAGES.—CLASSICAL: *Professors* Dorison, Royer.
ROMANCE : *MM.* Lame, Roy.
LITERATURE : *Professor* Legras.
COMPARATIVE PHILOLOGY: *M.* Lambert.
PHILOSOPHY : *Professor* Boirac.
HISTORY : *Professor* Gaffarel ; *MM.* Kleinclausz, Stouff.
GEOGRAPHY : *Professor* Gaffarel.

FACULTÉ DES SCIENCES DE DIJON.
Professors and Lecturers.

SCIENCE.
MATHEMATICS AND ASTRONOMY : *Professors* Duport, Méray.
CHEMISTRY : *Professor* Recoura ; *M.* Pigeon.
PHYSICS : *MM.* Bagard, Brunhes.
MINERALOGY AND GEOLOGY : *Professor* Collot.
BIOLOGY : *Professors* Émery, Jobert ; *M.* Bataillon.

FACULTÉ DE DROIT DE DIJON.
Professors and Lecturers.

POLITICAL SCIENCE : *Professor* Mongin ; *M.* Truchy.
LAW : *Professors* Bailly, Bonneville, Deslandres, Desserteaux, Duverdier-de-Suze, Gaudemet, Gény, Louis-Lucas, Renardet, Roux, Tissier ; *MM.* Mongin, Moulin, Stouff.

ÉCOLE PRÉPARATOIRE DE MÉDECINE ET DE PHARMACIE DE DIJON.
Professors and Lecturers.

MEDICINE.
Professors Broussolle, Brunhes, Collette, Deroye, Gautrelet, Laguesse, Misset, Parizot, Pauffard, Pigeon, Tarnier, Viallanes ; *MM.* Bellier, Bonnabeaud, Cottin, Dubard, Lagoutte, Vincent.

GRENOBLE, France.
UNIVERSITÉ DE GRENOBLE.

This university, founded in 1339, comprises the Faculties of Arts, Science and Law, and a preparatory School of Medicine and Pharmacy. The number of students is 499.

The *Comité de Patronage des Étudiants Étrangers* organised

in 1898 a holiday course in French language, literature and history, especially for foreigners. The course consists of daily lectures and conferences and lasts from July 1st to October 31st, but students may attend for one month only. The fees for lectures for four weeks are 20 fr. ($4), for the four months 50 fr. ($10). For further particulars apply to M. MARCEL REYMOND, place de la Constitution, 4, Grenoble.

FACULTÉ DES LETTRES DE GRENOBLE.
Professors and Lecturers.

ARTS.

LANGUAGES.—CLASSICS: *Professors* Bertrand, Dugit; *MM.* Bardot, Chabert.
ENGLISH: *M.* Mathias.
ROMANCE: *Professor* Morillot; *M.* Hauvette.
LITERATURE: *Professor* Besson.
PHILOSOPHY: *Professor* Dumesnil.
HISTORY AND GEOGRAPHY: *Professor* de Crozals.

FACULTÉ DES SCIENCES DE GRENOBLE.
Professors and Lecturers.

SCIENCE.

MATHEMATICS AND ASTRONOMY: *Professors* Astor, Collet; *M.* Cousin.
PHYSICS: *Professor* Pionchon; *M.* Beaulard.
CHEMISTRY: *Professor* Raoult; *M.* Chavastelon.
MINERALOGY AND GEOLOGY: *Professor* Kilian.
BIOLOGY: *Professors* Lachmann, Pruvot.

FACULTÉ DE DROIT DE GRENOBLE.
Professors and Lecturers.

POLITICAL SCIENCE: *M.* Reboud.
LAW: *Professors* Balleydier, Beaudouin, Beudant, Capitant, Fournier, Guétat, Gueymard, de Lapradelle, Michoud, Pillet, Tartari, Testoud; *MM.* Cuche, Hitier.

ÉCOLE PRÉPARATOIRE DE MÉDECINE ET DE PHARMACIE DE GRENOBLE.
Professors and Lecturers.

MEDICINE.

Professors Allard, Berlioz, Bordier, Douillet, Flandrin, Gallois, Girard, Labatut, Nicolas, Pegoud, Pionchon, Porte, Turel, Verne; *MM.* Baboin, Cibert, Deschamps, G. Dodero, D. Dodero, Salva.

LILLE, France.

UNIVERSITÉ DE LILLE.

This is a large university, founded in 1808, and comprises Faculties of Arts, Science, Law and Medicine; there are also free or

Catholic Faculties in the same subjects, and a Faculty of Catholic Theology.

FACULTÉ DES LETTRES DE LILLE.
Professors and Lecturers.

ARTS.

LANGUAGES. — CLASSICAL: *Professors* Dufour, Thomas; *MM.* Chamard, Couvreur, Dautremer, Fougères.
ENGLISH: *Professor* Angellier; *MM.* Chevrillon, Derocquigny.
GERMANIC: *Professor* Pinloche.
ROMANCE: *Professors* Dupont, Langlois, Moy.
SLAVONIC: *M.* Haumant.
PHILOSOPHY: *Professor* Penjon; *M.* Lefèvre.
HISTORY: *Professors* Fabre, Flammermont; *M.* Petit-Dutaillis.
ARCHÆOLOGY: *M.* Fougères.
GEOGRAPHY: *Professor* Ardaillon.

FACULTÉ DES SCIENCES DE LILLE.
Professors and Lecturers.

SCIENCE.

MATHEMATICS AND ASTRONOMY: *Professors* Demartres, Petot, Souillart; *MM.* Padé, Thybaut.
PHYSICS: *Professor* Damien; *MM.* Camichel, Swyngedauw.
CHEMISTRY: *Professors* Buisine, Willm; *M.* Pélabon.
MINERALOGY: *Professor* Gosselet.
GEOLOGY: *Professor* Gosselet; *M.* Barrois.
BIOLOGY: *Professors* Betrand, Hallez; *MM.* Prouho, Queva.
AGRICULTURE: *Professor* Buisine.

FACULTÉ DE DROIT DE LILLE.
Professors and Lecturers.

POLITICAL SCIENCE: *Professor* Bourguin.
LAW: *Professors* Bourguin, Collinet, Drumel, Féder, de Folleville, Garçon, Jacquey, Lacour, Mouchet, Vallas, Wahl; *MM.* Jacquelin, Margat, Peltier.

FACULTÉ MIXTE DE MÉDECINE ET DE PHARMACIE DE LILLE.
Professors and Lecturers.

MEDICINE.

Professors Barrois, Baudry, Calmette, Castiaux, Charmeil, Combemale, Curtis, Debierre, Doumer, Dubar, Folet, Gaulard, Laguesse, Lambling, de Lapersonne, Lemoine, Leroy, Lescoeur, Lotar, Moniez, Morelle, Surmont, Wertheimer; *MM.* Ausset, Carlier, Oui, Phocas.

FACULTÉ LIBRE DES LETTRES DE LILLE.
Professors and Lecturers.

LANGUAGES. — CLASSICAL: *Professors* Hérengt, Rambure.
ROMANCE: *Professor* Charaux.
LITERATURE: *Professors* Gahide, Looten.
RHETORIC: *Professor* Baunard.
COMPARATIVE PHILOLOGY: *Professor* Cliquennois.
PHILOSOPHY: *Professor* de Margerie.
HISTORY AND GEOGRAPHY: *Professor* Canet.

FACULTÉ LIBRE DES SCIENCES DE LILLE.

Professors and Lecturers.

SCIENCE.

MATHEMATICS AND ASTRONOMY: *Professors* de Salvert, Villié; *M.* Stoffaes.
PHYSICS: *Professors* Delenser, Witz.
CHEMISTRY: *Professor* Schmitt.
MINERALOGY AND GEOLOGY: *Professor* Bourgeat.
BIOLOGY: *Professors* Boulay, Maurice, Van-Oye.

FACULTÉ LIBRE DE DROIT DE LILLE.

Professors and Lecturers.

POLITICAL SCIENCE: *Professor* Béchaux.
LAW: *Professors* Arthaud, de Corbie, Delachenal, Duthoit, Gand, Groussau, Lamache, Moureau, Ory, Pillet, Rothe, Selosse, Trolley de Prévaux, Vanlaer, de Vareilles-Sommières; *MM.* Boissard, Cavrois, Duquesne, Maurice Vanlaer.

FACULTÉ LIBRE DE MÉDECINE ET DE PHARMACIE DE LILLE.

Professors and Lecturers.

MEDICINE.

Professors Augier, Baltus, Bernard, Bouchaud, Boulay, Carrez, Delassus, Desplats, Dujardin, Duret, Eustache, Faucon, Guermonprez, Lemière, Lenoble, Lienhart, Monnet, Rédier, Rogie, Schmitt, Thilliez, Toison, Voituriez, Witz.

FACULTÉ LIBRE DE THEOLOGIE DE LILLE.

Professors and Lecturers.

THEOLOGY: *Professors* Baunard, Chollet, Didiot, Moureau, Pannier, Pillet, Quilliet, Rohart, Salembier.

LYONS, France.

UNIVERSITÉ DE LYON.

This university, founded in 1808, is large and important, comprising state faculties of Arts, Science, Law, and a Faculty of Medicine, founded in 1876, which, with its large hospitals and excellent laboratories, is second only to that of Paris. There are also Catholic Faculties of Arts, Science, Law and Theology, situated at Lyons.

A branch of the *Comité de Patronage des Étudiants Étrangers* has been formed at Lyons: secretary, PROFESSOR THALLERS.

FACULTÉ DES LETTRES DE LYON.
Professors and Lecturers.

ARTS.

LANGUAGES.—INDO-IRANIAN: *Professor* Regnaud.
CLASSICAL: *Professors* Allègre, Fabia, Jullien; *M.* Legrand.
ENGLISH: *M.* Legouis.
GERMANIC: *M.* Gruber.
ROMANCE: *Professors* Clédat, Fontaine; *M.* Texte.
LITERATURE: *Professors* Firmery, Texte; *M.* Maigron.

COMPARATIVE PHILOLOGY: *Professor* Regnaud; *M.* Durand.
PHILOSOPHY: *Professor* Bertrand; *M.* Hannequin.
HISTORY: *MM.* Mariéjol, Waddington.
ART AND ARCHÆOLOGY: *Professors* Bloch, Coville; *MM.* Clédat, Holleaux, Legrand, Loret.
EGYPTOLOGY: *M.* Moret.
GEOGRAPHY: *MM.* Depéret, Schirmer.
ETHNOLOGY: *M.* Chantre.
PEDAGOGY: *M.* Chabot.

FACULTÉ DES SCIENCES DE LYON.
Professors and Lecturers.

SCIENCE.

MATHEMATICS AND ASTRONOMY: *Professors* André, Flamme, Lafon, Vessiot; *MM.* Autonne, Cartan, Gonnessiat.
PHYSICS: *Professor* Gouy; *MM.* Busquet, Houllevigue, Liénard.

CHEMISTRY: *Professors* Barbier, Vignon; *MM.* Bouveault, Couturier.
MINERALOGY: *Professor* Offret.
GEOLOGY: *Professor* Depéret; *M.* Douxami.
BIOLOGY: *Professors* Dubois, Gérard, Koehler; *MM.* Caullery, Sauvageau.
AGRICULTURE: *Professor* Vignon.

FACULTÉ DE DROIT DE LYON.
Professors and Lecturers.

POLITICAL ECONOMY: *Professors* Rougier, Souchon.
LAW: *Professors* Ch. Appleton, Audibert, Bartin, Berthélemy, Caillemer, Cohendy, Flurer, Garraud, Mabire, Pic; *MM.* Jean Appleton, Bonnecarrère, Bouvier, Galland, Lacassogne, Lambert, Lameire, Souchon.

FACULTÉ MIXTE DE MÉDECINE ET DE PHARMACIE DE LYON.
Professors and Lecturers.

MEDICINE.

Professors Arloing, Augagneur, Bard, Bondet, Cazeneuve, Crolas, Florence, Fochier, Gailleton, Gayet, Hugounenq, Lacassagne, Lépine, Lortet, Mayet, Monoyer, Morat, Ollier, Pierret, M. Pollosson, Poncet, Renaut, Soulier, Teissier, Testut, Tripier; *MM.* Barral, Beauvisage, Bordier, Boyer, Causse, Chandelux, Collet, Condamin, Courmont, Devic, Doyon, Durand, Gangolphe, Laroyenne, Moreau, Aug. Pollosson, Rochet, Rollet, Roque, Roux, Siraud, Vallas, Weill.

FACULTÉ LIBRES DES LETTRES DE LYON.
Professors and Lecturers.

ARTS.

LANGUAGES. — CLASSICAL: *Professors* Devaux, Forest, Gonnet.
ROMANCE: *Professors* Condamin, Delmont.
LITERATURE: *Professor* Frintz.

COMPARATIVE PHILOLOGY: *Professor* Lepitre.
PHILOSOPHY: *Professor* Reure.
HISTORY AND ARCHÆOLOGY: *Professor* Léotard.

FACULTÉ LIBRE DES SCIENCES DE LYON.

Professors and Lecturers.

SCIENCE.
MATHEMATICS AND ASTRONOMY: *Professors* Berloty, Magnus de Sparre, Onofrio, Valson.

PHYSICS: *Professor* Chassy.
CHEMISTRY: *Professor* Lepercq.
GEOLOGY: *Professor* Morin.
BIOLOGY: *Professors* Donnadieu, Morin.

FACULTÉ LIBRE DE DROIT DE LYON.

Professors and Lecturers.

POLITICAL SCIENCE: *Professor* Rambaud.
LAW: *Professors* Beaune, Boucaud, Gairal, Hostache, Jacquier, de Lajudie, Mouterde, Perrin, Poidebard, Richard, Roux, Wies; *MM.* Brun, Rivet, Roux, Voron, Wies.

FACULTÉ LIBRE DE THÉOLOGIE DE LYON.

Professors and Lecturers.

THEOLOGY.
Professors Belon, Blanc, Bourchany, Chambost, Chevallier, Dumas, Jacquier, Lémann, Vernet.

MONTPELLIER, France.

UNIVERSITÉ DE MONTPELLIER.

This university, founded in the twelfth century, comprises Faculties of Arts, Science, Law and Medicine, and is large and important. There are good laboratories and hospitals and some scientific institutes.

The branch of the *Comité de Patronage des Étudiants Étrangers* has arranged free practical courses for the benefit of foreigners. The secretary of the *Comité* is Professor Flahaut.

FACULTÉ DES LETTRES DE MONTPELLIER.

Professors and Lecturers.

ARTS.
LANGUAGES. — CLASSICAL: *Professors* Bonnet, Maury; *M.* Reynaud.
GERMANIC: *M.* Fécamp.
ROMANCE: *Professor* Rigal; *MM.* Chabaneau, Vianey.
LITERATURE: *Professor* Castets.

COMPARATIVE PHILOLOGY: *M.* Grammont.
PHILOSOPHY: *Professor* Milhaud; *M.* Bouglé.
HISTORY: *Professor* Gachon; *M.* Pelissier.
ARCHÆOLOGY: *MM.* Berthelé, Lechat.
GEOGRAPHY: *M.* Malavialle.

FACULTÉ DES SCIENCES DE MONTPELLIER.
Professors and Lecturers.

SCIENCE.

MATHEMATICS AND ASTRONOMY: *Professors* Dautheville, Fabry; *M.* Le Roux.
PHYSICS: *Professors* Crova, Meslin.
CHEMISTRY: *Professors* de Forcrand, Oechsner, de Coninck; *M.* Giran.
MINERALOGY: *Professor* Delage; *M.* Curie.
GEOLOGY: *Professor* Delage.
BIOLOGY: *Professors* Flahault, Sabatier; *MM.* Pavillard, Soulier.

FACULTÉ DE DROIT DE MONTPELLIER.
Professors and Lecturers.

POLITICAL SCIENCE: *Professor* Gide; *MM.* Brouilhet, Chauvin.
LAW: *Professors* Brémond, Charmont, Chausse, Glaize, Laborde, Laurens, Meynial, Valabrègue, Vigié; *MM.* Barde, Declareuil, Valéry.

FACULTÉ DE MÉDECINE DE MONTPELLIER.
Professors and Lecturers.

MEDICINE.

Professors Bertin-Sans, Bosc, Carrieu, Ducamp, Estor, Forgue, Gilis, Granel, Grasset, Grynfeltt, Hamelin, Hedon, Imbert, Mairet, Rauzier, Rodet, Sarda, Tédenat, Truc, Vialleton, Ville; *MM.* Baumel, Brousse, Delezenne, Espagne, Estor, François, Galavielle, Itié, Lapeyre, Lecercle, Moitessier, Mouret, Puech, de Rouville, Vallois.

NANCY, France.

UNIVERSITÉ DE NANCY.

This university, founded in 1572, comprises the Faculties of Arts, Science, Law and Medicine, a School of Pharmacy, and a Professional School. There is an influential branch of the *Comite de Patronage des Étudiants Étrangers* at Nancy, which has done much for the benefit of foreign students.

FACULTÉ DES LETTRES DE NANCY.
Professors and Lecturers.

ARTS.

LANGUAGES. — CLASSICAL: *Professors* Thiaucourt, Martin; *MM.* Collignon, Couve
GERMANIC: *M.* Lichtenberger.
ROMANCE: *Professor* Krantz; *M.* Étienne.
LITERATURE: *Professor* Grucker.
COMPARATIVE PHILOLOGY: *M.* Cousin.
PHILOSOPHY: *M.* Souriau.
HISTORY: *Professors* Diehl, Pfister; *M.* Pariset.
ARCHÆOLOGY: *Professor* Diehl.
GEOGRAPHY: *Professor* Auerbach.

FACULTÉ DES SCIENCES DE NANCY.

Professors and Lecturers.

SCIENCE.

MATHEMATICS AND ASTRONOMY: *Professors* Floquet, Molk; *MM.* Lacour, Vogt.
PHYSICS: *Professors* Bichat, Blondlot; *M.* Perreau.
CHEMISTRY: *Professors* Arth, Haller, Petit; *MM.* Guntz, Müller.
MINERALOGY: *Professor* Thoulet.
GEOLOGY AND GEOGRAPHY: *MM.* Millot, Nicklés.
BIOLOGY: *Professors* Friant, Le Monnier; *MM.* Cuénot, Gain, Saint-Remy.
AGRICULTURE: *Professor* Petit.

FACULTÉ DE DROIT DE NANCY.

Professors and Lecturers.

POLITICAL SCIENCE: *Professor* Garnier; *M.* Liégeois.
LAW: *Professors* Beauchet, Binet, Blondel, Bourcart, Chrétien, Gardeil, Gavet, Lombard, Lederlin, Liégeois, Carré de Malberg, May; *M.* Melin.

FACULTÉ DE MÉDECINE DE NANCY.

Professors and Lecturers.

MEDICINE.

Professors Baraban, Bernheim, Charpentier, Chrétien, Demange, Garnier, Gross, Herrgott, Heydenreich, Macé, Meyer, Nicolas, Prenant, Schmitt, Simon, Spillmann, Vuillemin, Weiss; *MM.* Étienne, Février, Froelich, Guérin, Guilloz, Haushalter, Jacques, Parisot, Rohmer, Schuhl, Zilgien.

POITIERS, France.

UNIVERSITÉ DE POITIERS.

This university, founded in 1431, comprises Faculties of Arts, Science and Law, and a Preparatory School of Medicine and Pharmacy.

FACULTÉ DES LETTRES DE POITIERS.

Professors and Lecturers.

ARTS.

LANGUAGES.—CLASSICAL: *Professors* Ernault, Hild.
ENGLISH: *M.* Castelain.
ROMANCE: *MM.* Arnould, Laumonier.
LITERATURE: *Professor* Parmentier.
COMPARATIVE PHILOLOGY: *M.* Audouin.
PHILOSOPHY: *Professor* Luguet; *M.* Mauxion.
HISTORY: *Professor* Carré; *M.* Boissonade.
ARCHÆOLOGY: *M.* Lièvre.

MINERALOGY AND GEOLOGY: *Professor* Lartet; *M.* Caralp.
BIOLOGY: *Professors* Leclerc du Sablon, Moquin-Tandon, Roule; *MM.* Jammes, Prunet.
AGRICULTURE: *M.* Fabre.

FACULTÉ DE DROIT DE TOULOUSE.

Professors and Lecturers.

POLITICAL SCIENCE: *Professor* Hoques-Fourcade.
LAW: *Professors* Bonfils, Bressolles, Brissaud, Campistron, Deloume, Despiau, Hauriou, Mérignhac, Paget, Rouard de Card, Timbal, Vidal, Wallon; *M.* Fraissaingea.

FACULTÉ MIXTE DE MÉDECINE ET DE PHARMACIE DE TOULOUSE.

Professors and Lecturers.

MEDICINE.

Professors Abélous, André, Braemer, Caubet, Chalot, Charpy, Crouzat, Dupuy, Frébault, Herrmann, Jeannel, Labéda, Mossé, Pénières, Rémond, Saint-Ange, Tapie, Tourneux; *MM.* Aldibert, Audry, Bézy, Biarnès, Garrigou, Gérard, Guilhem, Guiraud, Lamic, Marie, Maurel, Morel, Rispal, Secheyron, Soulié, Suis, Vieusse.

FACULTÉ LIBRE DES LETTRES DE TOULOUSE.

Professors and Lecturers.

ARTS.

LANGUAGES. — CLASSICAL: *Professors* Gimazanes, Montaut, Morlais; *M.* Valentin.
ROMANCE: *Professor* Arnaud.
MODERN: *Professor* de Suplicy.
LITERATURE: *Professor* Couture.
COMPARATIVE PHILOLOGY: *Professors* Couture, Samouilhan.

PHILOSOPHY: *Professor* Montagne.
ARCHÆOLOGY: *Professor* Saint-Raymond.

SCIENCE.

MATHEMATICS: *Professors* Domec, Thomas.
PHYSICS AND CHEMISTRY: *Professor* Senderens.

GERMANY.

The universities of Germany are state institutions, supported by the Government and subject to the Ministers of Education of the several States in which they are situated. They have, however, an independent legal personality, and are to a great extent self-governing. At most of the universities the Minister of Education is represented by the Curator, Chancellor, or Vice-Chancellor, whose duty it is to look after the state interests and to manage the finances of the university. When this official is wanting the universities are directly under the Ministers.

Each university comprises four Faculties, namely, the Faculties of Philosophy (Arts and Science), Law, Medicine, and Theology; by each of these Faculties courses of lectures, seminary, and laboratory work are provided, and the degree of Doctor is given to matriculated students who have passed the final examination and fulfilled certain requirements, which vary slightly with the different universities. It is the custom for students to go from one university to another, returning for their degrees to the university of their choice.

There are in Germany twenty universities, the largest and most important being the universities of Berlin, Leipzig and Munich. A German student when applying for permission to matriculate at a university is expected to hold the *Gymnasialabiturienten Zeugniss*, the certificate that he has attended the specified course in a *Gymnasium* and passed the final examination. Foreign students must give proof of an equal degree of preparation.

Women are as a rule admitted only as hearers to courses in the Philosophical Faculty of the several universities, although in some cases they have also attended lectures in the Faculties of Law and Medicine.*

The Degree of Doctor of Philosophy has been granted to women by the Universities of Berlin, Freiburg, Göttingen, Heidelberg and Tübingen, and at these universities women have a certain recognised position as hearers, although they are not allowed to matriculate. At most of the universities in Prussia properly qualified women are permitted to attend courses in the Philosophical Faculty if they obtain the permission of the Rector of the university and of the individual professors whose courses they desire to hear. They have, however, no rights, and are not counted as students. Any particular application for admission may be refused. The other universities of Germany vary in regard to the admission of women.

The reading-rooms of the university libraries are as a rule open to women as part of the general public on the same conditions as to men. Women who are studying at the various universities are in every case permitted to take books out of the libraries upon the same conditions as men.

The academic year begins in October and is divided into two semesters, the winter semester which extends from the middle of October to the middle of March, and the summer semester which extends from the middle of April to the middle of August. The lectures do not, however, generally begin until a week or ten days after the date officially announced as the beginning of the semester.

The list of courses to be given in one semester is not published until the end of the preceding semester. Official lists of lectures (*Vorlesungsverzeichnissen*) of the universities are sold at the bookshops, they are are not distributed by the uni-

---

* Wherever courses in Law and Medicine have been opened to women, special mention is made of the fact under the head of the separate universities.

versities themselves. The *Deutscher Universitäts-Kalender*, published each semester in Berlin, gives the courses offered during the semester at all the German universities.

The fees paid at German universities are of two kinds, those paid to the universities themselves and those paid to the individual professors. Each university charges students a small fee on entering for matriculation; 18 M. ($4.50) for first matriculation, 9 M. ($2.25) for students coming from another university; on leaving, for a certificate of work done 14 M. ($3.50), in addition to a fee each semester for the right to hear lectures (5 M., $1.25). For each course attended a fee is also paid to the professor giving the course, except in those cases where the course is expressly stated to be free (3–5 M., $.75–$1.25, for one hour a week during one semester). A much larger fee is paid to the university for a Doctor's degree (300–400 M., $75–$100).*

The fees paid by women vary in the different universities. Where women are officially admitted they may pay the university fee for those privileges which they enjoy. Where they attend lectures by the permission of the individual professors without the sanction of the Ministry, they pay the fees to the professors.

<small>The whole question of the admission of women to the universities has given rise to much discussion in Germany and is still far from being settled. Many Germans regard the higher education of women as undesirable and there is a strong objection manifested by a large number of the professors and students alike to the admission of women to the universities. In the last few years, however, great advances have been made and the foundation of several *gymnasia* for girls on exactly the same plan as those for boys has made it possible for German women to obtain adequate preparation for the universities.

The seriousness of purpose and the ability of individual women who have studied in Germany has, it is believed, done much towards destroying the prejudice against women students in the minds of the professors under whom they have worked. Each woman who applies for permission to attend lectures should bear in mind the great responsibility she incurs in thus becoming, as it were, a test case, by which other similar cases in the future will be judged. If she is insufficiently prepared or lacking in seriousness of purpose in her work she cannot fail to do harm to the cause of women's education in Germany. Women students should also bear in mind that the conditions of German</small>

---

* The above figures are approximate.

life are very different from the conditions of American life, and that any failure to observe the established customs of the people among whom they are living and whose hospitality they are enjoying, is likely to bring women students as a class into discredit.

BERLIN, Prussia.
KÖNIGL. FRIEDRICH-WILHELMS-UNIVERSITÄT.

Until within the last few years the University of Berlin, which was founded in 1809, was entirely closed to women, and no degrees had ever been granted by it to women. At present individual women are in general permitted by the University to attend lectures as *gastzuhörerinnen*, provided that they can prove that they are properly prepared.

The application to be allowed to attend lectures, accompanied by the passport and testimonials of the applicant, should be left at the *Kuratorium*. After the applicant receives notice from the authorities that she is admitted she should go to the *Universitäts-Sekretariat* for the *Rektorats-Erlaubniss-Schein*. After the individual professors have given the applicant permission to attend their lectures the Quaestor of the University registers and regularly admits the student.

Women students are sometimes admitted to lectures when, on account of lack of space, entrance to the seminaries and laboratories is refused them, but some professors have opened both their seminaries and their laboratories to individual women.

Practically all the courses offered by the Philosophical Faculty are now open to women, and courses in Law and Physiology have been attended by women, but in Anatomy and Medicine the classes are in general closed.

In 1898-99 two hundred and forty-one women were studying at the University of Berlin; a room in the University building has been set apart for their use. One woman has recently obtained the degree of Doctor in the Philosophical Faculty.

For information as to dates of semesters, fees, etc., see pp. 62-64.

Professors and Lecturers.

ARTS.
LANGUAGES. — SEMITIC : *Professors* Barth, Dieterici, Sachau, Schrader ; *Docents* Erman, Sethe, Winckler.

INDO-IRANIAN : *Professors* Geldner, Weber ; *Docents* Oppert, Sieg.
CLASSICAL : *Professors* Diels, Hübner, Kirchhoff, Vahlen, v. Wilamo-

witz Möllendorff, Winter; *Docents* Kübler, Rothstein, Schöne, Thomas.
ENGLISH: *Professor* Brandl; *Reader* Harsley.
GERMANIC: *Professors* Brückner, Heusler, Hoffory, Roediger, E. Schmidt, Weinhold; *Docents* Cornicelius, Herrmann, Meyer.
ROMANCE: *Professors* Geiger, Tobler; *Docent* Schultz-Gora; *Readers* Hecker, Pariselle.
CHINESE: *Professor* Grube.
MONGOLIAN AND HISTORY OF BUDDHISM: *Docent* Huth.
ORIENTAL LANGUAGES SEMINAR: *Professors* Arendt, Berneker, Hassan Djelaled-din Fischer, Foy, Güssfeldt, Hartmann, Lange, Amin Maârbes, Mitsotakis, de Mugica. Neuhaus, Senga, Sid Gilani Schirkawi, Hsüeh Shen, Steinbach Vacha, Velten, Warburg, Abder-rahman Zaghlul.
COMPARATIVE PHILOLOGY: *Professor* John Schmidt.
PHILOSOPHY: *Professors* Dilthey, Paulsen, Runze, Stumpf, Zeller; *Docents* Dessoir, Döring, Hoppe, Lasson, Simmel, Schumann, Thiele.
POLITICAL SCIENCE: *Professors* Boeckh, Lass, v. Martitz, Meitzen, Reinhold, Schmoller, Sering, Wagner; *Docents* v. Halle, Hoeniger, Jastrow, v. Kaufmann, v. Wenckstern.
HISTORY: *Professors* Breysig, Delbrück, Hirschfeld, Köhler, Lenz, Mommsen, Scheffer-Boichorst, Schiemann; *Docents* Dessau, Hintze, Höniger, Klebs, Koepp, Koser, Kübler, Lehmann, Liesegang. Meinecke, Naudé, Oncken, Roloff, Seler, Spahn, Sternfeld, Tangl.
ART AND ARCHÆOLOGY: *Professors* Erman, Frey, Grimm, Kekulé, Winnefeld, Winter; *Docents* Dessau, Goldschmidt, Graef, Helmert, Kalkmann, Kern, Pernice, Schmid, Sethe.
PEDAGOGY: *Professor* Münch.
GEOGRAPHY: *Professors* v. Drygalski, v. Richthofen; *Docents* Dove, Kretschmer.

SCIENCE.

MATHEMATICS AND ASTRONOMY: *Professors* Bauschinger, Foerster. Frobenius, Fuchs, Hensel, Hettner, Knoblauch, Lehmann-Fi hés Planck, Scheiner, Schwarz; *Docents* Battermann, Hoppe, Marcuse.
PHYSICS: *Professors* v. Bezold, Blasius, Neesen, Planck, Warburg; *Docents* Arons, Assmann, du Bois, Krigar-Menzel, Pringsheim.
CHEMISTRY: *Professors* Biedermann, Fischer, Fock, Gabriel, Landolt, Liebermann, Pinner, Rammelsberg, Schneider, Sell, Tiemann, Van t'Hoff, Wichelhaus, Will; *Docents* v. Buchka, Harries, Hayduck, Jacobson, Jahn, Marckwald, Meyerhoffer, Reissert, Rosenheim, Schöpff, Schotten, Thoms, W. Traube, Windisch, Wohl.
MINERALOGY: *Professor* Klein; *Docents* Fock, Tenne, H. Traube.
GEOLOGY: *Professors* Berendt, Dames; *Docent* Jaekel.
BIOLOGY: *Professors* Ascherson, Engler, Garcke, Kny, Magnus, v. Martens, Moebius, Schulze, Schwendener, Wittmack; *Docents* Gilg, Heymons, Holtermann, Karsch, Kolkwitz, Lindau, von Luschan, Plate, Reinhardt, Schaudinn, Schumann, Volkens, Warburg, Zimmermann.
AGRICULTURE: *Professor* Orth.

LAW.

Professors Aegidi, Berner, Bornhak, Brunner, Dambach, Dernburg, Eck, Gierke, Hübler, Kahl, Kohler, Oertmann, Pernice, Rehme, Seckel, Zeumer; *Docents* Burchard, Heilborn, Jacobi, Kaufmann, Preuss, Schwartz, Stölzel.

MEDICINE.

Professors A. Baginsky, v. Bergmann, Bernhardt, Brieger, Busch, von Coler, Ehrlich, Engelmann, Eulenburg, Ewald, Fasbender, B. Fränkel, Fritsch, Gerhardt, Goldscheider, Gurlt, Gusserow, Henoch, Hertwig, Heubner, Hildebrand, Hirschberg, Horstmann, Israel, Jolly, Koch, König, Köppen, Lesser, Lewin, Leyden, Liebreich, Lucae, Mendel, Miller, Moeli, H. Munk. I. Munk, Nagel, Olshausen, Rose, Rubner, Salkowski, Schoe'er, Schweigger, Schweninger, Senator, Silex, Skrzeczka, Sonnenburg, Strassmann, Thierfelder, Trautmann, H. Virchow, R. Virchow, Wa'deyer, J. Woff,

M. Wolff; *Docents* B. Baginsky, Behrend, Benda, Boedeker, C. du Bois-Reymond, R. du Bois-Reymond, Bonhoff, Casper, Dührssen, A. Fraenkel, Gebhard, Gluck, Grawitz, Greeff, Grunmach, Günther, Guttstadt, Hansemann, Herter, Heymann, Hirschfeld, Jacobson, Jansen, Joachimstahl, Katz, Klemperer, Kobanck, König, R. Krause, W. Krause, Krönig, Laehr, Landau, Langerhans, Langgaard, Lassar, Lewinski, Lexer, Litten, Loewy, Martin, Mendelsohn, Meyer, Michaelis, Mitscherlich, I. Munk, Nagel, Neumann, Nitze, Oestreich, Ohlmüller, Oppenheim, Pagel, Perl, Pfeiffer, Posner, Puppe, Rabl-Rückhard, Rawitz, Remak, Riess, Rosenheim, Rosin, Ruge, de Ruyter, Salomon, Schelske, Schüller, Schultz, Stadelmann, Strassmann, Strauss, Tobold, Westphal, Wolpert, Zinn.

THEOLOGY.

Professors Benzinger, Deutsch, Gunkel, Harnack, Kaftan, Kleinert, Müller, Pfleiderer, Seeberg, von Soden, Strack, Weiss, Wobbermin; *Docents* Gennrich, Holl, Plath.

MUSIC.

Professors Bellermann, Fleischer; *Docent* Friedländer.

BONN, Prussia.

RHEINISCHE FRIEDRICH-WILHELMS-UNIVERSITÄT.

The university was founded in 1818 and is under the same general regulations as all the universities of Germany; see pp. 62–64.

Twenty-six women were attending courses in the university as hearers in the winter semester of 1898–99.

Holiday courses for women teachers are given in August by the university professors. The subjects are chiefly philosophical and philological.

Professors and Lecturers.

ARTS.

LANGUAGES.—SEMITIC: *Professor* Prym; *Docent* Nix.
 CLASSICAL: *Professors* Buecheler, Elter, Usener; *Docents* Brinkmann, Radermacher, Solmsen.
 INDO-IRANIAN: *Professor* Jacobi; *Docent* Solmsen.
 ENGLISH: *Professor* Trautmann.
 GERMANIC: *Professors* Franck, Litzmann, Wilmanns; *Docent* Drescher.
 ROMANCE: *Professor* Foerster; *Reader* Gaufinez.
 COMPARATIVE PHILOLOGY: *Professor* Jacobi.
 PHILOSOPHY: *Professors* Bender, Elter, Meyer, Neuhaeuser; *Docents* Erdmann, Wentscher.
 POLITICAL SCIENCE: *Professors* Dietzel, Gothein.
 HISTORY: *Professors* v. Bezold, Meister, Nissen, Ritter, Schmitt, Wiedemann; *Docents* Meister, Strack.
 ART AND ARCHÆOLOGY: *Professors* Justi, Küppers, Loeschke; *Docents* Clemen, Firmenich-Richartz.
 GEOGRAPHY: *Professor* Rein; *Docents* Philippson, Reinhertz.
 MUSIC: *Professor* L. Wolff.

SCIENCE.

MATHEMATICS: *Professors* Deichmüller, Lipschitz, Küstner, Kortum, Study; *Docents* Heffter, Mönnichmeyer.
 PHYSICS: *Professors* Kayser, Lorberg; *Docent* Pflüger.
 CHEMISTRY: *Professors* Anschütz, Partheil, Rimbach; *Docents* Binz, Heusler, Löb, Schroeter.
 MINERALOGY: *Professor* Laspeyres; *Docent* Kaiser.

GEOLOGY: *Professors* Pohlig, Schlüter; *Docent* Rauff.
BIOLOGY: *Professors* Borgert, Ludwig, Strasburger; *Docents* Fischer, König, Noll, Strubell, Voigt.
AGRICULTURE: *Docent* von der Goltz.

LAW.

Professors Bergbohm, Cosack, Crome, Hübner, Hüffer, Krüger, Landsberg, Loersch, Pflüger, v. Schulte, Seuffert, Zitelmann.

MEDICINE.

Professors Binz, Doutrelepont, Finkelnburg, Finkler, Fritsch, Fuchs, Geppert, la Valette St. George, Koester, Leo, v. Mosengeil, Nussbaum, Pelmann, Peters, Pflüger, Saemisch, Schede, Schiefferdecker, Schultze, Ungar, Walb, Witzel; *Docents* Bleibtreu, Boennecken, Bohland, Burger, Dreser, Eschweiler, Graff, Hummelsheim, Jores, J. Kocks, W. Kocks, Krukenberg, Kruse, Petersen, Pletzer, Rieder, Schmidt, Schöndorff, Schröder, Schultze, Thomsen, Wendelstadt, Wolters.

THEOLOGY, PROTESTANT.

Professors Bratke, Goebel, Grafe, Kamphausen, Meinhold, Ritschl, Sachsse, Sell, Sieffert; *Docents* Meyer, Simons.

THEOLOGY, CATHOLIC.

Professors Englert, Esser, Felten, Kellner, Kaulen, Kirschkamp, Langen, Schrörs; *Docent* Rauschen.

BRESLAU, Prussia.

KÖNIGLICHE UNIVERSITAT.

The University of Breslau, founded in 1506, admits women under the same restrictions as the University of Berlin. No degrees have as yet been granted by women by this University. Women who hold the *Gymnasialabiturientenzeugniss* are allowed to attend all the medical courses, including those in anatomy, but no one is admitted who does not hold the certificate in question. Thirty-one women were attending courses in the University in the winter semester of 1898–99. The general regulations are same as those of other German universities; see pp. 62–64.

Professors and Lecturers.

ARTS.

LANGUAGES.—SEMITIC: *Professors* Delitzsch, Fraenkel.
INDO-IRANIAN: *Professors* Hillebrandt, Hoffmann; *Docents* Brockelmann, Liebich.
CLASSICAL: *Professors* Förster, Müller, Norden, Skutsch, Zacher; *Docents* Cohn, Kroll, Wünsch.
ENGLISH: *Professor* Kolbing; *Lecturer* Pughe.
GERMANIC: *Professors* Nehring, Vogt; *Docents* Bobertag, Jiriczek, Koch.
ROMANCE: *Professor* Appel; *Lecturer* Pillet.
RUSSIAN: *Lecturer* Abicht.
COMPARATIVE PHILOLOGY: *Professors* Fick, Hillebrandt.
HISTORY OF LITERATURE: *Professor* Koch.
PHILOSOPHY: *Professors* Baeumker, Ebbinghaus, Freudenthal, Stern.
POLITICAL SCIENCE: *Professors* Auhagen, Sombart, Wolf.
HISTORY: *Professors* Caro, Grünhagen, Kaufmann, Schulte, Wilcken.
ART AND ARCHÆOLOGY: *Professor* Muther; *Docent* Semrau.

SCIENCE.

MATHEMATICS AND ASTRONOMY: *Pro-*

GERMANY. 69

fessors Franz, Rosanes, Sturm; *Docent* London.
PHYSICS: *Professors* Heydweiller, O. E. Meyer.
CHEMISTRY: *Professors* Ahrens, Ladenburg, Poleck, Weiske; *Docents* Küster, Scholtz.
MINERALOGY: *Professor* Hintze; *Docent* Milch.
GEOLOGY: *Professor* Frech; *Docents* Gürich, Milch.
GEOGRAPHY: *Professor* Partsch; *Docent* Leonhard.
BIOLOGY: *Professors* Brefeld, Chun, Ferdinand, Kükenthal, Pax, Stutzer; *Docents* Braem, Mez, Rohde, Rosen, Weberbauer.
ENGINEERING: *Docent* Beyer.
AGRICULTURE: *Professors* Ahrens, Holdefleiss, Luedecke, von Kümker, Stutzer; *Docents* Beyer, von Nathusius, Strauch.
FORESTRY: *Docent* Kayser.
VETERINARY SURGERY: *Professor* Metzdorf; *Docent* Strauch.

LAW.

Professors Beling, Brie, Bruck, Dahn, Fischer, Jörs, Leonhard, Schott; *Docent* Heymann.

MEDICINE.

Professors Born, Cohn, Czerny, Filehne, Flügge, Hasse, Hirt, Kast, Kolaczek, Küstner, Lesser, Magnus, Mikulicz, Neisser, Partsch, Ponfick, Richter, Röhmann, Uhthoff, Wernicke; *Docents* Alexander, Bonhoeffer, Bruck, Buchwald, Fränkel, Groenouw, Henke, Henle, Hiller, Hürthle, Jacobi, v. Kader, Kaiser, Keilmann, Kionka, Krienes, Kühnau, Kümmel, Mann, Peter, Pfannensteil, Reichel, Riegner, Sachs, Schäfer, Stern, Tietze.

THEOLOGY.

PROTESTANT: *Professors* Arnold, Cornill, Hahn, Kawerau, Löhr, Müller, Schmidt, Wrede; *Docents* Juncker, Schulze.
CATHOLIC: *Professors* Commer, König, Krawutzcky, Lämmer, Müller, Nikel, Nürnberger, Pohle, Probst, Schaefer, Scholz, Sdralek; *Docents* von Tessen-Wesierski.

ERLANGEN, Bavaria.

KGL. FRIEDRICH-ALEXANDERS-UNIVERSITÄT.

This university was founded in 1743, and the general regulations are the same as those of other German universities; see pp. 62–64.

Women are in general allowed to attend lectures at the three Bavarian Universities and also to take degrees in their philological and scientific departments. Nevertheless, a woman, who, after passing the final examinations of a gymnasium, wished to study medicine at this university has been refused permission to attend lectures in anatomy.

Five women were attending courses at the university during the winter semester of 1898–99.

Professors and Lecturers.

ARTS.

LANGUAGES.—SEMITIC: *Professor* Abel.
CLASSICAL: *Professors* Heerdegen, Römer.
GERMANIC: *Professors* Geiger, Steinmeyer.
ROMANCE: *Professor* Schneegans.
MODERN: *Professor* Varnhagen.

SANSKRIT AND COMPARATIVE PHILOLOGY: *Professor* Geiger.
PHILOSOPHY: *Professors* Class, Falckenberg.
POLITICAL SCIENCE: *Professors* Eheberg, Neuburg.
HISTORY: *Professors* Fester, von Hegel, Pöhlmann.
GEOGRAPHY: *Professor* Pechuel-Loesche; *Docent* Blanckenhorn.
ART AND ARCHÆOLOGY: *Professor* Flasch.
PEDAGOGY: *Professor* Römer.

SCIENCE.

MATHEMATICS AND ASTRONOMY: *Professors* Gordan, Nöther.
PHYSICS: *Professor* Wiedemann; *Docent* Schmidt.
CHEMISTRY: *Professors* Busch, Fischer, Paal.

MINERALOGY: *Professor* Lenk; *Docents* Blanckenhorn, v. Elterlein.
GEOLOGY: *Professor* Lenk.
BIOLOGY: *Professors* Fleischmann, Reess; *Docent* Schmidt.

LAW.

Professors Allfeld, Gengler, Hellwig, Jäger, Kipp, Rehm, Sehling.

MEDICINE.

Professors Eversbush, Fleischer, Frommel, Leo Gerlach, Graser, Hauser, Heim, von Heineke, Hermann, Kiesselbach, Penzoldt, Rosenthal, Specht, v. Strümpell; *Docents* Gessner, Heinz, v. Kryger, Müller, Schneider, Spuler.

THEOLOGY.

Professors Caspari, Ewald, Ihmels, Kolde, Lotz, Müller, Zahn; *Docent* Wiegand.

FREIBURG IM BREISGAU, Baden.

GROSHERZ. BAD. ALBERT-LUDWIGS-UNIVERSITÄT.

The University of Freiburg, founded in 1457, is one of the three universities of Germany that have granted the degree of Doctor to women. Women are admitted to university lectures under the same restrictions as at the University of Heidelberg. (See p. 75.) For the general regulations see pp. 62–64.

Professors and Lecturers.

ARTS.

LANGUAGES.—SEMITIC: *Professor* Reckendorf.
INDO-IRANIAN: *Professors* Holtzmann, Thumb.
CLASSICAL: *Professors* Hense, Kalbfleisch, Schmidt, Steup, Thurneysen.
ENGLISH: *Professor* Schröer.
GERMANIC: *Professors* Kluge, Meyer, Panzer, Weissenfels.
ROMANCE: *Professors* Baist, Green, Levy, Paufler.
COMPARATIVE PHILOLOGY: *Professors* Thumb, Thurneysen.
PHILOSOPHY: *Professors* Cohn, Grosse, Rickert, Riehl.

POLITICAL ECONOMY: *Professors* Fuchs, v. Schulze-Gaevernitz.
HISTORY: *Professors* Bienemann, Dove, Fabricius, Finke, Michael, v. Simson.
ART AND ARCHÆOLOGY: *Professor* Puchstein, Studniczka, Sutter; *Docent* Cornelius.
GEOGRAPHY: *Professor* Neumann.
PEDAGOGY: *Docent* Zürn.
MUSIC: *Docent* Hoppe.

SCIENCE.

MATHEMATICS AND ASTRONOMY: *Professors* Loewy, Lüroth, Rebman, Stickelberger.
PHYSICS: *Professors* Himstedt, Meyer.

CHEMISTRY: *Professors* Claus, Willgerodt; *Docents* Edinger, Fromm.
MINERALOGY: *Professors* Graeff, Steinmann.
GEOLOGY: *Professor* Boehm
BIOLOGY: *Professors* Gruber, Häcker, Oltmanns, Weismann; *Docent* Fritze.
AGRICULTURE: *Professor* v. Schulze-Gaevernitz.

LAW.

Professors Eisele, Merkel, von Rohland, Rosin, Rümelin, Schmidt, Stutz; *Docents* Schmezer, Sieveking.

MEDICINE.

Professors Bartels, Bass, Bloch, Bäumler, Emminghaus, Goldmann, Hegar, Hildebrand, v. Kahlden, Keibel, Killian, Kiliani, Kirn, Knies, Korn, Kraske, von Kries, Jacobi, Manz, Müller, Schinzinger, Schottelius, Sonntag, Wiedersheim, Wiedow, Ziegler; *Docents* Autenrieth, Bulius, Clemens, v. Dungern, Gaupp, Nagel, Reerink, Ritschl, Roos, Schüle, Sellheim, Treupel.

THEOLOGY.

Professors Baumgartner, Braig, Heiner, Hoberg, Keppler, Kraus, Krieg, Künstle, Rückert, Trenkle, Weber.

GIESSEN, Hesse.

GROSSHERZOGL. HESSISCHE LUDWIGS-UNIVERSITÄT.

This University was founded in 1607, and the general regulations are the same as those of other German universities; see pp. 62–64.

It is the first university in Germany to take action in regard to admitting women on the same footing as men. In January, 1899, the Senate decided by a large majority to admit women who have obtained the *Reifezeugniss* of a gymnasium or of a *Realschule* of the first order as *matriculated* students in the Faculties of Philosophy and Law. Up to the present no women have been admitted to the university.

Professors and Lecturers.

ARTS.

LANGUAGES.—INDO-IRANIAN: *Professor* Bartholomæ.
  CLASSICAL: *Professors* A. Dieterich, Gundermann.
  ENGLISH: *Professors* Pichler, Wetz.
  GERMANIC: *Professor* Behagel; *Docents* Collin, Pichler, Strack.
  ROMANCE: *Professors* Behrens, Pichler.
PHILOSOPHY: *Professor* Siebeck; *Docent* Kinkel.
POLITICAL SCIENCE: *Professor* Laspeyres.
HISTORY: *Professors* Höhlbaum, Oncken; *Docents* J. R. Dieterich, Kernemann.

ART AND ARCHÆOLOGY: *Professor* Sauer.
GEOGRAPHY: *Professor* Sievers.
PEDAGOGY: *Professor* Schiller.

SCIENCE.

MATHEMATICS AND ASTRONOMY: *Professors* Fromme, Netto, Pasch; *Docent* Haussner.
PHYSICS: *Professors* Fromme, Scholl, Wiener.
CHEMISTRY: *Professors* Elbs, Naumann; *Docents* Eidmann, Rhode, Schön, Schwarzmann.

MINERALOGY : *Professor* Brauns.
BIOLOGY : *Professors* Hansen, Spengel, v. Wagner.
AGRICULTURE : *Professors* Hess, v. Minden, Thaer, Wimmenauer.

LAW.

Professors Biermann, Braun, Frank, Günther, Heimburger, Jung, Leist, Schmidt.

MEDICINE.

Professors Bose, Bostroem, Eckhard, Fuhr, Gaehtgens, Gaffky, Geppert, Löhlein, Poppert, Riegel, Sommer. Steinbrügge, Sticker, Strahl, Vossius, Walther; *Docents* Baur, Henneberg, Köppe.

THEOLOGY.

PROTESTANT : *Professors* Baldensperger, Holtzmann, Kattenbusch, Köstlin, Krüger, Stade.

GÖTTINGEN, Prussia.
GEORG-AUGUSTS-UNIVERSITÄT.

The University of Göttingen, founded in 1737, is one of the four universities in Germany that have granted the degree of Doctor to women. In 1893 its doors were first opened to women students, and from the beginning a certain official position has been given to them, although they are not allowed to matriculate, and the application of any individual candidate for admission may be refused at the option of the university authorities.

The university library, reading rooms and the special reading rooms for separate subjects are open to women students as freely as to men students and upon the same conditions. Four women have obtained the degree of Doctor of Philosophy in this university within the last few years. Twenty-one women were attending courses in the University as hearers during the summer semester of 1898.

The mathematical seminary has issued a programme of study to aid students in choosing the most profitable arrangement of lectures, etc.

Fees are paid to the Quaestor of the University. The general regulations are the same as for other German Universities; see pp. 62–64.

Professors and Lecturers.

ARTS.
LANGUAGES. — SEMITIC : *Professors* Pietschmann, Rahlfs, Smend, Wellhausen ; *Docents* Lüders, Schulthess.
INDO-IRANIAN : *Professor* Kielhorn.

CLASSICAL : *Professors* Dilthey, Kaibel, Leo, Meyer ; *Docents* Schulten, Schulze, Wentzel.
ENGLISH : *Professor* Morsbach ; *Lector* Tamson.

GERMANIC: *Professors* Heyne, Roethe; *Docent* Meissner.
ROMANCE: *Professor* Stimming; *Lector* Sechehaye.
COMPARATIVE PHILOLOGY: *Professor* Schulze.
PHILOSOPHY: *Professors* Baumann, Müller, Peipers, Rehnisch.
POLITICAL SCIENCE: *Professors* Cohn, Ehrenberg, Lexis.
HISTORY: *Professors* Kehr, Krauske, Lehmann, Willrich; *Docent* Busold.
ART AND ARCHÆOLOGY: *Professor* Vischer.
GEOGRAPHY: *Professor* Wagner.
MUSIC: *Professor* Freiberg.

SCIENCE.

MATHEMATICS AND ASTRONOMY: *Professors* Hilbert, Klein, Schur, Voigt; *Docents* Ambronn, Bohlmann, Brendel, Sommer.
PHYSICS: *Professors* Des Coudres, Nernst, Riecke, Voigt; *Docents* Simon, Wiechert.
CHEMISTRY: *Professors* Fischer, Nernst, Polstorff, Wallach; *Docents* Abegg, Coehn, Koetz, Lorenz.
MINERALOGY: *Professor* Liebisch.

GEOLOGY: *Professor* von Koenen.
BIOLOGY: *Professors* Berthold, Ehlers, Peter; *Docents* Henking, Rhumbler.
AGRICULTURE: *Professors* Bürger, Fleischmann, Griepenkerl, Lehmann, E. Meyer, v. Seelhorst, Tollens.

LAW.

Professors André, von Bar, Detmold, Dove, Ehrenberg, Frensdorff, v. Hippel, Merkel, Planck, Regelsberger, v. Savigny.

MEDICINE.

Professors Aschoff, Beneke, Borattam, Braun, Bürkner, Cramer, Damsch, Droysen, Ebstein, Esmarch, Esser, Heitmüller, Hildebrand, Husemann, Jacobi, Kallius, König, Lohmeyer, Marmé, Meissner, Merkel, Meyer, Nicolaier, Orth, Rosenbach, Runge, Schmidt-Rimpler, Sultan; *Docents* v. Reichenbach, Schreiber.

THEOLOGY.

Professors Althaus, Bonwetsch, Knoke, Schäder, Schultz, Schürer, Smend, Tschackert, Wiesinger, Zorn; *Docents* Achelis, Bousset, Hackmann, Otto, Rahlfs, Wellhausen.

GREIFSWALD, Prussia.
KÖNIGLICHE UNIVERSITÄT.

The University of Greifswald, founded in 1456, admits women under the same restrictions as the University of Berlin. No degrees have as yet been granted to women by this university. A summer course in literature, philosophy, etc., is held from July 10th to July 28th. It is open to foreigners, both men and women and is largely attended.

The general regulations are the same as those of other German universities; see pp. 62–64.

Professors and Lecturers.

ARTS.
LANGUAGES.—SEMITIC: *Professor* Kessler.
ORIENTAL: *Professors* Ahlwardt, Zimmer; *Docent* Heller.
CLASSICAL: *Professors* Gercke, Körte.
ENGLISH: *Professor* Quiggin.

GERMANIC: *Professors* Bruinier, Reifferscheid, Siebs; *Docent* Stengel; *Reader* Conlet.
ROMANCE: *Professor* Brandin.
COMPARATIVE PHILOLOGY: *Professor* Zimmer.

PHILOSOPHY: *Professors* Rehmke, Schmekel, Schuppe.
POLITICAL SCIENCE: *Professors* Biermer, Stock, Struck, Waentig; *Docent* Schmoele.
HISTORY: *Professors* Bernheim, Pyl, Seeck, Ulmann; *Docents* Altmann.
ART AND ARCHÆOLOGY: *Professor* Preuner.
GEOGRAPHY: *Professors* Credner.

SCIENCE.
MATHEMATICS AND ASTRONOMY: *Professors* Study, Thomé.
PHYSICS: *Professors* Holtz, Richarz; *Docent* Schreber.
CHEMISTRY: *Professors* Limpricht, Schwanert; *Docents* Posner, Semmler.
MINERALOGY: *Professor* Cohen.
GEOLOGY: *Professor* Deecke.

BIOLOGY: *Professor* Schütt; *Docents* Moeller, Müller.

LAW.
Professors Bierling, Frommhold, Krückmann, Pescatore, Stampe, Stoerk, Weismann; *Docents* v. Marck, Medem.

MEDICINE.
Professors Arndt, Ballowitz, Beumer, Bier, Bonnet, Grawitz, Krabler, Landois, Löffler, Mosler, Peiper, Pernice, Rosemann, O. Schirmer, Schulz, Solger, Strübing, Tilmann, Triepel; *Docents* Busse, Gerulanos, Helferich, Hoffmann, Leick, Stoewer, v. Preuschen.

THEOLOGY.
Professors Bosse, Cremer, Haussleiter, Lütgert, v. Nathusius, Oettli, Schultze, Zöckler; *Docents* Lezius, Volck.

HALLE, Prussia.
VEREINIGTE FRIEDRICHS-UNIVERSITÄT HALLE-WITTENBERG.

In order to attend lectures at the University of Halle women students must obtain permission from the Prussian Minister of Education and from the individual professors whose courses they desire to hear.

In making application to the Minister the candidate must state the course of study to be pursued and, in so far as is possible, the names of the professors under whom she wishes to work. Fifteen women were attending courses as hearers during the winter semester of 1898–99; six of these attended the courses in medicine and were admitted to the lectures on anatomy.

The doctors and students attached to the hospitals in Halle have protested against the action of the medical faculty in admitting women to courses in medicine.

The general regulations are the same as for other German universities; see pp. 62–64.

Professors and Lecturers.
ARTS.
LANGUAGES.—SEMITIC: *Professor* Prätorius; *Docents* Fischer, Jacob.

INDO-IRANIAN: *Professors* Pischel, Zachariae; *Docent* Schmidt.

CLASSICAL: *Professors* Bechtel, Blass, Dittenberger, Wissowa; *Docents* Ihm, Maurenbrecher.
ENGLISH: *Professor* Wagner; *Reader* Thistlethwaite.
GERMANIC: *Professors* Burdach, Haym, Riehl, Strauch; *Docents* Bremer, Collitz, Meier, Saran, Schultze.
ROMANCE: *Professor* Suchier; *Docents* Heuckenkamp, Simon, Wechssler, Wiese.
COMPARATIVE PHILOLOGY: *Professors* Bechtel, Zachariae.
PHILOSOPHY: *Professors* Erdmann, Haym, Uphues, Vaihinger; *Docents* Husserl, Schwarz.
POLITICAL SCIENCE: *Professors* Conrad, Friedberg, Kähler.
HISTORY: *Professors* Droysen, Ewald, Hertzberg, Lindner, Meyer, Rachfahl; *Docents* Brode, von Heinemann, von Ruville, Sommerlad.
GEOGRAPHY: *Professor* Kirchhoff; *Docents* Schenck, Ule
ART AND ARCHÆOLOGY: *Professor* Robert; *Docents* Kautzsch, Wernicke.
PEDAGOGY: *Docent* Fries.
MUSIC: *Professor* Reubke.

SCIENCE.

MATHEMATICS AND ASTRONOMY: *Professors* Cantor, Eberhard, Gutzmer, Wangerin.
PHYSICS: *Professor* Schmidt; *Docent* Roloff.
CHEMISTRY: *Professors* Doebner, Volhard; *Docents* Baumert, Chess, Erdmann, Vorländer.

MINERALOGY: *Professor* Luedecke; *Docents* v. Kraatz-Koschlau.
GEOLOGY: *Professor* v. Fritsch.
BIOLOGY: *Professors* Grenacher, Klebs, O. Taschenberg; *Docents* Brandes, Schulz.
AGRICULTURE: *Professors* Albert, Kuehn, Maercker, Wüst; *Docents* Cluss, Disselhorst, Falke, Fischer, Freytag, Holdefleiss, Knoch, Lorenz, v. Mendel-Steinfels, Müller.

LAW.

Professors Arndt, Boretius, v. Bruenneck, van Calker, Endemann, Fitting, Heck, v. Hollander, Lastig, Liepmann, v. Liszt, Loening, Rietschel, Rosenfeld, Schulte, Stammler, Stein.

MEDICINE.

Professors Bernstein, v. Bramann, Bunge, Eberth, Fehling, Fränkel, Genzmer, Harnack, v. Hippel, Hitzig, Kohlschütter, v. Mering, Oberst, Pott, Roux, Schwarz, Schwartze, Seeligmüller, Weber; *Docents*, Braunschweig, Eisler, Endres, Grunert, Haasler, Heilbronner, v. Herff, Hessen, Hessler, Jensen, Koerner, Kromayer, Leser, Mehnert, Reineboth, Sobernheim, Vahlen.

THEOLOGY.

Professors Beyschlag, Eichhorn, Haupt, Hering, Kaehler, Kautzsch, Koestlin, Loofs, Reischle, Rothstein, Warneck; *Docents* Beer, Clemen, Ficker, Scheibe, Stange, Steuernagel.

HEIDELBERG, Baden.

GROSSHERZOGLICHE RUPRECHT-KARLS-UNIVERSITÄT.

The University of Heidelberg, founded in 1386, has granted the degree of Doctor to several women. Women who obtain the permission of the Dekan of the Faculty in question and of the individual professors may attend lectures at the university. The seminaries and laboratories of certain professors have been opened to individual women. Twelve women were attending courses in the university as hearers during the winter semester of 1898-99.

Permission to take the Doctor's examination is granted by the Philosophical Faculty, each case being considered separately by the Faculty.

Fees are paid to the Quaestor of the University. The general regulations are the same as for other German universities; see pp. 62-64.

Professors and Lecturers.

ARTS.

LANGUAGES.—INDO-IRANIAN: *Professors* Bezold, Brünnow, Lefmann, Osthoff, Sütterlin.

CLASSICAL: *Professors* Crusius, Osthoff, Schöll; *Docent* Baumstark.

ENGLISH: *Professors* Hoops, Ihne.

GERMANIC: *Professors* Braune, Kahle, Meyer, von Waldberg, Wunderlich; *Docents* Ehrismann, Waag.

ROMANCE: *Professor* Neumann; *Docents* Schneegans, Vossler.

COMPARATIVE PHILOLOGY: *Professors* Brandt, Lefman.

PHILOSOPHY: *Professors* K. Fischer, Hensel; *Docent* Arnsperger.

POLITICAL SCIENCE: *Professors* Leser, Weber; *Docent* Kindermann.

GEOGRAPHY: *Professors* Hettner, Wolf.

HISTORY: *Professors* v. Domaszewski, Erdmannsdörffer, Kleinschmidt, Koch, Neumann, Schäfer, Scherrer; *Docent* Cartellieri.

ART AND ARCHÆOLOGY: von Duhn, Eisenlohr, Thode, Zangemeister.

PEDAGOGY: *Professor* Uhlig.

MUSIC: *Professor* Wolfrum.

SCIENCE.

MATHEMATICS AND ASTRONOMY: *Professors* Cantor, Eisenlohr, Koehler, Königsberger, Landsberg, Valentiner, Wolf.

PHYSICS: *Professor* Quincke; *Docent* Precht.

CHEMISTRY: *Professors* Auwers, Bornträger, Brühl, Bunsen, Curtius, Gattermann, H. Goldschmidt, Horstmann, Jannasch, Knövenagel, Krafft; *Docent* Dittrich.

MINERALOGY: *Professors* v. Goldschmidt, Osann, Rosenbusch.

GEOLOGY: *Professors* Rosenbusch, Salomon, Sauer, Schmidt.

BIOLOGY: *Professors* Askenasy, Bütschli, Haller, Koch, Pfitzer, Schuberg; *Docent* Lauterborn.

AGRICULTURE: *Professor* Stengel.

LAW.

Professors Bekker, Buhl, Jellinek, Karlowa, von Kirchenheim, v. Lilienthal, Meyer, Schröder, Seng, Strauch; *Docents* Affolter, Hatschek, His, Mittermaier, Schmidt.

MEDICINE.

Professors Arnold, v. Beck, Cramer, Czerny, Dinkler, Erb, Ernst, Ewald, Fleiner, Gegenbaur, Gottlieb, Bessel-Hagen, Hoffmann, Jordan, Jurasz, Kaiser, Kehrer, Klaatsch, Knauff, Kraepelin, Kühne, Leber, Lossen, Maurer, Oppenheimer, Passow, Schottländer, Vierordt, Weiss; *Docents* Aschaffenberg, Bettmann, Brauer, Cohnheim, Fischer, Göppert, Hammer, v. Hippel, Marwedel, Nissl, Petersen, Schaeffer, Schmidt, Vulpius.

THEOLOGY.

Professors Bassermann, Deissmann, Grützmacher, Hausrath, Kneucker, Lemme, Merx, Rohrhurst, Troeltsch; *Docent* Schmitthenner.

JENA, Saxe-Weimar.
GROSSHERZOGL. UND HERZOGL. SÄCHSISCHE GESAMT-UNIVERSITÄT.

This university, founded in 1558, is under the same general regulations as other German universities; see pp. 62-64.

Women are not allowed to attend lectures at the university, but are admitted as candidates for the Doctor's degree provided they have attended a university as matriculated students for at least six semesters and have had the required previous training.

Holiday courses for women teachers and others are held by the university professors in August. The subjects are philosophy, philology, the natural sciences, pedagogy, history of religion, and there are courses in the German language and literature for foreigners.

Professors and Lecturers.

ARTS.

LANGUAGES.—SEMITIC: *Professor* Wilhelm; *Docent* Hilgenfeld.
 INDO-IRANIAN: *Professors* Cappeller, Delbrück, Schrader, Vollers, Wilhelm.
 CLASSICAL: *Professors* Gelzer, Götz, Hirzel; *Docent* Schlösser.
 GERMANIC: *Professors* Leitzmann, Michels.
 ENGLISH: *Reader* Keller.
 ROMANCE: *Professor* Cloëtta.
COMPARATIVE PHILOLOGY *Professors* Delbrück, Schrader.
PHILOSOPHY: *Professors* Eucken, Liebmann; *Docent* Dinger.
POLITICAL SCIENCE: *Professor* Pierstorff; *Docent* Anton.
HISTORY: *Professors* Gelzer, Liebenam, Lorenz; *Docents* Keutgen, Mentz, S. Stoy.
GEOGRAPHY: *Professor* Dove.
ART AND ARCHÆOLOGY: *Professors* Gaedechens, Noack; *Docent* Weber.
PEDAGOGY: *Professor* Rein; *Docent* Stoy.

SCIENCE.

MATHEMATICS AND ASTRONOMY: *Professors* Abbe, Frege, Schäffer, Thomae; *Docent* Knopf.
PHYSICS: *Professors* Auerbach, Schäffer, Winkelmann; *Docents* Duden, Straubel.
CHEMISTRY: *Professors* Knorr, Wolff; *Docent* Gaenge.
GEOLOGY: *Professors* Linck, Walther; *Docent* Steuer.
BIOLOGY: *Professors* Detmer, Haeckel, Pick, Stahl, Ziegler.
AGRICULTURE: *Professors* Edler, Pfeiffer, Settegast.

LAW.

Professors Danz, Kniep, Langenbeck, Leist, Löning, Rosenthal, Schoen, Schultze, Thon.

MEDICINE.

Professors v. Bardeleben, Biedermann, Binswanger, Engelhardt, Fürbringer, Gärtner, Kessel, Krehl, Matthes, Müller, Riedel, Schillbach, Schultze, Seidel, Skutsch, Stintzing, Verworn, Wagenmann, Ziehen; *Docents* Braus, Gumprecht, Hertel, Schulz, Witzel.

THEOLOGY.

Professors Drews, Hilgenfeld, Nippold, Seyerlen, Siegfried, Wendt; *Docents* Baentsch, von Dobschütz.

KIEL, Prussia.
KÖNIGLICHE CHRISTIAN-ALBRECHTS UNIVERSITÄT.

The University of Kiel was founded in 1665. The general regulations are the same as those of other German universities; see pp. 62-64.

Eleven women were attending courses in the university as hearers during the winter semester of 1898–99.

KÖNIGSBERG.

Professors and Lecturers.

ARTS.

LANGUAGES.—SEMITIC: *Professor* Hoffmann; *Docent* Lidzbarski.
INDO-IRANIAN: *Professor* Oldenberg.
CLASSICAL: *Professors* Bruns, Schöne.
ENGLISH: *Professor* Sarrazin; *Reader* Gough.
GERMANIC: *Professors* Gering, Kauffmann; *Docents* Groth, Stosch, Uhl, Wolff.
ROMANCE: *Professor* Körting; *Reader* Schenk.
COMPARATIVE PHILOLOGY: *Professor* Oldenberg; *Docent* Cauer.
PHILOSOPHY: *Professors* Deussen, Martius; *Docents* Adickes.
POLITICAL SCIENCE: *Professors* Hasbach, Seelig; *Docent* Tönnies.
GEOGRAPHY: *Professor* Krümmel.
HISTORY: *Professors* Rodenberg, Schirren, Volquardsen; *Docent* Unzer.
ART AND ARCHÆOLOGY: *Professors* Milchhoefer, Matthaei; *Docents* Ehrenberg.
MUSIC: *Docent* Stange.

SCIENCE.

MATHEMATICS AND ASTRONOMY: *Professors* Harzer, Kreutz, Pochhammer, Stäckel.
PHYSICS: *Professors* Ebert, Karsten, Lenard, Weber.
CHEMISTRY: *Professors* Claisen, Rügheimer; *Docents* Berend, Biltz, Emmerling, Stoehr.
MINERALOGY: *Professor* Lehmann.
GEOLOGY: *Professors* Haas, Lehmann; *Docent* Stolley.
BIOLOGY: *Professors* Brandt, Reinke; *Docents* Apstein, Karsten, Lohmann, Schneidemühl, Vanhoffen.
AGRICULTURE: *Profes or* Rodewald.

LAW.

Professors Frantz, Hänel, Kleinfeller, Niemeyer, Pappenheim, Schlossmann, Weyl; *Docents* Leidig, Thomsen.

MEDICINE.

Professors Bier, Bockendahl, Falck, Fischer, Flemming, Heller, Hensen, Hoppe-Seyler, Petersen, Quincke, v. Spee, v. Starck, Völckers, Werth; *Docents* Doehle, Fricke, Glaevecke, Heermann, Hochhaus, Hölscher, Jessen, Kirchhoff, Klein, Meves, Nicolai, Paulsen, Seeger.

THEOLOGY.

Professors Baumgarten, Bosse, Klostermann, Mühlau, v. Schubert, Titius; *Docent* Riedel.

KÖNIGSBERG, Prussia.

KÖNIGLICHE ALBERTUS-UNIVERSITÄT.

The University of Königsberg was founded in 1544. The general regulations are the same as those of other German universities; see pp. 62–64. Thirty-four women were attending courses in the university as hearers in the winter semester, 1898–99.

Professors and Lecturers.

ARTS.

LANGUAGES.—SEMITIC: *Professor* Jahn; *Docents* Peiser, Rost.
INDO-IRANIAN: *Professor* Franke.
CLASSICAL: *Professors* Brinkmann, Friedländer, Jeep, Ludwich, Rossbach; *Docent* Tolkiehn.
ENGLISH: *Professors* Kaluza, Kissner.
GERMANIC: *Professors* Baumgart, Schade; *Docent* Uhl.
ROMANCE: *Professor* Kissner; *Reader* Scharff.
COMPARATIVE PHILOLOGY: *Professor* Bezzenberger.

PHILOSOPHY: *Professors* Busse, Walter.
POLITICAL SCIENCE: *Professors* Diehl, Gerlach, Umpfenbach.
HISTORY: *Professors* Erler, Lohmeyer, Prutz, Rühl, Schubert; *Docent* Immich.
GEOGRAPHY: *Professor* Hahn.
ART AND ARCHÆOLOGY: *Professor* Händcke; *Docent* Ehrenberg.

SCIENCE.

MATHEMATICS AND ASTRONOMY: *Professors* Franz Meyer, Saalschütz, Schoenflies, Struve, Volkmann; *Docents* Cohn, Rahts, Vahlen.
PHYSICS: *Professors* Pape, Volkmann; *Docent* Wiechert.
CHEMISTRY: *Professors* Blochmann, Klinger, Lossen; *Docents* Gutzeit, Löwenberg, Löwenherz.
MINERALOGY: *Professor* Mügge; *Docents* Jentzsch, Schellwien.
GEOLOGY: *Docents* Jentzsch, Schellwien.
BIOLOGY: *Professors* Braun, Luerssen; *Docent* Lühe.

AGRICULTURE: *Professors* Backhaus, Gisevius; *Docent* Rörig.

LAW.

Professors Gareis, Gradenwitz, Güterbock, Salkowski, Schirmer, Zorn; *Docent* Hubrich.

MEDICINE.

Professors Berthold, Braun, Caspary, v. Eiselsberg, v. Esmarch, Falkenheim, Grünhagen, Hermann, Jaffe, Kuhnt, Lichtheim, Meschede, Münster, Nauwerck, Neumann, Samuel, Schneider, Schreiber, Seydel, Stieda, Winter, Zander; *Docents* M. Askanazy, S. Askanazy, Braatz, Cohn, Döbbelin, Gerber, Hallervorden, Heisrath, Hilbert, Jäger, Kafemann, Lange, Leutert, Münster, Prutz, Rosinski, Stamer, Stetter, Valentini, Weiss.

THEOLOGY.

Professors Benrath, Dalmer, Dorner, Giesebrecht, Jacoby, Sommer, Voigt; *Readers* Hoffmann, Lackner, Pelka.

LEIPZIG, Saxony.

UNIVERSITÄT.

The University of Leipzig, founded in 1409, is not officially open to women, although women have for a number of years been permitted to attend certain courses at the university. They have no standing as students and are in no cases granted degrees. Permission to attend lectures must be obtained from the Minister of Education in Saxony. In many cases the seminaries and laboratories have been opened to women students.

In the Medical Faculty nearly all the courses except clinical courses and all laboratories except the anatomical laboratory have been attended by women.

The general regulations are the same as those of other German universities; see pp. 62-64.

Professors and Lecturers.

ARTS.

LANGUAGES.—INDO-IRANIAN: *Professors* Lindner, Socin, Windisch; *Docent* Stumme.

ORIENTAL: *Professors* Conrady, Zimmern; *Docents* Bloch, Schwarz.
CLASSICAL: *Professors* Cichorius, Im-

misch, Lipsius, Marx, Schmitt, Wachsmuth, Zarncke.
ENGLISH : *Professor* Wülker ; *Reader* Lake.
GERMANIC AND SLAVONIC : *Professors* v. Bahder, Elster, Hirt, Holz, Köster, Hasse, Leskien, Mogk, Scholvin, Sievers, Witkowski, Wollner.
ROMANCE: *Profe sors* Birch-Hirschfeld, F. Settegast, Weigand ; *Reader* Duchesne.
COMPARATIVE PHILOLOGY : *Professor* Brugmann ; *Docent* Hirt.
PHILOSOPHY : *Professors* Barth, Heinze, Strümpell, Wundt ; *Docents* Mentz, Richter, Störring, H. Wolff.
POLITICAL SCIENCE : *Professors* Bücher, Fricker, Hasse, Stieda ; *Docents* Lambert, Pohle, Richter, Walcker.
HISTORY : *Professors* Biedermann, Buchholz, Cichorius, Gardthausen, Lamprecht, Marcks, Seeliger ; *Docents* Brandenburg, Daenell, Götz, Kaerst, Salomon, Sörensen, Weissbach.
ART AND ARCHÆOLOGY : *Professors* Brockhaus, Schmarsow, Schneider, Schreiber, Steindorff, Studniczka; *Docent* Kautzsch.
GEOGRAPHY : *Professors* Ratzel, Sieglin; *Docents* Fischer, Hassert.
PEDAGOGY : *Professors* Barth, Richter, Volkelt.

SCIENCE.

MATHEMATICS AND ASTRONOMY : *Professors* Bruns, Engel, Hölder, Karl Mayer, Neumann, von Oettingen, Scheibner ; *Docents* Hausdorff, Nieper.
PHYSICS : *Professors* Drude, Wiedeburg, Wiener ; *Docents* O. Fischer, Knoblauch, Mentz.
CHEMISTRY : *Professors* Beckmann, Le Blanc, Ostwald, Weddige, Wislicenus; *Docents* Euler, Rassow, Stobbe, Wagner.

GEOLOGY : *Professors* Credner, Felix.
BIOLOGY : *Professors* Ambronn, Chun, A. Fischer, Fraisse, Looss, Marshall, Pfeffer, Schmidt, Simroth ; *Docent* zur Strassen.
MINERALOGY : *Professor* Zirkel.
AGRICULTURE: *Professors* Eber, Fischer, Howard, Kirchner, Strecker.

LAW.

Professors Binding, Burchard, v. Degenkolb, Friedberg, Goetz, Haepe, Hölder, Rieker, Schmidt, Sohm, Stein, Strohal, Voigt, Wach ; *Docents* Engelmann, Kloeppel, Stintzing, Triepel.

MEDICINE.

Professors Altmann, Barth, Birch-Hirschfeld, Boehm, Carus, Curschmann, Eigenbrodt, Fick, Fischer, Flechsig, Friedrich, Hagen, Held, Hennig, Hering, Hesse, Wilhelm His, Friedrich Albin Hoffmann, Franz Hofmann, Kockel, Kölliker, Romberg, Riehl, Sänger, Sattler, Schmidt, Schoen, Schroeter, Schwarz, Siegfried, Soltmann, Tillmanns, Trendelenburg, Winter, Zweifel ; *Docents* Dolega, Ficker, Friedheim, Friedländer, E. P. Friedrich, Garten, Haake, Heymann, Wilhelm His, Jr., F. B. Hofmann, Kaestner, Kollmann, Kroenig, Krückmann, Küster, Lange, von Lesser, Menge, Naumann, Pässler, Perthes, Schütz, Tschermak, Wagner, Wilms, Windscheid.

THEOLOGY.

Professors Brieger Dalman, Fricke, Gregory, Guthe, Hauck, Heinrici, Hofmann, Kirn, Kittel, Luthardt, Rietschel, Schnedermann, Thieme; *Docents* Bohmer, Hölscher, Kunze, Seesemann.

MUSIC.

Professor Kretzschmar; *Docents* Prüfer, Riemann.

MARBURG, Prussia.

UNIVERSITÄT.

The University of Marburg, founded in 1527, is open to women under the same restrictions as the University of Berlin; see p. 65.

GERMANY.

Twenty-three women were attending courses in the university as hearers during the summer semester, 1898, and ten during the winter semester, 1898-99.

The general regulations are the same as those of other German universities; see pp. 62-64.

Professors and Lecturers.

ARTS.

LANGUAGES.—SEMITIC: *Professor* Jensen.
  CLASSICAL: *Professors* Birt, Maass; *Docent* Thiele.
  ENGLISH: *Professor* Vietor; *Reader* Tilley.
  GERMANIC: *Professor* Schroeder; *Docent* Wrede.
  ROMANCE: *Professor* Koschwitz; *Reader* Doutrepont.
SANSKRIT AND COMPARATIVE PHILOLOGY: *Professors* Justi, Kretschmer, *Docent* Finck.
PHILOSOPHY: *Professors* Bergmann, Cohen, Natorp; *Docent* Kühnemann.
POLITICAL SCIENCE: *Professors* Oldenberg, Rathgen; *Docent* Waentig.
HISTORY: *Professors* v. Below, Brandi, Könnecke, Niese, von der Ropp; *Docents* Diemar, Judeich, Wenck.
GEOGRAPHY: *Professor* Fischer.
ART AND ARCHÆOLOGY: *Professors* von Drach, von Sybel.

SCIENCE.

MATHEMATICS AND ASTRONOMY: *Professors* Feussner, Hess, Schottky; *Docent* v. Dalwigk.

PHYSICS: *Professors* Feussner, Melde.
CHEMISTRY: *Professors* Fittica, Rathke, Schmidt, Zincke; *Docents* Fritsch, Gadamer, Schaum, Schenck.
MINERALOGY: *Professor* Bauer.
GEOLOGY: *Professor* Kayser.
BIOLOGY: *Professors* Kohl, Korschelt, Meyer; *Docent* Brauer.

LAW.

Professors Enneccerus, Lehmann, Leonhard, Sartorius, Träger, Wochenfeld, Westerkamp; *Docent* Meyer.

MEDICINE.

Professors Ahlfeld, Behring, Disse, Enderlen, Gasser, Hess, v. Heusinger, Kossel, Küster, Lahs, Mannkopff, Marchand, Meyer, Müller, Nebelthau, Ostmann, Tuczek, Wernicke; *Docents* Albrecht, Buchholz, Heine, Kühne, Saxer, Zumstein.

THEOLOGY.

Professors Achelis, von Baudissin, Cremer, Herrmann, Jülicher, Mirbt, Weiss, Werner; *Docents* Bauer, Kraetzschmar.

MUNICH, Bavaria.

KONIGL. LUDWIG-MAXIMILIANS-UNIVERSITÄT.

The university was founded in 1472, and is under the same general regulations as the other German universities; see pp. 62-64.

Advanced women students are allowed to attend certain lectures at the university as hearers provided that they can prove that they are sufficiently prepared. Application for admission should be made to the Minister of Education in Munich.

Professors and Lecturers.

ARTS.

LANGUAGES.—SEMITIC: *Professor* Hommel; *Docent* Dyroff.
INDO-IRANIAN: *Professors* Kuhn, von der Schulenberg; *Docents* Schermann, Simon.
CHINESE: *Docent* von der Schulenberg.
CLASSICAL: *Professors* v. Christ, v. Müller, v. Woelfflin; *Docents* Drerup, Oehmichen, von der Pfordten, Traube, Weyman.
BYZANTINE AND MODERN GREEK: *Professor* Krumbacher.
ENGLISH: *Professor* Schick; *Docent* Sieper; *Reader* Blinkhorn.
GERMANIC: *Professors* Muncker, Paul; *Docents* Borinski, Woerner.
ROMANCE: *Professor* Breymann; *Docent* Hartmann; *Reader* Pirson.
HISTORY OF MODERN LITERATURE: *Professor* Woerner.
COMPARATIVE PHILOLOGY: *Professor* Kuhn.
PHILOSOPHY: *Professors* Güttler, von Hertling, Lipps; *Docent* Cornelius.
POLITICAL SCIENCE: *Professors* Brentano, Gayer, Lotz, v. Mayr; *Docent* Wasserrab.
HISTORY: *Professors* Friedrich, Grauert, v. Heigel, Oberhummer, Riezler, Simonsfeld; *Docents* Doeberl, Mayr, Traube.
GEOGRAPHY: *Professor* Oberhummer.
ART AND ARCHÆOLOGY: *Professors* Furtwängler, Riehl, Riggauer; *Docents* Bulle, Weese.

SCIENCE.

MATHEMATICS AND ASTRONOMY: *Professors* Bauer, Ebermayer, Lindemann, Pringsheim, Seeliger; *Docents* Anding, Brunn, Doehlemann, Erk, Korn, v. Weber.
PHYSICS: *Professors* Graetz, von Lommel; *Docent* Donle.
CHEMISTRY: *Professors* v. Baeyer, Hofmann, Hilger, Koenigs, Muthmann, Thiele; *Docents* Bergeat, Dieckmann, Rothmund, Willstätter.
MINERALOGY: *Professor* Groth.
GEOLOGY: *Professors* Rothpletz, von Zittel; *Docents* Pompeckj, Weinschenk.
BIOLOGY: *Professors* Goebel, Hartig, Hertwig, Radlkofer, Ranke, Selenka; *Docents* Giesenhagen, Hefele, Hofer, Maas, Pauly, Solereder, v. Tubeuf.
AGRICULTURE: *Professors* Ebermayer, Endres, Mayer, Pauly, Weber

LAW.

Professors v. Amira, v. Bechmann, Birkmeyer, Grueber, Harburger, Hellmann, Loewenfeld, v. Maurer, v. Planck, Seuffert, v. Seuffert, v. Seydel, v. Sicherer, v. Stengel, Ullmann.

MEDICINE.

Professors J. Amann, Angerer, Bauer, Bezold, Bollinger, Hans Buchner, L. A. Buchner, Bumm, Emmerich, Herzog, Klausner, v. Kupffer, Messerer, Moritz, Oeller, Oertel, v. Pettenkofer, Posselt, v. Ranke, Rieder, v. Rothmund, Rückert, Schech, Seitz, v. Strümpell, Tappeiner, v. Voit, v. Winckel, v. Ziemssen; *Docents* J. A. Amann, Barlow, Brandl, Cremer, Dürck, Fessler, Frank, Gudden, Hahn, Haug, Hecker, Hofer, Klein, Kopp, Krummacher, Lange, v. Liebig, May, Mollier, Neumayer, Passet, Port, Salzer, Schloesser, Schmauss, Schmitt, Schönwerth, Seydel, v. Sicherer, Sittmann, v. Stubenrauch, Stumpf, Trumpp, Voit, Wolfsteiner, Ziegenspeck, Ziegler.

THEOLOGY.

Professors Atzberger, Bach, Bardenhewer, Knoepfler, Andreas Schmid, Alois Ritter v. Schmid, Schoenfelder, Silbernagl, Wirthmüller; *Docents* Dausch, Holzhey.

MUSIC.

Docents Sandberger, v. d. Pfordten.

GERMANY.

ROSTOCK, Mecklenberg.
GROSSHERZOGLICHE UNIVERSITÄT.

The University of Rostock has in individual cases permitted women who make teaching a profession to attend certain lectures of the Philosophical Faculty. Permission must be obtained from the Rector, the Vice-Chancellor and the professor concerned. The Ministry has asked for information in regard to these women students, and for the present the question of the admission of women to the university remains in abeyance.

The university was founded in 1419 and is under the same general regulations as the other German universities; see pp. 62–64.

Professors and Lecturers.

ARTS.

LANGUAGES.—INDO-IRANIAN: *Professor* Philippi.
CLASSICAL: *Professors* v. Arnim, Kern.
GERMANIC: *Professor* Golther.
ROMANCE: *Professors* Lindner, Zenker; *Docent* Robert.
PHILOSOPHY: *Professor* Ehrhardt.
POLITICAL SCIENCE: *Professor* Waentig.
HISTORY: *Professor* Schirrmacher; *Docent* Schäfer.
ART AND ARCHÆOLOGY: *Professor* Körte.

SCIENCE.

MATHEMATICS AND ASTRONOMY: *Professor* Staude.
PHYSICS: *Professors* Matthiessen, Wachsmuth.
CHEMISTRY: *Professor* Michaelis; *Docent* Stoermer.

MINERALOGY: *Professor* Geinitz.
GEOLOGY: *Professor* Geinitz.
BIOLOGY: *Professors* Falkenberg, Seeliger, Will; *Docent* Hegler.
AGRICULTURE: *Professor* Heinrich.

LAW.

Professors Bernhöft, v. Blume, Geffcken, Lehmann, Matthiass, Sachsse.

MEDICINE.

Professors Axenfeld, Barfurth, Garré, Gies, Kobert, Körner, Langendorff, Lubarsch, Martius, Pfeiffer, Schatz, Schuchardt, Albert Thierfelder, Theodor Thierfelder; *Docents* Reinke, Ricker.

THEOLOGY.

Professors Hashagen, Koenig, Nösgen, Schulze, Walther.

STRASSBURG, Alsace.
KAISER-WILHELMS-UNIVERSITÄT.

The University of Strassburg, founded in 1567, is not officially open to women. By the special permission of certain professors and without the sanction of the Ministry one or two advanced women students have been admitted, as a great exception, to certain of the university courses.

The general regulations are the same as those of other German universities; see pp. 62–64.

Professors and Lecturers.

ARTS.

LANGUAGES.—SEMITIC: *Professors* Euting, Keil, Landauer, Nöldeke; *Docent* Schwally.
INDO-IRANIAN: *Professor* Leumann.
CLASSICAL: *Professors* Friedländer, Keil, Michaelis, Reitzenstein, Schwartz, Thrämer; *Docents* Heinze, Miller.
ENGLISH: *Professor* Koeppel; *Reader* Robertson.
GERMANIC: *Professors* Henning, Martin; *Docents* Joseph, Röhrig.
ROMANCE: *Professor* Gröber; *Reader* Lopez.
COMPARATIVE PHILOLOGY: *Professor* Hubschmann.
PHILOSOPHY: *Professors* Windelband, Ziegler.
POLITICAL SCIENCE: See Law and Political Science.
HISTORY: *Professors* Bresslau, Neumann, Varrentrapp, Wiegand; *Docents* Bloch, Kromayer, Ludwig, Sackur.
GEOGRAPHY: *Professor* Gerland; *Docent* Hergesell.
ART AND ARCHÆOLOGY: *Professor* Dehio, Michaelis; *Docents* Heinze, Leitschuh, Spiegelberg.

SCIENCE.

MATHEMATICS AND ASTRONOMY: *Professors* Becker, Krazer, Reye, Roth, Timerding, Weber, Wellstein, Wislicenus; *Docents* Kobold.
PHYSICS: *Professors* Braun, Cohn; *Docent* Cantor.

CHEMISTRY: *Professors* Erlenmeyer, Fittig, Rose, Schaer; *Docent* Cantor.
MINERALOGY: *Docent* Bruhns.
GEOLOGY: *Professors* Benecke, Bücking; *Docent* Tornquist.
BIOLOGY: *Professors* Döderlein, Goette, Jost, Solms-Laubach.

LAW AND POLITICAL SCIENCE.

LAW: *Professors* van Calker, Heimberger, Laband, Lenel, Mayer, Merkel, Schultze, Sickel, v. Tuhr, Wlassak, Zimmermann.
POLITICAL SCIENCE: *Professors* Knapp, von Mayr, von Waltershausen; *Docent* Wittich.

MEDICINE.

Professors Bayer, Cahn, Ewald, F. E. Fischer, F. Fischer, Forster, W. A. Freund, Fürstner, Goltz, Hofmeister, Kohts, Kuhn, Laqueur, Lederhose, Levy, Madelung, Minkowski, Naunyn, Pfitzner, v. Recklinghausen, Schmiedeberg, Schwalbe, Stilling, Ulrich, Wolff; *Docents* Dreyfuss, Ehret, H. Freund, Gerhardt, Hoche, Jacobj, Jessen, Klein, Manasse, Schmidt, Siegert.

THEOLOGY.

Professors Budde, Ficker, Holtzmann, Lobstein, Lucius, Mayer, Nowack, Smend, Spitta; *Docent* Anrich.

MUSIC.

Professor Jacobsthal.

TÜBINGEN, Württemberg.

KONIGLICHE EBERHARD-KARLS UNIVERSITÄT.

The University of Tübingen was founded in 1477. The general regulations are the same as those of other German universities; see pp. 62–64.

Permission to attend lectures at the university is, in exceptional cases, granted to women by the Minister of Education in Stuttgart on application from the Academic Senate. As regards granting the Doctor's degree to women, the faculty and Chancellor decide in special cases. One woman has obtained the degree of Doctor in the department of Natural Science.

Professors and Lecturers.

ARTS.

LANGUAGES.—SEMITIC: *Docent* Seybold.
INDO-IRANIAN: *Professor* Garbe.
CLASSICAL: *Professors* von Herzog, Schmid.
ENGLISH: *Professor* Franz.
GERMANIC: *Professors* Fischer, Lange; *Docent* Bohnenberger.
ROMANCE: *Professors* Pfau, Voretzsch.
COMPARATIVE PHILOLOGY: *Professor* Garbe.
PHILOSOPHY: *Professors* v. Pfleiderer, v. Sigwart, Spitta; *Docent* Maier.
POLITICAL SCIENCE: *Professors* Anschütz, von Jolly, Leemann, Lorey, v. Neumann, von Schönberg, Speidel, Tröltsch.
HISTORY: *Professors* Busch, v. Heinemann; *Docents* Ernst, Günter, Marquart.
ART AND ARCHÆOLOGY: *Professors* Lange, von Schwabe.
PEDAGOGY: *Docent* Treuber.

SCIENCE.

MATHEMATICS AND ASTRONOMY: *Professors* v. Brill, Maurer, Stahl, Waitz.
PHYSICS: *Professors* Oberbeck, Waitz.
CHEMISTRY: *Professors* v. Hüfner, Paul, v. Pechmann; *Docents* Bülow, Küster, Mayer.

MINERALOGY: *Professor* Koken; *Docent* Wülfing.
GEOLOGY: *Professor* Koken.
BIOLOGY: *Professors* Blochmann, Hegelmaier, Vöchting; *Docents* Correns, Hesse, Mayer, Schmid.
AGRICULTURE: *Professors* Bühler, Leemann.

LAW.

Professors v. Franklin, Gaupp, Geib, v. Mandry, v. Meyer, Rümelin, v. Seeger, v. Thudichum, Wendt.

MEDICINE.

Professors v. Baumgarten, v. Bruns, Dennig, Döderlein, Froriep, Grützner, von Jürgensen, v. Liebermeister, v. Lenhossek, Oesterlen, Schleich, Siemerling, Vierordt, Winternitz, Wagenhaeuser; *Docents* Burker, Dietrich, Grünert, Henke, Hofmeister, Küttner, Qurin, Sarway, Walz, Wickel.

THEOLOGY.

PROTESTANT: *Professors* von Buder, Gottschick, Grill, Häring, Hegler, Schlatter, v. Weizsäcker; *Docent* Metzger.
ROMAN CATHOLIC: *Professors* Belser, von Funk, Koch, Sägmuller, Schanz, Vetter; *Docent* Möhler.

WÜRZBURG, Bavaria.

KÖNIGLICHE JULIUS-MAXIMILIANS UNIVERSITÄT.

The University of Würzburg was founded in 1402. Women are not generally admitted to the university, but in special cases may attend lectures if they obtain the consent of the Minister of Education and of the professor whose courses they wish to hear.

The general regulations are the same as those of other German universities; see pp. 62–64.

Professors and Lecturers.

ARTS.

LANGUAGES.—INDO-IRANIAN: *Professor* Jolly.
CLASSICAL: *Professors* Grasberger, Schanz, Sittl.
ENGLISH: *Professor* Förster.
GERMANIC: *Professor* Brenner; *Docent* Rötteken.
ROMANCE: *Professor* Stürzinger; *Docent* Hartmann; *Reader* Soisky.
COMPARATIVE PHILOLOGY: *Professor* Jolly.
PHILOSOPHY: *Professors* Külpe, Stölzle; *Docents* Marbe, Neudecker.
POLITICAL SCIENCE: (See Law and Political Science).
HISTORY: *Professors* Chroust, Henner, Unger.
GEOGRAPHY: *Professor* Regel; *Docent* Ehrenburg.
PEDAGOGY: *Professor* Grasberger.

SCIENCE.

MATHEMATICS AND ASTRONOMY: *Professors* Prym, Selling, Voss; *Docent* Haussner.
PHYSICS: *Professors* Medicus, Röntgen, Zehnder; *Docent* Wien.
CHEMISTRY: *Professors* Hantzsch, Medicus, Tafel, Wislicenus; *Docent* Reitzenstein.
GEOLOGY: *Professor* Beckenkamp.
BIOLOGY: *Professors* Boveri, Kraus; *Docents* Hauptfleisch, Spemann.

LAW AND POLITICAL SCIENCE.

LAW: *Professors* v. Burckhard, Mayer, Meurer, Piloty, Oetker, Schollmeyer; *Docents* Binder, Knapp.
POLITICAL SCIENCE: *Professor* Schanz.

MEDICINE.

Professors Fick, Geigel, Helfreich, Hoffa, Hofmeier, Kirchner, v. Kölliker, Lehmann, v. Leube, Matterstock, v. Michel, Riedinger, Rieger, v. Rindfleisch, Rosenberger, Schönborn, Schultze, Seifert, Stöhr; *Docents* Arens, Bach, Borst, Dieudonné, v. Franqué, Heidenhain, Michel, Müller, Nieberding, Schenck, Sobotta, Stubenrath.

THEOLOGY.

Professors Abert, Braun, Göpfert, Kihn, Merkle, Schell, Scholz, Stahl, Weber.

GREAT BRITAIN AND IRELAND.

ENGLAND AND WALES.

There are six universities in England and Wales: Cambridge, Durham, London, Oxford, Victoria and the University of Wales. These are in the main examining bodies and confer degrees on the results of examinations held by the examiners on their staff. Candidates are prepared for these examinations by colleges affiliated with the different universities. In British universities the candidate for the Bachelor's and Master's degrees may usually choose whether he will take the 'pass' or 'honours' examinations. The honours examinations vary greatly from the pass examinations both in standard and in the amount of specialisation required. At the universities of Oxford and Cambridge the honours examinations for the degree of B.A. are entirely special, the candidate being examined in mathematics, or in classics, or in natural science or in whatever branch he may select. There seems to be a tendency, at any rate at Cambridge, to reduce the amount of specialisation; a few years ago the mathematical 'Tripos' or honours examination was widened by the addition of some physical subjects. A proposal to require some knowledge of art and literature in the classical tripos has, however, just been defeated. At Oxford and Cambridge the universities appoint professors and lecturers who give lectures open to all students, but the greater part of the teaching is arranged for by the college authorities. London is at present merely an examining university, but after long discussion it has been decided to make it also a teaching university.

CAMBRIDGE, England.
THE UNIVERSITY OF CAMBRIDGE.

The University of Cambridge, founded in the 12th century, is a corporation which provides instruction in the various branches of knowledge and confers degrees in arts, science, law, medicine, theology and music on candidates who have fulfilled certain conditions in regard to residence at specified colleges and passed certain examinations. There are in Cambridge seventeen colleges and two public hostels for men students and there are a few non-collegiate students. Each college and hostel has its own staff of lecturers and tutors, and though university lectures given by university professors and lecturers are open to members of all the colleges, college lectures are in some cases open to students of specified colleges only. Preparation for the degree of B.A. occupies, in general, three years, only half of each year being spent in residence. A student who has obtained the B.A. degree undergoes no further examination for the degree of M.A. Persons over twenty-one years of age who present a diploma or certificate of graduation at a university are admitted as "Advanced Students" and permitted to pursue courses of advanced study or research under the guidance of the Degree Committee. They are allowed to take Tripos examinations after a shorter period of residence than is required of ordinary undergraduate students and may proceed to obtain a degree or a "certificate of research." They must apply to the registrary before the first of October for permission to become advanced students, and must be members of a college or hostel or of the body of non-collegiate students.

Women who desire to attend lectures in Cambridge must enter as students one of the two colleges for women in Cambridge, Girton College or Newnham College, residence at which confers certain privileges.

Women students who reside at Girton College (see p. 91), Newnham College (see pp. 92–93), or in Cambridge, as "out-students" of one of these colleges, are admitted, with a few exceptions, to all the university lectures, to certain of the college lectures and to most of the laboratories and museums. Women are, by special permission, allowed to read in the university library.

Women who have fulfilled, in connection with one of the above mentioned colleges, the conditions respecting length of residence and standing which men students are required to fulfil have been admitted, since 1881, to the Previous and Tripos (*i. e.*, honours) examinations of the university.

After each examination the examiners publish a list of the successful candidates, arranged either in classes and divisions or numbered in order of merit. The names of the men and women students are on separate lists, but the position taken by the women with reference to the men is shown and the standard is the same for each.

The question of granting degrees to women who have passed these examinations was brought before the Senate in 1896, and after a long discussion of the evidence collected by a syndicate appointed by the Senate it was proposed that women who had fulfilled the ordinary requirements for the B. A. and M. A. and higher degrees should be granted the *titles* of these degrees. This proposal was voted on on May 21st, 1897, and rejected by 1707 votes to 661.

The regulations regarding advanced students do not technically include women students, but there is a hall of residence for women graduate students (see pp. 94–95).

All applications for admission to the university lectures, etc., are made by the authorities of Girton and Newnham colleges on behalf of the students, and all fees are paid and arrangements made by these authorities.

There are three terms in each year: the Michaelmas term, beginning in the middle of October and lasting nine weeks; the Lent term, beginning in the middle of January, lasting eight weeks; and the Easter term, beginning in the middle of April, lasting eight weeks.

University Professors and Lecturers and College Lecturers.

ARTS.

LANGUAGES.—SEMITIC AND INDO-IRANIAN: *Professors* Bevan, Cowell, Giles, Kirkpatrick, Rieu; *Drs.* Barnes, Schechter; *Messrs.* Aldridge, Browne, Chapman, Frost, Kennett, McLean, Neil, Sherlock, Strong, Towers, Wyatt.

CLASSICAL: *Professors* Jebb, Mayor; *Drs.* Jackson, Peile, Postgate, Reid, Sandys; *Messrs.* Abbott, Adam, Archer-Hind, Cooke, Davies, Dimsdale, Edwards, Giles, Gill, Graves, A. Gray, J. H. Gray, Hadley, Hicks, Leaf, Lendrum, Levin, Miles, Neil, Rackham, Roberts, Shuckburgh, Sikes, Thompson, Tottenham, Wardale, Wedd, Whibley, Wyse.

ENGLISH: *Professors* Dowden, Skeat; *Messers.* Comber, Giles, Gollancz, Morier Hinde, Magnússon, Wyatt.

GERMANIC: *Dr.* Breul; *Mr.* Wolstenholme.

RUSSIAN: *Mr.* Schnurmann.

ROMANCE: *Messrs.* Boquel, Braunholtz, Comber, Morier Hinde, Kastner, Oelsner, Tilley, Wyatt.

COMPARATIVE PHILOLOGY: *Dr.* Postgate; *Messrs.* Breul, Chadwick, Giles.

PHILOSOPHY: *Professors* Sidgwick, Ward; *Dr.* Keynes; *Messrs.* Johnson, Levin, McTaggart, Rivers, Russell, Stout.

POLITICAL SCIENCE: *Professors* Marshall, Sidgwick; *Messrs.* Berry, Browning, Foxwell, Green, Levin.

HISTORY: *Professors* Lord Acton, Gwatkin, Maitland, Westlake; *Drs.* Cunningham, Walker; *Messrs.* Archbold, Browning, Corbett, Dickinson, Evans, Figgis, Hammond, Heitland, Leathes, Miles, Moriarty, Mullinger, Oldham, Reddaway, Shuckburgh, Tanner, Thornely, Tilley, Whitney.

ART AND ARCHÆOLOGY: *Professors* Ridgeway, Waldstein; *Messrs.* E. A. Gardner, Haddon, Roberts.

SCIENCE.

MATHEMATICS AND ASTRONOMY: *Professors* Sir R. S. Ball, Darwin, Forsyth; *Drs.* Glaisher, Hobson, Lachlan; *Messrs.* Baker, Bennett, Berry, Coates, Herman, Hinks, Lamb, Love, Munro, Pendlebury, Richmond, Webb, Whitehead.

PHYSICS: *Professors* Ewing, Sir G. G. Stokes, Thomson; *Messrs.* Bryan, Capstick, W. E. Dalby, D'Arcy, Fitzpatrick, Glazebrook, Griffiths, Larmor, Munro, Peace, Shaw, Skinner, Walker, Whetham, Wilberforce.

CHEMISTRY: *Professors* Dewar, Liveing; *Messrs.* Adie, Dickson, Easterfield, Fenton, Heycock, R. M. Lewis, Morrell, Neville, Pattison Muir, Ruhemann, Scott, Sell, Spivey.

MINERALOGY: *Professor* Lewis; *Mr.* Hutchinson.

GEOLOGY: *Professor* Hughes; *Messrs.* Harker, Marr, Oldham, Seward, Woods.

BIOLOGY, PHYSIOLOGY, ETC.: *Professors* Foster, Macalister, Newton, Ward; *Drs.* Barclay-Smith, Gaskell, Hill, Langley, Melsome, Rivers, Shore; *Messrs.* Blackman, Burkill, Cunningham, Darwin, Duckworth, Eichholz, Ellis, Gadow, Gardiner, Hardy, Harmer, Higgins, Hopkins, Kempson, Lister, Sedgwick, Seward, Shipley, Warburton, Woods.

ENGINEERING: *Professor* Ewing; *Messrs.* Hartree, Lamb, Peace, Peel.

AGRICULTURE: *Messrs.* Easterfield, Wood.

LAW.

Professors Clark, Maitland, Sir R. West, Westlake; *Drs.* Anningson, Bate, Bond, Gordon Campbell, Kenny, Lawrence, Walker, Waraker; *Messrs.* Barlow, Buckland, Harris, Higgins, Monro, Whittaker, Wright.

MEDICINE.

Professors Allbutt, Bradbury, Kanthock; *Drs.* Anningson, Barlow, Cory, Macalister; *Messrs.* Douty, Griffiths, Marshall, Pigg, Stabb, Wherry.

THEOLOGY.

Professors Gwatkin, Kirkpatrick, Mason, Robinson, Ryle, Stanton, Swete;

Drs. Barnes, Chase, Watson; *Messrs.* Barlow, Bethune-Baker, Blenkin, Boughey, Brooke, Chapman, Foakes-Jackson, Fulford, Gore, Gray, Harris, Headlam, Jackson, Knight, McLean, McNeile, Murray, Parry, Forbes Robinson, Srawley.

MUSIC.

Professor Stanford; *Drs.* Garrett, Wood.

GIRTON COLLEGE, CAMBRIDGE.

This college, which took its origin in a home for women students opened in 1869 by Miss Emily Davies at Hitchin, about eighteen miles from Cambridge, is open to women only, and provides instruction for the Previous and Tripos examinations of the University of Cambridge. (See pp. 88–89.) There is one large hall of residence, situated about one and a half miles from Cambridge, providing accommodation for the mistress, Miss Welsh, seven resident lecturers and about one hundred students.

Students are not admitted under the age of eighteen, and before entering they are required to pass the Girton College entrance examination or an equivalent examination.

Though no definite regulation is made in regard to the matter, duly qualified American women have been occasionally admitted, when space permitted, without examination and without undertaking the whole three years' course.

Some Tripos examinations may be taken after two; others only after three years of residence, but students are expected to reside in the college for three years. There are three terms in each year corresponding to the university terms (see p. 89).

The charge for board, lodging and tuition is £35 ($175) a term, and this covers all university and college charges. Each student has a bedroom and sitting room, or one large room divided. Students who desire to reside at the college during the long vacation may do so during July and August at a charge of £14 ($70), for four weeks or £20 ($100) for six weeks.

There are numerous scholarships varying in value from £17 12s. ($88) to £80 ($400) a year for three or four years. These are awarded on the results of special examinations.

For further information apply to the secretary, MISS SHORE NIGHTINGALE, 11 Queensborough Terrace, Bayswater, London, W.

Lecturers.

In addition to the university lectures attended by students of Girton College in Cambridge (see p. 90), lectures and individual instruction were given during 1897-98 at the college by the following lecturers:

ARTS.

LANGUAGES.—CLASSICAL: *Dr.* Postgate; *Messrs.* Adam, Conway, Cooke, Dickinson, Duff, Earp, Graves, Hicks, Leaf, Lendrum, Miles, Moulton, Pretor, Sikes; *Mrs.* Adam; *Misses* Alford, Jex-Blake, Taylor.

MEDIÆVAL AND MODERN: *Drs.* Braunholtz, Breul, Boquel; *Misses* Hensley, Kennedy, Steele Smith.

PHILOSOPHY AND POLITICAL SCIENCE: *Mr.* Johnson; *Miss* Constance Jones.

HISTORY: *Miss* McArthur; *Messrs.* Clapham, Dickinson, Green.

SCIENCE.

MATHEMATICS: *Messrs.* Dodds, Love, Munro, Whitehead, Young; *Misses* Hardcastle, Meyer.

BIOLOGY, CHEMISTRY, ETC.: *Misses* Dale, Greenwood, Marshall, Saunders, Sedgwick.

THEOLOGY.

Miss Taylor, *Mr.* Graves.

MUSIC.

Dr. Wood.

NEWNHAM COLLEGE, CAMBRIDGE.

This college, which took its origin in a home for women students opened by Miss Clough in 1871, is open to women only and provides instruction for the Previous and Tripos examinations of the University of Cambridge (see pp. 88-89). It consists of three halls of residence, situated about five minutes' walk from the centre of Cambridge, and accommodating about 150 students in addition to the principal, vice-principals and resident lecturers. The principal is Mrs. Henry Sidgwick; the vice-principals and heads of the different halls are Miss Katharine Stephen, Miss Mary E. Rickett and Miss B. A. Clough.

Students are not admitted under the age of eighteen, except in special cases; they are required to give satisfactory references and to pass, before entering, the Newnham College entrance examination or an equivalent examination. In exceptional cases women who do not reside in the college are admitted as out-students.

Though no definite regulation is made in regard to the matter, duly qualified American women are admitted, when space permits, without examination and without undertaking the whole three years' course.

The year is divided into three terms, corresponding to the university terms (see p. 89).

The fees for board, lodging and tuition vary from twenty-five guineas ($131.25) to thirty-two guineas ($168) a term. These do not include fees for laboratories or for university examinations.

Students residing in the college, by the advice of the principal, during the long vacation, pay a guinea ($5.25) a week for board and lodging. This does not include tuition.

Various scholarships of £35 ($175), £40 ($200) and £50 ($250) a year for one, two or three years are awarded under special conditions and in general on the results of examinations. There are two studentships of £75 ($375) and £80 ($400) a year awarded, one to a student who has passed the Natural Science Tripos with credit, the other to a student who has finished her college course and shows ability to carry on advanced independent work. There is also a research fellowship, the Geoffrey Fellowship, of £100 ($500) a year for three years, open to women who have obtained honours in a Cambridge Tripos examination or in the Oxford Final Schools.

For further information apply to the hon. secretary, MISS M. G. KENNEDY, Shenstone, Cambridge, from whom a pamphlet giving a detailed account of the Tripos examinations may be obtained.

Lecturers.

In addition to the university lectures attended by students of Newnham College in Cambridge (see p. 90), lectures and individual instruction were given during 1897-98 at Newnham College by the following lecturers:

ARTS.

LANGUAGES.—CLASSICAL: *Mr.* Archer-Hind, *Mrs.* Archer-Hind, *Messrs.* A. B. Cook, Davies, Moulton, Rackham, *Misses* Sharpley, White, *Mr.* Willson, *Mrs.* Verrall, *Mr.* Wedd.

MEDIÆVAL AND MODERN: *Messrs.* Boquel, Braunholtz, Breul, Chadwick, *Misses* J. E. Kennedy, Macleod Smith, *Mr.* Magnússon; *Misses* Steele Smith, Tuke, *Mr.* Wyatt.

PHILOSOPHY AND POLITICAL SCIENCE: *Mr.* Johnson, *Miss* Jones; *Mrs.* Marshall, *Mrs.* Ward.

HISTORY: *Miss* Bateson; *Mr.* Clapham, *Miss* Gardner; *Mr.* Reddaway.

SCIENCE.

MATHEMATICS: *Mr.* Carson, *Misses* Collier, Fawcett, *Messrs.* Godfrey, Gunston, *Misses* Johnson, Rickett.

NATURAL SCIENCES: *Misses* Alcock, Durham, Freund, Gostling, Greenwood, *Mr.* Kerr, *Misses* Klaassen, Marshall, Philipps, Saunders, Sheldon, Skeat, *Mr.* Wade.

WOMEN'S HALL OF RESIDENCE, CAMBRIDGE.
[For Students Engaged in Post-Graduate Work.]

The Women's Hall of Residence was opened in October, 1897, under the direction of Miss E. A. McArthur, with a view to meeting the desire felt by an increasing number of students engaged in post-graduate work to secure the advantages of association with other students and of assistance, if required, in the pursuit of their studies. During the academic year, 1896–7, a private experiment of this kind was undertaken by Miss E. A. McArthur with sufficiently satisfactory results to warrant a trial on a more formal basis.

Students are, in general, required to have taken a degree of some university, or to have passed an examination qualifying for such a degree, and must present testimonials satisfactory to the Committee. They must also furnish a statement both of their previous course of study and of the line of work which they propose to pursue.

The inclusive charge for board and residence during the academic year (three terms of nine weeks each) is from £50 ($250) to £60 ($300), according to the rooms chosen, and is payable in advance. This does not include fees for lectures or any other form of tuition. In exceptional cases students will be received for one or two terms upon payment at a slightly higher rate. Provision may also be made, when necessary, for residence during the vacations.

A Studentship of the value of £50 ($250) to be held at the Hall will, it is hoped, be awarded by the Committee yearly, provided that, in the opinion of the Committee, a candidate of sufficient merit present herself.

Any woman who has taken a university degree, or has passed an examination qualifying for such a degree, or who submits satisfactory testimonials of fitness to profit by the work is eligible for the Studentship. Each candidate is required to describe the course of study or research which she intends to pursue, and to give two references as to ability and character.

The student will be elected in the first instance for one year, and will be required to report to the Committee upon the work in which she has been engaged It is understood that the student will not undertake paid work during the tenure of the Studentship without the special permission of the Committee. The tenure of the Studentship will be from October 1st, and it will be paid terminally in advance.

Applications for the Studentship should be sent before July 10th to Miss ELLEN A. MCARTHUR, Girton College, Cambridge, from whom further particulars in regard to the Hall may be obtained.

COMMITTEE.

Rev. W. Cunningham, D. D., Fellow and Lecturer of Trinity College; Hon. Fellow of Gonville and Caius College (*Chairman*).

Arthur Berry, M. A., Fellow and Assistant Tutor of King's College.

Miss E. C. Jones, Vice-Mistress and Lecturer of Girton College.

Miss M. G. Kennedy, Hon. Secretary of Newnham College.

Miss Ellen A. McArthur, late Vice-Mistress of Girton College; Head Lecturer in History, Girton College.

R. D. Roberts, M. A., late Fellow of Clare College; Secretary for Lectures to the Local Examinations and Lectures Syndicate.

DURHAM, England.

THE UNIVERSITY OF DURHAM.

This university, opened in 1833, is situated in Durham, and is an examining body, conferring degrees in Arts, Science, Law, Medicine, Theology and Music. In 1895 a supplementary charter was granted enabling the university to grant degrees to women in all the faculties except that of Theology.

The colleges and halls in Durham are colleges for men to which women are not admitted. Men students are expected to reside in one of the halls or colleges or to reside in some house approved by the Warden and Proctors. Attendance at the classes of the Durham School of Medicine in Newcastle and at the classes of the Durham College of Science in Newcastle is allowed, with certain restrictions, to count as residence at Durham, and to qualify students to enter for the degrees of the university. The degree of

B. Litt. was instituted recently and may be obtained after two years' residence. The degree of B.A. is not generally taken in less than three years, though residence for more than six terms is not required.

Arrangements have now been made for admitting women to lectures at the University of Durham. A hostel was opened in October, 1896, and women were enabled to go into residence at once. All students wishing to qualify for a degree must reside for at least two years in Durham or Newcastle and attend lectures either at the University of Durham, the Durham College of Science in Newcastle or the Durham School of Medicine in Newcastle. Up to the present women are working in Durham for the degrees of B.A. and M.A. only. Women are admitted as students in music at the University of Durham. Those working for degrees in Science, Literature and Medicine (B.Sc., B.Litt., M.B., M.D., etc.) are studying at Newcastle. The Durham College of Science in Newcastle (see under Local Colleges, pp. 105–106) is open to women.

The year is divided into three terms of eight or nine weeks' duration, beginning in October, January and the end of April.

The fees are very low; entrance fee £2 ($10), tuition fees £7 ($35) per term, fees for examination from £1 ($5) to £10.10 ($52.50). A composition fee of £70 ($350) is charged for the complete five years' course in Medicine.

The terms for board and residence at one of the women's hostels are from £1.1 ($5.25) to £1.5 ($6.25) a week. There is a hall of residence for women medical students, Eslington Tower, Newcastle-on-Tyne; Principal, Miss Perry. The charge for board and residence is from £42 ($210) for the session.

Further information may be obtained from the Rev. J. R. SHORTT, M.A., the University, Durham, or from the registrar.

LONDON, England.

THE UNIVERSITY OF LONDON.

Burlington House, Vigo Street, London, W.

London University, founded in 1826, is an examining body, conferring degrees in Arts (B. A., M. A., D. Lit.); Science (B. Sc.,

D. Sc.); Law (LL. B., LL. D.); Medicine (M. B., B. S., M. S., M. D.); Music (B. Mus., D. Mus.). The university also gives a certificate, called the "Teacher's Diploma," to each candidate who has passed the examination in teaching.

A proposal to found a teaching university in connection with the University of London has been under consideration for some years and a scheme has at last been adopted.

In 1867 the university offered certain special certificates to women; in 1878 it opened all degrees, honours and prizes to students of both sexes on equal terms, and in 1882 it was resolved by the governing body, Convocation, "that female graduates be admitted to Convocation."

The degrees are conferred on candidates that have passed a prescribed series of examinations held by examiners appointed by the university. The examinations must be taken in a prescribed order and, in general, an interval of at least one academic year must elapse between two consecutive examinations. For the Bachelors' degrees in Arts, Science, Medicine and Law two examinations of widely different standards, "pass" and "honours," are held in each subject, and candidates are at liberty to choose which they will take.

Prizes, exhibitions and scholarships, varying in value from £5 ($25) to £50 ($250) a year for two years, are awarded to the candidates that most distinguish themselves in the different honours examinations.

The fees for the examinations are from £2 ($10) to £10 ($50).

Candidates for degrees are free to reside and study where they please, but preparation for the examinations may be obtained at the numerous colleges affiliated with the University. See University College, London (pp. 98–99); King's College, London (p. 100); Bedford College for Women, London (pp. 103–104); Royal Holloway College, Egham (p. 104) and pp. 105–106.

All particulars may be obtained from the "London University Calendar," which is published yearly and contains the examination papers for the preceding year.

Communications should be addressed to the registrar of the University of London, Burlington Gardens, London, W.

DAVY-FARADAY RESEARCH LABORATORY OF THE ROYAL INSTITUTION.

21 Albemarle Street, London, West.

This laboratory was endowed and given to the Royal Institution in 1897 by Dr. Ludwig Mond. It is open, at the discretion of the committee, to all persons, irrespective of sex or nationality, who have done scientific research work, or are judged capable of undertaking it.

Any person who obtains permission to attend the laboratory for a certain term may do so free of charge and will, in general, be supplied with all materials, chemicals, gas, electricity, etc., necessary for his work, but these may in special cases be refused. The worker will be eligible for readmission after the expiration of the term for which he has been admitted.

The year is divided into three terms: Michaelmas term from the first Monday in October to the Saturday nearest the 18th of December; Lent term from the Monday nearest to the 15th of January to the second Saturday in April; Easter term from the first Monday in May to the fourth Saturday in July.

For further information apply to the Secretary of the Royal Institution.

Directors of the Laboratory: LORD RAYLEIGH, PROFESSOR DEWAR.

UNIVERSITY COLLEGE.

Gower Street, London, W. C.

University College, London, separated from the University of London in 1836 and given a charter in 1869, prepares for the examinations of London University in Arts, Science, Medicine and Law. Students do not reside in the college (for hall of residence for women, see p. 99). All classes in the Faculties of Arts, Science and Law are open to women as to men, *except* classes in engineering, histology and physiology. (For courses for women in medicine, see under the School of Medicine for Women, pp. 102–103.)

Women wishing to enter as students must present satisfactory references and should call on the lady superintendent, Miss Morison, whose recommendation is required for admittance. Miss Morison may be seen at her office in the college during the first week of the term.

The session is divided into three terms, dates for 1898–99: October 4th till December 16th, January 10th till March 24th, April 18th till June 30th.

The fees vary from £1.1 ($5.25) to £7.7 ($36.75) per class for the session.

There are numerous prizes and scholarships open, with few exceptions, to women as to men. They vary in value from £10 ($50) to £150 ($750) a year.

For further information, see "University College, London, Calendar." Communications should be addressed to the secretary.

Hall of Residence.—College Hall, Byng Place, Gordon Square, is a hall of residence for women students attending University College and the London School of Medicine for Women. No student is admitted under 17 years of age. The expenses for board and residence vary from £51 ($255) to £80 ($400) for the University College session of 33 weeks, and from £58 ($290) to £90 ($450) for the session of the London School of Medicine of 37 weeks. Further information may be obtained from the principal, MISS GROVE.

Professors.

ARTS.

LANGUAGES. — SEMITIC: *Professors* Marks, Ross, Schechter, Strong.
INDO-IRANIAN*: *Professors* Bendall, Blumhardt, Rhys Davids.
CLASSICAL: *Professors* Housman, Platt.
ENGLISH: *Professor* Ker.
GERMANIC: *Professor* Priebsch.
ROMANCE: *Professors* Butler, Lallemand.
COMPARATIVE PHILOLOGY: *Professor* Postgate.
PHILOSOPHY: *Professor* Sully.
POLITICAL ECONOMY: *Professor* Foxwell.
HISTORY: *Professor* Montague.
ART AND ARCHÆOLOGY: *Professors* Brown, E. A. Gardner, Petrie.

ARCHITECTURE: *Professor* Roger Smith.

SCIENCE.

MATHEMATICS AND ASTRONOMY: *Professors* M. J. M. Hill, Karl Pearson.
PHYSICS: *Professsor* Callendar.
CHEMISTRY: *Professor* Vaughan Harley, Ramsay.
GEOLOGY: *Professor* Bonney.
BIOLOGY, PHYSIOLOGY, ETC.: *Professors* Martin, Oliver, Schäfer, Weldon.
ENGINEERING: *Professors* Hudson Beare, Chadwick, Fleming, Vernon-Harcourt.

LAW.

Professors Bate, Birrell, Carter, Murison, Neil, Raleigh.

*There is a school of Modern Oriental studies established by the Imperial Institute in connection with University College and King's College. For particulars see "University College Calendar."

KING'S COLLEGE.
Strand, London, S. W.

This college is for men only and prepares for the examinations of the University of London; it is similar in its organisation to University College and its medical school is important.

There is a separate "Department for Ladies" at 13 Kensington Square, London, W., giving instruction in Arts, Science, Law, Theology and Music. The professors and lecturers are, with some exceptions, professors at King's College. The classes organised are of a very elementary nature, but more advanced classes can in some cases be arranged when desired. Students do not reside in the college; a hall of residence for women, King's Hall, has recently been opened, fees for board and residence 2½ guineas ($13.12) and 2 guineas ($10.50) a week. For further information apply to Miss E. Faithfull, 28 Kensington Square.

The academic year is divided into three terms: Michaelmas term, beginning Monday, October 14th, and ending Friday, December 20th; Lent term, beginning January 20th and ending March 27th; Easter term, beginning April 17th and ending July 3rd.

The fees are one or two guineas ($5.25 to $10.50) per term for each class.

Further information can be obtained from Miss Lilian M. Faithfull, vice-principal and secretary, 13 Kensington Square, London, W.

Professors and Lecturers.

ARTS.

LANGUAGES.—CLASSICS: *Professor* Warr; *Miss* Pater.
ENGLISH: *Professors* Heath, Knight, Shuttleworth; *Miss* Faithfull, *Mr.* de Selincourt.
GERMANIC: *Professor* Buchheim; *Miss* Buchheim, *Mr.* Menken.
ROMANCE: *Professors* Perini, Ramirez, Spiers; *Mr.* Esclangon.
PHILOSOPHY: *Professors* Caldecott, Mayor, Knight; *Miss* Meyer.
POLITICAL ECONOMY: *Professors* Cunningham, Hewins, Shuttleworth.
HISTORY: *Professors* Laughton, Shuttleworth, Warr.
ART AND ARCHÆOLOGY: *Messrs.* Vicat Cole, Holden, Pownall, Speight.

SCIENCE.

MATHEMATICS: *Mr.* Dale; *Miss* Barwell.
CHEMISTRY: *Professor* J. M. Thomson; *Mr.* Jackson; *Mrs.* McKillop.
GEOLOGY: *Professor* Seeley.
BIOLOGY: *Professors* Beale, Bottomley; *Miss* Lulham.

LAW.

Professor John Cutler.

THEOLOGY.

Professors Knowling, Robertson.

MUSIC.

Professor Vernham; *Dr.* Hamilton Robinson.

THE LONDON SCHOOL OF ECONOMICS AND POLITICAL SCIENCE.

10 Adelphi Terrace, London, W. C.

This school was founded in 1895, its object being to organise economic and political studies in England. During the first year 300 students, of whom 75 were women, joined the school. The students are chiefly graduates of British and foreign universities, government officials, railway officials, bank managers and clerks, and persons engaged in public work who require the guidance of experts on particular subjects. The school is also a centre of information for foreigners visiting England for purposes of investigation, and guidance and advice has been given to students from Belgium, France, Germany, the United States and other countries.

Research studentships varying in value from £25 ($125) to £100 ($500) for the encouragement of special investigations are given on the result of examinations. A Studentship of the value of £100 ($500) a year for two years was awarded in July, 1897, and others will be awarded in July, 1899. The selected candidate is expected to give a short course of lectures on the result of his investigations.

An excellent special library has been collected, and the publication of a series of studies on Political Science commenced.

The academic year, which begins at the end of October and ends about June 22nd, is divided into three terms. The fee for full membership of the school, admitting to all lectures and classes is £3 ($15) a year or £1 ($5) a term. The fee for one course of 20 lectures is 15s. ($3.75).

Further information may be obtained from the DIRECTOR, MR. W. A. S. HEWINS, 10 Adelphi Terrace, London, W. C.

Lecturers in 1898-99.

ECONOMICS: *Dr.* Cunningham; *Messrs.* Cannan, von Halle, Hewins, Hobson, Mackinder, Sargent, Sydney Webb.
STATISTICS: *Messrs.* Bowley, Edgeworth, Hewins, Sanger.
LOCAL GOVERNMENT: *Messrs.* Glen, Gomme, Hirst, Hobhouse, Kemp.
PALÆOGRAPHY AND DIPLOMATIC: *Mr.* Hubert Hall, Sir E. Maunde Thompson.
RAILWAYS: *Mr.* Acworth.
BANKING: *Messrs.* Foxwell, Palgrave.
COMMERCIAL LAW: *Mr.* Barlow.
CONSTITUTIONAL LAW: *Professor* Dicey; *Dr.* Schuster; *Mr.* Whittuck.
POLITICAL SCIENCE: *Messrs.* Dickinson, Gomme; *Dr.* von Halle, Sir Courtenay Ilbert; *Miss* McArthur; *Mr.* Graham Wallas.

LONDON SCHOOL OF MEDICINE FOR WOMEN.
8 Hunter Street, Brunswick Square, London, W. C.

This school, opened about 1875, provides, in association with the Royal Free Hospital, Gray's Inn Road, instruction for women in all medical subjects. Students do not reside in the school; for a hall of residence in connection with it see p. 99.

The courses of the London School of Medicine for Women include all the medical subjects required for the degrees and diplomas of the University of London, the Royal University of Ireland, the Irish and Scotch colleges, and the Society of Apothecaries, London.

Before entering on medical studies students are required to have passed a qualifying examination in Arts. After passing this they should register as soon as possible at the office of the General Medical Council, which requires all medical practitioners to have taken a five years' course, dating from the time of registration. The course comprises five years of study at the school and attendance for four years on the courses of clinical instruction at the Royal Free Hospital. Women may however, by permission of the Executive Council, attend certain of the classes without having passed the examination in Arts and without entering on the complete course of study. Graduates of foreign and colonial universities can occasionally be admitted to the hospital practice when the accommodation permits.

Besides the Royal Free Hospital, the Brompton Consumption Hospital, the New Hospital for Women, the Clapham Maternity Hospital, the London Fever Hospital, the Hospital for Sick Children, Great Ormond Street, the National Dental Hospital, and several other hospitals, are open to students of the school. There are two sessions: winter session, October 1st to April 1st; summer session, May 1st to August 1st.

The fees for the separate classes vary from one to eight guineas ($5.25 to $42) for the session. The cost of a medical education varies considerably according to the requirements of the different examining boards. The "compounder's fee" for the school and hospital courses for four years is, if paid in one sum, £125 ($625).

There are several prizes and scholarships varying in value from £5 to £100 ($25 to $500) a year for three or four years.

Further information and a prospectus can be obtained from the secretary, MISS DOUIE, 8 Hunter street, Brunswick Square, W. C.

Lecturers and Demonstrators.

Drs. (*Mrs.*) Garrett Anderson, F. W. Andrewes, (*Miss*) Cock, Dupré, (*Miss*) Evans, Manson, (*Miss*) McCall, Sainsbury, (*Mrs.*) Scharlieb, Starling; *Miss* Appel; *Messrs.* Barrow, Berry, Bodmer, Stanley Boyd; *Mrs.* Dowson, *Mrs.* Evans; *Misses* Forrest, Hooper; *Mrs.* Keer, Macdonald; *Messrs.* Mackinlay, Mercier; *Misses* Poole, Smith, Turner, Webb, Welby.

Medical Officers.

Drs. (*Miss*) Aldrich-Blake, Carr, Cockle, Crawfurd, Evans, Fawcett, Hayes, Marsden, Roughton, Sainsbury, West; *Miss* Appel; *Messrs.* Barrow, Battle, Berry, Dodd, Gant, Legg, Mackinlay, Rose; *Miss* Rowse; *Messrs.* Todd, Wakley.

BEDFORD COLLEGE (for Women).

8 and 9 York Place, Baker Street, London, W.

Bedford College, founded in 1849, is open to women only, and provides instruction in Arts and Science. Students are prepared for all the examinations of the University of London in these subjects; there is also a training department and an art school in connection with the college. A course of scientific instruction in hygiene, bacteriology, etc., preparing women for posts as Sanitary Inspectors, is a special feature of the college.

The session is divided into three terms, the first beginning on October 6th and ending on December 20th; the second beginning on January 19th and ending on March 28th; the third beginning on April 20th and ending on June 28th.

The fees for the separate classes vary from one to three guineas ($5.25 to $15.75) a term.

Students may reside in the college, the charge for board being from 58 to 68 guineas ($304.50 to $357.00) a year. The inclusive average fees for residence and tuition are $472.50 to $565.75. There are several scholarships varying in value from 30 guineas to £48 ($157.50 to $240.00).

For further information apply to MISS ETHEL HURLBATT, principal of the college, Bedford College, 8 and 9 York Place, Baker street, London, W.

Lecturers.

ARTS.
LANGUAGES.—CLASSICAL: *Messrs.* A. Bernard Cook, Platt; *Misses* Fitzgerald, Weir.
ENGLISH: *Dr.* G. Foster; *Miss* G. A. Howell.
GERMANIC: *Mr.* W. F. Bentinck Smith.
ROMANCE: *Mr.* Victor Oger.
PHILOSOPHY: *Miss* Edgell.
HISTORY: *Messrs.* Allen, Cook.

ART: *Mr.* Thompson.
PEDAGOGY: *Miss* H. Robertson.

SCIENCE.
MATHEMATICS: *Mr.* Harding; *Miss* A. E. Lee.
PHYSICS: *Mr.* Womack, *Miss* A. E. Lee.
CHEMISTRY: *Mr.* Crompton.
GEOLOGY: *Miss* Raisin.
BIOLOGY: *Drs.* Drysdale, Tims; *Mr.* Edkins; *Miss* Raisin.
HYGIENE: *Mr.* W. C. C. Pakes.

ROYAL HOLLOWAY COLLEGE (for Women).

Egham, Surrey (near London).

Royal Holloway College, opened in 1886, has beautiful buildings and grounds situated about twenty miles from London, is open to women only and provides the instruction necessary for London University degrees in Arts and Science, for the London preliminary M. B., and for pass and honours examination of the University of Oxford. Candidates for admission must be over 17 years of age and are required to pass an entrance examination or to have passed its equivalent.

The college session extends from the beginning of October to the beginning of July, and is divided into three terms of about eleven weeks each.

The fees for board, residence and instruction are £30 ($150) per term, or £90 ($450) a year. Numerous scholarships of £30 ($150) to £75 ($375) a year are awarded on the results of examinations. For information apply to the secretary, MISS MARGARET SIM.

Professors and Lecturers.

ARTS.
LANGUAGES.—CLASSICS: *Professor* Donkin; *Miss* ——; *Mr.* Allen.
ENGLISH: *Misses* Guinness, Kimpster, Bentinck Smith, Mr. Boas.
GERMANIC: *Misses* Corry, Skeat, Bentinck Smith.
ROMANCE: *Misses* Péchinet, Skeat, M. Berthon.
PHILOLOGY: *Miss* ——.
PHILOSOPHY: *Mr.* Solomon.

HISTORY: *Miss* Penrose.
ART: *Mr.* Carey.

SCIENCE.
MATHEMATICS: *Professors* Cassie, Loney; *Miss* C. Frost.
PHYSICS: *Professor* Cassie.
CHEMISTRY: *Miss* Field.
BIOLOGY: *Misses* Benson, Durham.

MUSIC.
Miss Daymond, *Mr.* Burnett, *Miss* Glazebrook.

LOCAL COLLEGES AFFILIATED TO THE UNIVERSITY OF LONDON AND OTHER UNIVERSITIES.

In addition to University College, King's College and Bedford College (see pp. 98–104), there are numerous local colleges affiliated to the different universities in England and Wales. These colleges prepare principally for the degrees of B.A. and B.Sc. given by these universities; the courses they offer are arranged to prepare students for the degree examinations, and are on the same. general plan as those offered by University College, London; many distinguished professors are on their faculties, but no lists are given here on account of lack of space. They offer few courses which may properly be called graduate. They admit women, as a rule, to the Arts and Science classes on the same terms as men. No students are admitted under 16 years of age. No requirements are made as to residence, but there are halls of residence for women in connection with most of the colleges.

The college session, beginning in October, is usually divided into three terms, each of about eleven weeks' duration.

The fees for the different classes vary from 1 to 3 guineas ($5.25 to $15.75) per term, the cost of one of the ordinary degree courses for the year being about £20 ($100). The cost of board and residence in the halls for women students is usually from £40 to £50 ($200 to $250) a session.

Numerous prizes and scholarships of considerable value are open to students of the different colleges.

For further information about any particular college application should be made to the registrar. The following is a list of the most important:

*Aberystwyth, University College of Wales; * Bangor, University College of North Wales; Birmingham, The Mason College; Bristol, University College; * Cardiff, University College of South Wales and Monmouthshire; † Leeds, The Yorkshire College; † Liverpool, University College; † Manchester, The Owens Col-

---

* Affiliated to the University of Wales.
† Affiliated to Victoria University.

lege; ‡ Newcastle-on-Tyne, Durham College of Science; Nottingham, University College; Sheffield, Firth College.

MANCHESTER, England.
VICTORIA UNIVERSITY.
The Owens College, Manchester.

This university, founded in 1880, and having its seat at the Owens College, Manchester, is an examining body with power to confer degrees in Arts, Science, Law, Medicine and Music. The general scheme of the examinations is similar to that of London University and they are open to women on the same conditions as to men.

All candidates must have been regular students of one of the colleges of the university. These colleges are: The Owens College, Manchester; University College, Liverpool; The Yorkshire College, Leeds (see p. 105). Graduates of other colleges and universities are also allowed to take the examinations under special conditions.

Enquiries should be addressed to the registrar of the Victoria University, Manchester, and information may be obtained from the calendar of the university, price, 1s ($0.25).

OXFORD, England.
THE UNIVERSITY OF OXFORD.

The University of Oxford, founded in the twelfth century, is a corporation which provides instruction in the various branches of knowledge and confers degrees in Arts, Law, Medicine, Theology and Music on men who have since matriculation fulfilled certain conditions as to residence and passed certain examinations. Research degrees are also granted under somewhat different arrangements. There are in Oxford twenty-one colleges, one public and three private halls. Members of the university must be members of one of these or of the body of non-collegiate students. Each college has its own staff of teachers and its affairs are administered by its Head and Body of Fellows. University lectures given by

---

‡ Affiliated to the University of Durham.

professors and readers are open to all members of the university; college lectures, which supply a great part of the teaching, are, by arrangement, generally open to the members of colleges other than that in which they are given.

Women are not admitted to matriculation or graduation, but are allowed to enter for all the public examinations for the degrees in Arts and Music without being required to fulfil precisely the same conditions as men. Names of candidates must be sent in through the Secretary to the Delegates of Local Examinations, H. T. GERRANS, 8 Clarendon Building, Oxford, from whom the special regulations affecting women students can be obtained. The requirements of the university for the degree course can be ascertained from the Student's Hand-book (price 2s. 8d. ($0.66)), or from the Examination Statutes (price 1s. 2d. ($0.29)), to be obtained at the Clarendon Press Depot, 116 High street, Oxford. The names of successful women candidates are officially published in supplementary lists and they receive a certificate signed by the examiners. No preliminary residence or study in Oxford is required, but an examination in two languages and elementary mathematics must be passed before admission to any of the higher examinations. Graduates of colleges included in the Association of Collegiate Alumnæ are excused from this examination. Certain examinations are arranged by the Delegates of Local Examinations for women only.

The year is divided into three terms, each of eight weeks' duration, beginning respectively about the middle of October, middle of January and middle of April.

Women who desire to attend lectures in Oxford should put themselves in communication with the "Association for Promoting the Education of Women in Oxford" (see pp. 109–111), and should apply for information to the hon. secretary, MISS ROGERS, Clarendon Building, Oxford.

Professors and Lecturers.

The list of lecturers for each year is published in the "Oxford University Gazette." The following list is compiled from the Gazette for January, 1899:

ARTS.

LANGUAGES.—SEMITIC: *Professors* Driver, Margoliouth, Nicholl, Sayce; *Messrs.* Allen, Burney, G. A. Cooke, Neubauer, Stenning.

INDO-IRANIAN: *Professors* Legge, Macdonnell, Mills; *Messrs.* Bellairs, Blumhardt, Platts, Pope, St. John, Wells.

CLASSICAL: *Professors* Bywater, Ellis; *Messrs.* Abbott, Bailey, Baker, Barton, Blakiston, Burge, Clark, Cookson, Cooper, Ellis, Farnell, Ferard, Fox, Godley, Greene, Haigh, Hall, Inge, Jackson, Lindsay, Lys, Matheson, Moore, Owen, de Paravicini, Phelps, Phillimore, Phillips, Pickard-Cambridge, Pope, Poynton, Prickard, Raper, Richards, Rushforth, Scott, Sidgwick, Smith, Snow.

ENGLISH: *Professors* Napier, Earle; *Messrs.* Firth, de Selincourt.

GERMANIC: *Professor* Rhys; *Mr.* Macdonell.

CHINESE: *Professor* Bullock.

RUSSIAN: *Mr.* Morfill.

CELTIC: *Professor* Rhys.

ROMANCE: *Messrs.* de Arteaga, Berthon, Bué, Coscia, Moore.

COMPARATIVE PHILOLOGY: *Professor* Max Müller, *Deputy Professor* Wright.

PHILOSOPHY: *Professors* Case, Stewart, Cook Wilson; *Messrs.* Ball, Bate, Benecke, Blunt, Caird, Fairbrother, Hadow, Wright Henderson, Hobhouse, Joachim, Joseph, Prichard, Rashdall, Richards, Schiller, Smith, Spooner, Storr, Underhill, Walker, Warner, Wood, Wylie.

POLITICAL SCIENCE: *Professor* Edgeworth; *Messrs.* Carlyle, Hughes, Marriott, Phelps, Smith, Pogson Smith, Williams.

DIPLOMATIC: *Mr.* R. Lane Poole.

HISTORY: *Professors* Montagu Burrows, Pelham, York Powell; *Messrs.* Abbott, Case, Strachan-Davidson, Davis, Edwards, Fisher, Fletcher, Fowler, Greenidge, Grundy, Hall, Hardy, Hassall, Haverfield, Henderson, How, Hutton, Johnson, Stuart Jones, Leigh, Macan, Marriott, Medley, Mee, Montague, Myres, Munro, Oman, Owen, Poole, Robertson, Smith, Tracey, Underhill, Urquhart, Wakeling, Walker, Ward, Wells, Wood.

ARCHÆOLOGY: *Professors* Gardner; *Messrs.* Farnell, Myres.

POETRY: *Professor* Courthope.

MUSIC: *Professor* Stainer; *Drs.* Mee, Parry.

SCIENCE.

MATHEMATICS: *Professors* Elliott, Esson, Love, Turner; *Messrs.* Campbell, Dixon, Gerrans, Haselfoot, Hayes, Leudesdorf, Pedder, Russell, Sampson, Thompson.

PHYSICS: *Professors* Clifton; *Messrs.* Alsop, Baynes, Craig, Hudson, Plummer, Smith, Walker.

CHEMISTRY: *Professor* Odling; *Messrs.* Elford, Fisher, Vernon Harcourt, Marsh, Nagel, Veley, Watts, Wilderman.

GEOLOGY: *Professor* Sollas.

MINERALOGY: *Professor* Miers; *Mr.* Bowman.

GEOGRAPHY: *Mr.* Mackinder.

BIOLOGY: *Professors* Gotch, Tylor, Vines; *Messrs.* Bourne, Burch, Goodrich, Haldane, Jenkinson, Mann, Ramsden, Thompson.

AGRICULTURE: *Professor* ——.

LAW.

Professors Dicey, Goudy, Holland, Sir F. Pollock, Sir W. R. Anson; *Messrs.* Burnham, Carter, Davis, Hazel, Holdsworth, Jenks, Sir W. Markby, Montague, Moyle, Pottinger, Prankerd, Smith, Wakeling, Williams, Wilson.

MEDICINE.

Professors Burdon-Sanderson, Clifton, Gotch, Odling, Thomson, Vines; *Messrs.* Brooks, Farmer, Haldane, Jerome, Mann, Ritchie, Winkfield.

THEOLOGY.

Professors Bright, Cheyne, Driver, Ince, Lock, Moberly, Sanday; *Messrs.* Allen, Bate, Bebb, Bennett, Burney, Bussell, Carlyle, Clayton, Henderson, de la Hey, Kidd, Lake, Lovell, Maude, Moore, Pullan, Spooner, Stenning, Strong, Turner, White, Wild, Wilson, Wright.

THE ASSOCIATION FOR PROMOTING THE EDUCATION OF WOMEN IN OXFORD.

The teaching of women is organised and directed by the Council of the Association for promoting the education of Women in Oxford, founded in 1879; President, the Master of Balliol College; Secretaries, Mr. A. Sidgwick, Miss Rogers. Lectures are provided and arrangements made for the admission of women to lectures given in the University, names being sent in through the Secretary and the fees paid through the Treasurer. About one hundred and fifty professors and lecturers admit women thus recommended to their lectures, and facilities are also granted to them for work in the University Laboratories. Students, whether men or women, find little difficulty in obtaining permission to read in the Bodleian and other University Libraries. Further information can be obtained from Miss Rogers, Clarendon Building, Broad Street, Oxford. Women coming to Oxford for regular study are requested to put themselves in communication with her rather than to apply direct to the lecturers and will find it to their advantage to do so. As a rule they are expected to register as students of the Association the fee for which is for students of a Hall or College 5s. ($1.25), for Home Students 10s. ($2.50). Private tuition which forms an important part of the Oxford system of education is arranged through Miss Rogers. Professors' lectures are usually free, the fees for other lectures vary from 12s. ($3) to two guineas ($10.50), the course. Private teaching from is £2 ($10) to £4 ($20) for a course of eight lessons. The Association has a small library, kept in a room in one of the University Buildings which is used as an office. Students taking the full degree course with Honours receive a special diploma from the Council of the Association, other certificates are given for other courses of study. For all these residence is required. These may be looked upon as temporary substitutes for degrees. A movement for opening the B. A. degree to women made in 1896 was unsuccessful, but it is probable that a further attempt will be made, as there is a strong party in Oxford in favour of it.

The lists of lectures are not published till the beginning of the term in which they are given but earlier information can be obtained from the Secretary to the Association, or from one of the special tutors appointed in each subject.

Residence.—There are three Halls and one College for women students each governed by its own Council and having its own staff represented on the Council of the Association by its Principal and one member of its Council. Details of the students' education are arranged by a Committee of the Association Council of which the Principals are members. Registered students not belonging to any of these Societies are called Home Students, are under the charge of a Committee and a Principal, and enjoy the same privileges of admission to lectures, use of libraries, etc., as students of the Halls and College.

Lady Margaret Hall.—Oxford, opened in 1879, has accommodation at present for about fifty students. Students who desire to enter must have passed an examination in two languages and elementary mathematics, and must give satisfactory references to the principal. Students coming from another college or university must present a letter of recommendation from its authorities.

Fees for board and residence are £75 ($375) a year. Fees for tuition are paid to the association; (see p. 109).

Several scholarships, varying in value from £25 to £50 ($125 to $250) a year for three or four years, are given annually on the results of an examination held in June.

Further information may be obtained from the lady principal, MISS WORDSWORTH, or from the secretary, MISS LODGE, Lady Margaret Hall, Oxford. Tutors: Miss Sellar, Miss Pearson.

Somerville College.—Woodstock Road, Oxford, opened in 1879, provides accommodation for seventy-two students; no student is admitted under the age of seventeen, and students are required to give satisfactory references to the principal and to satisfy her that they are qualified to profit by the course of study at Oxford.

The inclusive charges for board, lodging and tuition are £30 15s. 4d. ($153.83), £28 13s. 4d. ($143.33) or £26 ($130) per term, to be paid in advance.

A research studentship of £50 ($250) a year for two years has recently been founded.

Further information may be obtained from the principal, Miss MAITLAND, or the vice-principal, the HON. ALICE BRUCE, Somerville College, Oxford. Resident tutors: Miss Lees, Miss Lorimer, Miss M. Pope, Miss Sheavyn.

St. Hugh's Hall.—Oxford, founded in 1886, is intended for members of the Church of England. It provides accommodation for only a few students. Charges for board and residence, £45 to £66 ($225 to $330) a year.

St. Hilda's Hall.—Oxford, founded in 1893, is conducted according to the principles of the Church of England, with liberty for members of other denominations. Further particulars may be obtained from the principal, MRS. BURROWS.

Home Students.—Students who do not reside in a hall are called "Home Students" and are under the care of a principal, MRS. A. H. JOHNSON, 8 Merton street, Oxford, from whom particulars may be obtained. Students may be received as boarders in a private family at a charge of from £1 5s. to £2 12s. 6d. ($6.25 to $13.12) a week. The cost of lodging in Oxford is from 12s. ($3.00) a week upwards, and board may be reckoned at 12s. ($3.00) a week.

The "Calendar" of the Association may be obtained from the office, Clarendon Building, Oxford; price, 6d. ($0.12).

Lecturers and Tutors.

ARTS.

LANGUAGES.–CLASSICAL: *Messrs.* Haigh, Lys; *Misses* Lorimer, Rogers, Sellar; *Mr.* Sidgwick.
ENGLISH: *Messrs.* Edwards, Firth, de Sélincourt; *Misses* Lee, Sheavyn, Wardale.
MODERN: *Mr.* Carlyle; *Misses* Pope, A. M. Todd, Wardale; *Mr.* Wright.
PHILOSOPHY: *Mr.* Hadow.

MODERN HISTORY: *Mr.* Armstrong; *Misses* Burrows, Lees, Lodge; *Messrs.* Hutton, Marriott, *Mrs.* Marriott, *Messrs.* Smith, Wakeling.
LAW: *Mr.* Burnham.

SCIENCE.

MATHEMATICS AND PHYSICS: *Mr.* Gerrans; *Miss* Pearson; *Mr.* Russell.
NATURAL SCIENCE: *Miss* Kirkaldy; *Mr.* Nagel.

OXFORD UNIVERSITY EXTENSION.

In recent years much attention has been paid to the development of the system of university extension lectures. A university extension college has been founded in Reading, Berkshire, and will, when fully organised, be similar to one of the university colleges affiliated to London University (see pp. 105–106).

The annual summer meeting will be held in Oxford from July 29th to August 23rd, 1899; it is divided into two parts, the first lasting from July 29th to August 9th and the second from August 9th to August 23rd. The subject of this year's course is the history, literature, art, etc., of the period 1837–1871. There are also classes in architecture, education, economics, languages and science. In the latter there are classes for practical work.

The fee for a ticket admitting to all the courses, concerts, conversaziones, etc., for the whole meeting is £1 10s. ($7.50), a ticket for either part costs £1 ($5). There are extra fees of 10s. ($2.50) for some of the special classes.

Full information may be obtained from MR. J. A. R. MARRIOTT, M.A., University Extension Office, Oxford.

Lecturers in 1899.

LANGUAGES.—CLASSICAL: *Mr.* H. G. Gibson.

ENGLISH: *Dr.* Henry Sweet.

LITERATURE: *Professor* York Powell; *Messrs.* Bailey, Bayne, Boas, Bodington, de Burgh, Churton Collins, Cotterill, Ashe King, Lummis, Myers, Oldershaw, Paul, de Sélincourt, Hudson Shaw, Shaw-Jeffrey, Arthur Sidgwick.

POLITICAL SCIENCE: Lord Farrer, *Messrs.* Birchenough, Geoffrey Drage, Masterman, Owen, Sargent.

HISTORY: Lords Farrer, Strathcona and Mount Royal, Sir Alfred Lyall, the Hon. G. C. Brodrick, the Hon. W. P. Reeves; *Professor* Dicey; *Messrs.* H. Belloc, Horsburgh, Jenks, Johnson, Marriott, Phillips, Russell, F. E. Smith, Souttar, Stride.

HELLENIC STUDIES: *Professors* Jebb, Ernest Gardner, Percy Gardner; *Messrs.* Sayce, Wells.

ARCHITECTURE: *Messrs.* Francis Bond, Marshall.

PEDAGOGY: *Professor* Barnes; *Messrs.* Hassall, Keatinge, Sadler.

SCIENCE: *Professors* Miers, Sollas; *Drs.* Farrar, Ransome; *Messrs.* Bourne, Brown, Burch, Dickson.

WALES.

THE UNIVERSITY OF WALES.

The University of Wales, constituted in 1894, is a Public Corporation representing the Counties and County Boroughs of Wales, the three University Colleges and other educational authorities. It confers degrees upon students who have pursued an approved course of study in one or other of the associated colleges, and have passed the university examinations corresponding thereto. For degrees in Theology a further course of study in a Theological College is necessary; the degree of Doctor is given by the University on the result of examination or in recognition of work.

The status of women in the university differs in no respect from that of men. They are admissible to every degree and eligible for every office in the university.

The three colleges of the University are:—The University College of Wales, the University College of North Wales, and the University College of South Wales and Monmouthshire. (See pp. 105-106.) The university itself is situated at Newport, Monmouthshire.

H. R. H. The Prince of Wales is the Chancellor of the University.

IRELAND.

There are two universities in Ireland, both situated in Dublin: the Royal University of Ireland, which is merely an examining body; and the University of Dublin (Trinity College), which is a college for men, conferring its own degrees, to which women are not admitted. Affiliated to the University of Ireland are three small local colleges: Queen's College, Belfast; Queen's College, Cork; and Queen's College, Galway. These colleges are undenominational; the question of founding a Catholic university in Ireland is being agitated.

DUBLIN, Ireland.
THE ROYAL UNIVERSITY OF IRELAND.

The Royal University of Ireland, founded in 1850, is an examining body conferring degrees in Arts (B.A., M.A., D. Lit.); Philosophy (D.Ph.); Science (B.Sc., D.Sc.); Engineering (B.E., M.E.); Law (LL.B., LL.D.); Medicine (M.B., M.D., B.Ch., M.Ch., B.A.O., M.A.O.); Music (B. Mus., D. Mus.).

All degrees, honours, exhibitions, prizes, scholarships, studentships and junior fellowships in the university are open to students of either sex.

The degrees are conferred on candidates that have passed a prescribed series of examinations held by examiners appointed by the university. The examinations must be taken in a prescribed order, and in general an interval of at least one academic year must elapse between two consecutive examinations.

The B.Sc. degree differs from that of the University of London in being conferred on the result of an examination taken after an interval of at least one academic year from the time of graduating in any faculty of the university.

Prizes, exhibitions, scholarships, and fellowships, varying in value from £12 ($60) to £200 ($1,000) a year, for four years are open to competition.

No conditions as to residence are imposed, and candidates for degrees may obtain their education where they please.

Colleges affiliated with the Royal University are the Queen's Colleges of Belfast, Cork and Galway; (see below).

Further information may be obtained from the Calendar of the Royal University of Ireland or from the registrar, The Royal University of Ireland, Dublin.

COLLEGES AFFILIATED TO THE ROYAL UNIVERSITY OF IRELAND.

Belfast, Cork, Galway.

The three colleges, Queen's College, Belfast; Queen's College, Cork; and Queen's College, Galway, prepare for the examinations of the Royal University of Ireland; they provide lectures, but do not provide for residence. Women are admitted on the same conditions as men to all the lectures, and by a recent decree all scholarships and prizes have been opened to them, so that women have now equal facilities with men.

The college session, beginning in October, is divided into three terms, each of about ten weeks' duration.

The fee for each course is £2 ($10) or £3 ($15) for the session. Further information may be obtained from the registrar of the particular college.

THE UNIVERSITY OF DUBLIN.

Trinity College, Dublin.

The University of Dublin consists of only one college, Trinity College, founded in 1591. It confers degrees in Arts, Science, Law, Medicine, Theology and Music.

No degrees are granted to women, and women are admitted only to those lectures that are open to the public and free. Public lectures are given in German, Hebrew, Irish, Biblical Greek, Ancient

History, Astronomy, Geology and Mineralogy, Law, Divinity and Oratory.

In 1895, with a view to testing the probable numbers and the ability of the women students who wished to be admitted to the honour examinations, the university framed the following new regulations applying to the years 1896, 1897 and 1898 only:

1. Women who have obtained at any of the Trinity College examinations either a junior or a senior certificate* may be examined in the same honour courses as the senior freshmen.

2. Those who have obtained a senior certificate may, under the same conditions, if they prefer it, be examined in any of the courses for moderatorships.

The university then decided that the rules were to remain in force for the years 1899 and 1900.

Women are permitted to use the university library for purposes of research on the same conditions as men.

There are three terms in the year: Michaelmas term, beginning October 10th and ending December 20th; Hilary term, beginning January 10th and ending March 25th; Trinity term, beginning April 15th and ending June 30th.

Full information is given in the Dublin University Calendar (Dublin), Hodges, Figgis & Co.; price, 4s. ($1.00). Enquiries may be addressed to the registrar, Trinity College, Dublin.

Professors and Lecturers.

ARTS.

LANGUAGES.—SEMITIC : *Professor* Abbott; *Messrs.* Beare, White, Wilkins.
INDO-IRANIAN : *Professor* Lane Poole.
CLASSICAL : *Professors* Bury, Purser, Tyrrell; *Mr.* Smyly.
ENGLISH : *Professor* Edward Dowden.
GERMANIC : *Professor* Selss.
ROMANCE : *Professor* Atkinson.
IRISH : *Professor* Murphy.

COMPARATIVE PHILOLOGY : *Professor* Atkinson.
PHILOSOPHY : *Professors* Beare, Johnston.
POLITICAL ECONOMY : *Professor* Bastable.
HISTORY : *Professors* Bury, Mahaffy.
ORATORY (Rhetoric) : *Professor* Dowden.

---

*The university arranges special "examinations for women" and successful candidates receive the junior certificate, the senior certificate, or a certificate of honour, according to the examination taken. These examinations cover the same range of subjects and are of about the same grade as ordinary English college entrance examinations.

SCIENCE.

MATHEMATICS AND ASTRONOMY: *Professors* Burnside, Joly, Arthur Panton.
PHYSICS: *Professors* Fitzgerald, Tarleton; *Messrs.* Joly, Thrift, Traill, Trouton.
CHEMISTRY: *Professor* Reynolds; *Messrs.* Bailey, E. A. Werner.
MINERALOGY AND GEOLOGY: *Professor* Joly.
BIOLOGY: *Professors* Mackintosh, Wright; *Mr.* Dixon.
ENGINEERING: *Professor* Alexander; *Mr.* Walter E. Lilly.

LAW.

Professors Hart, Leech, Thompson.

MEDICINE.

Professors Charles Bent Ball, Bennett, Cunningham, Little, O'Sullivan.

THEOLOGY.

Professors Bernard, Charles, Dickinson, Gwynn, Lawlor; *Dr.* Kennedy; *Messrs.* Berry, Carleton, Graham, Roberts, Walsh, White, Wilkins.

MUSIC.

Professor Ebenezer Prout.

SCOTLAND.

There are four universities in Scotland—Aberdeen, St. Andrews, Edinburgh and Glasgow. These are all teaching as well as examining bodies and confer degrees. Women are in every case admitted to the degrees in Arts, Science and Medicine, and at Aberdeen to the degrees in Law. The university lectures are as a rule open to women, but in some cases separate instruction is provided for them, and separate lectures are given by the university professors and lecturers.

University College, Dundee, affiliated to St. Andrews University, admits women to all its classes and prepares for the examinations of Edinburgh, Glasgow and London Universities. There are special medical schools for women at Edinburgh and Glasgow.

ABERDEEN, Scotland.

UNIVERSITY OF ABERDEEN.

The University of Aberdeen gives instruction and confers degrees in Arts, Science, Law, Medicine and Theology. Women are admitted to graduation in all these subjects with the exception of Theology, and all classes in Arts and Science are open to women, as are also, with some exceptions, the classes in Medicine.

The academic year is divided, in the Faculties of Arts, Science and Medicine, into two sessions, the winter session beginning in the middle of October and ending in the middle of March, and the summer session beginning in the end of April and ending about the middle of July.

The matriculation fee is one guinea ($5.25) and the class fees vary from one to three guineas ($5.25 to $15.75). There are numerous prizes and bursaries, the majority of which are open to women.

Women are permitted to use the same libraries and reading rooms as the men students.

A hall of residence for women students, Castleton House, Chanonry, Old Aberdeen, was opened in October, 1898, under the charge of a lady warden. Terms for board and lodging are £1 1s. ($5.25) a week.

For further information apply to the secretary, MR. DONALDSON ROSE THOM.

The Aberdeen University Calendar is published by A. King & Co., Aberdeen; price, 2s. 6d. ($0.62).

Professors and Lecturers.

ARTS.

LANGUAGES.—SEMITIC: *Professor* Gilroy.
CLASSICAL: *Professors* Harrower, Ramsay.
GERMANIC: *Mr.* Hein.
ENGLISH: *Professor* Grierson.
ROMANCE: *Dr.* Scholle.
PHILOSOPHY: *Professors* Davidson, Royce, Sorley; *Mr.* Stout.
HISTORY: *Mr.* Terry.
ELOCUTION: *Mr.* Macleod.
PEDAGOGY: *Mr.* Clarke.

SCIENCE.

MATHEMATICS: *Professor* Pirie; *Mr.* Clark.

PHYSICS: *Professor* Niven
CHEMISTRY: *Professor* Japp.
BIOLOGY: *Professors* MacWilliam, Nicholson; *Mr.* Brown.
BOTANY: *Professor* Trail.
AGRICULTURE: *Messrs.* Hendrick, Wilson.

LAW.

Professor J. D. Wilson; *Mr.* Duguid.

MEDICINE.

Professors Cash, Finlay, Hamilton, Hay, Ogston, Reid, Stephenson.

THEOLOGY.

Professors Cowan, Johnston, Paterson.

DUNDEE, Scotland.

UNIVERSITY COLLEGE.

This college provides instruction in Arts, Science and Medicine, and prepares students for graduation in these subjects at the Universities of St. Andrews, London, Edinburgh and Glasgow.

The classes are open to all persons without restrictions as to age or sex, but all candidates for graduation must take the preliminary examination or must have taken an equivalent examination. The entrance examinations of most American or European universities are considered equivalent.

The academic year is divided into a winter session, beginning on

October 12th and ending on March 22nd, and a summer session, beginning on April 25th and ending on June 30th.

The fees for each class are from one guinea ($5.25) to three guineas ($15.75). The matriculation fee is 10s. 6d. ($2.62).

Students do not reside in the college.

For further information see the college calendar, or apply to the secretary, MR. R. N. KERR.

Professors and Lecturers.

ARTS.

LANGUAGES.—CLASSICAL: *Mr.* Hannay.
ENGLISH: *Professor* M'Cormick.
GERMAN AND FRENCH: *Mr.* Durlac.

SCIENCE.

MATHEMATICS: *Professor* Steggall; *Dr.* M'Cowan.
PHYSICS: *Professor* Kuenen; *Dr.* M'Cowan.
CHEMISTRY: *Professor* Walker; *Dr.* Lumsden; *Mr.* Wood.

BIOLOGY: *Professors* Geddes, Mackay, Waymouth Reid, D'Arcy W. Thompson; *Mr.* Waite.
ENGINEERING: *Professor* Claxton Fidler; *Mr.* ———.

MEDICINE.

Professors MacEwan, Stalker; *Drs.* M'Gillivray, Rorie, Templeman, Whyte; *Mr.* Greig.

EDINBURGH, Scotland.

UNIVERSITY OF EDINBURGH.

This university, founded in 1582, is a teaching and examining body, giving instruction and conferring degrees in Arts, Science, Law, Medicine and Theology.

Students desiring to attend the classes must obtain a matriculation card and pay the matriculation fee of one guinea ($5.25). The matriculation fees, class fees, etc., amount to about ten guineas ($52.50) yearly. Fees for the separate classes are from one guinea ($5.25) to three guineas ($15.75) for the session.

All the Arts classes and some of the Science classes have been open to women since 1892, but some of the instruction in Science is given for women at the Edinburgh School of Medicine for Women, Surgeon Square, Edinburgh, and at the Medical College for Women, Chambers Street, Edinburgh.

All the degrees in Arts, Science and Medicine are open to women; women are, moreover, allowed to graduate in subjects in which the university has not provided for their teaching if they obtain instruction of a kind specified by the university.

A section of the university library is set apart for women and they have access to all the books.

The university scholarships are not generally open to women, but there are several scholarships open to women only.

The academic year is divided into two sessions—a winter session, beginning early in October and ending early in April; a summer session, beginning early in May and ending early in July.

There are no requirements as to residence, but there are three halls of residence for women students: Crudelius House, 6 Archibald Place, Edinburgh; terms for board and lodging from 18s. ($4.50) per week, including the use of a common sitting room, light, service, etc.; for particulars apply to the hon. secretary, MISS H. MCLEAN, 35 Howe Street, Edinburgh;—Masson Hall, 31 George Square, Edinburgh; terms may be had on application to the warden, MISS F. H. SIMPSON;—Muir Hall, 12 George Square, Edinburgh, for students of medicine; terms for board and lodging from 16s. 6d. ($4.12) per week; apply to the lady superintendent, MISS ROBERTSON.

Further information may be obtained from the Edinburgh University Calendar, published by James Thin, 55 South Bridge, Edinburgh, price, 3s. ($0.75); or from MISS LOUISA STEVENSON, hon. secretary of the Edinburgh Association for the University Education of Women, 13 Randolph Crescent, Edinburgh.

Professors and Lecturers.

ARTS.

LANGUAGES.—SEMITIC: *Professor* Kennedy.
  CLASSICAL: *Professors* Butcher, Hardie; *Messrs.* Mill, Thomson.
  ENGLISH: *Professor* Saintsbury; *Mr.* Smith.
  GERMANIC: *Dr.* Schlapp.
  ROMANCE: *Dr.* Sarolea.
  CELTIC: *Professor* Mackinnon.
COMPARATIVE PHILOLOGY: *Professor* Eggeling.
PHILOSOPHY: *Professors* Pattison, Seth; *Mr.* Hardie.
POLITICAL ECONOMY: *Professor* Nicholson.
HISTORY: *Professors* Kirkpatrick, Prothero.

PEDAGOGY: *Professor* Laurie.
ART AND ARCHÆOLOGY: *Professor* Brown; *Mr.* Kern.

SCIENCE.

MATHEMATICS AND ASTRONOMY: *Professors* Chrystal, Copeland; *Dr.* Knott; *Mr.* Tweedie.
PHYSICS: *Professor* Tait; *Dr.* Peddie.
CHEMISTRY: *Professor* Crum Brown; *Dr.* Dobbin.
MINERALOGY: *Dr.* Marshall.
GEOLOGY: *Professor* Geikie; *Mr.* Flett.
BIOLOGY: *Professors* I. B. Balfour, Ewart; *Mr.* Burrage.
ENGINEERING: *Professor* Armstrong.
AGRICULTURE: *Professor* Wallace; *Drs.* Aitken, Fream; *Colonel* Bailey.

LAW.

Professors Sir Ludovic Grant, Kirkpatrick, Sir H. D. Littlejohn, Mackintosh, Nicholson, Rankine, Wood; *Messrs.* Burnet, Cook.

MEDICINE.

Professors Annandale, Balfour, Brown, Chiene, Ewart, Greenfield, Fraser, Rutherford, Simpson, Sir T. Stewart, Sir Wm. Turner; *Drs.* Beard, Carlier, Carmichael, Clouston, Dobbin, Hepburn, M'Bride, Muir, Playfair; *Messrs.* Berry, Sillar.

THEOLOGY.

Professors Flint, Kennedy, Taylor, Thiele.

MUSIC.

Professors Niecks, Kirkpatrick.

EDINBURGH SUMMER SCHOOL OF MODERN LANGUAGES.

The object of this school is to extend the knowledge and advance the teaching of Modern Languages. In 1899 courses in French and English Language, Literature, History, Geography, etc., for both French and English students will be given in Edinburgh from August 1st to August 26th.

The inclusive fee is £2 2s. ($10.50) and students can board in one of the houses of University Hall for £1 5s. ($6.25) weekly. For further particulars apply to the secretary, Outlook Tower, Castlehill, Edinburgh.

Lecturers.

ENGLISH : *Professors* Geddes, Kirkpatrick; *Messrs.* Cran, Eyre-Todd, Kelman, Jr., Marr, Wyld.

FRENCH : *Professors* Seignobos; *MM.* Bazalgette, Delvolvé, Guyou, Mansion, Marillier.

EDINBURGH SCHOOL OF MEDICINE FOR WOMEN.

Surgeon Square, Edinburgh.

This school, in connection with the Royal Infirmary, Edinburgh, in which eighty beds are set apart for the clinical instruction of women, prepares for the medical examinations of the University of Edinburgh. The two years' residence required by the university can be kept at this school.

The year is divided into the winter session, beginning about October 10th and ending about April 1st, and the summer session, beginning about May 1st and ending about August 1st. The full course of study is five years. The school and hospital fees vary from £20 ($100) to £30 ($150) a year; the total expense of the five years' course is estimated to be about £160 ($800).

There are several scholarships and bursaries, varying in value from £25 ($125) to £50 ($250) a year.

There is as yet no hall of residence, but it is hoped that one will soon be founded.

For further information apply to MISS LA COUR, School of Medicine, Surgeon Square, Edinburgh, who will send copies of the school prospectus and of the Syllabus of the Medical Faculty of the University of Edinburgh, post free, for 6d. ($0.12).

Lecturers.

MEDICINE AND SURGERY.
Drs. Aitken, Bramwell, Graham Brown, Bruce, Clouston, Croom, Husband, Jamieson, Sophia Jex-Blake, Littlejohn, McBride, Muir, Noel Paton, Stockman; *Messrs.* Berry, Cathcart, Cotterill, Hardie, Leith; *Miss* Jessie M. McGregor; *Mr.* McLaren; *Miss* Marion Newbigin; *Messrs.* Thomson, Turnbull, Wood.

MEDICAL COLLEGE FOR WOMEN.
20 Chambers Street, Edinburgh.

The particulars given for the School of Medicine hold good for the Medical College. For further information apply to the secretary, MISS MACKAY.

Lecturers.

Drs. Ballantyne, Cathcart, Craig, Cumming, Gibson, Husband, Mackay, Macpherson, Noel Paton, Philip, Russell, Thomson, Tuke, Turner, Walker; *Messrs.* Berry, Brewis, Cadell, Littlejohn, Macadam, Murdoch, *Miss* Newbigin, *Messrs.* Thomson, Turnbull, Whitaker.

GLASGOW, Scotland.

UNIVERSITY OF GLASGOW.

This university, founded in 1451, is a teaching and examining body giving instruction and conferring degrees in the five Faculties of Arts, Science, Law, Medicine and Theology.

The requirements for admission to the university are the preliminary examinations, which are different for Arts, Science and Medicine, and must be passed by all the students who wish to take the degrees. The classes are also open, without any preliminary examinations, to students not desiring to take the degrees.

In 1892 the University Commissioners empowered the Scotch University Courts to provide instruction for women, and accordingly Queen Margaret College, a college for women only, was taken over by the university and formed into a women's department.

In Queen Margaret College lectures in Arts, Science, Mental Philosophy and Medicine are given for women only by the university professors, and these lectures qualify for the degrees of the university.

All degrees of the university are open to women on the same conditions as to men. After graduation women become members of the University Council.

In addition to the classes for women held in Queen Margaret College, women have been allowed to attend a few of the honours classes in the university in Moral Philosophy, Political Economy, History, Education, and Insanity.

In Medicine a complete course of five years' instruction is arranged by Queen Margaret College, and in the Royal infirmary 200 beds are appropriated to the exclusive instruction of women students. Women also study at the Royal Hospital for Sick Children, the Glasgow Maternity Hospital, the Royal Lunatic Asylum, Gartnavel; the Eye Hospital, Charlotte Street; and the City of Glasgow Fever Hospital.

The number of women students in 1897–98 was 257, of whom 67 took the courses in Medicine. Permission to attend courses in Law and Divinity has not yet been applied for by women.

Women students are allowed to borrow books from the university library, and there is a reading room in Queen Margaret College.

Queen Margaret College has in connection with it a hall of residence for women students, information in regard to which may be obtained from Mrs. Riddoch, honorary secretary, 34 Lawrence Place, Dowanhill, Glasgow. The terms for board and lodging are from £1 ($5) a week.

The college year is divided into two sessions: the winter session, beginning October 20th and ending March 23rd; the spring session, beginning, in Medicine and Science, on April 25th, and in Arts on May 2nd, lasting in each case ten weeks.

The fees are from one guinea ($5.25) to three guineas ($15.75) for each class for the session, and should be paid at the secretary's office, Queen Margaret College.

The majority of scholarships and fellowships are not open to women, but the university has been empowered to open to women any scholarships or fellowships that have been founded not more than twenty-five years.

Further information may be obtained from the Glasgow University Calendar, published by James Maclehose & Sons, 61 St. Vincent Street, Glasgow; price, 3s. ($0.75).

Professors and Lecturers

ARTS.

LANGUAGES.—SEMITIC: *Professor* Robertson.
  CLASSICAL: *Professors* Murray, Ramsay; *Messsrs.* Balgarnie, Brown, Macdonald.
  ENGLISH: *Professor* Bradley; *Mr.* Jack.
  GERMANIC: *Dr.* Tille.
  ROMANCE: *Mr.* Mercier.
PHILOSOPHY: *Professors* Adamson, Jones; *Messrs.* Duff, Smith
POLITICAL SCIENCE: *Professor* Smart.
HISTORY: *Professor* Lodge.
PEDAGOGY: *Dr.* Ross.

SCIENCE.

MATHEMATICS AND ASTRONOMY: *Professors* Becker, Jack; *Messrs.* Carslaw, Lindsay.
PHYSICS: *Professor* Lord Kelvin; *Messrs.* Blyth, Maclean.

CHEMISTRY: *Professor* Ferguson; *Messrs.* Gray, Lang.
BOTANY: *Professor* Bower.
BIOLOGY: *Professor* Young.
ENGINEERING: *Professors* Barr, Biles; *Mr.* Cormack.

LAW.

Professors Moir, Moody Stuart; *Messrs.* Irvine, Mackenzie, M'Kechnie, Miller.

MEDICINE.

Professors Anderson, Buchanan, Cameron, Cleland, Coats, Gairdner, Glaister, Macewen, M'Kendrick, Stockman; *Drs.* Anderson, Barr, Ramsay, Reid, Yellowles, Young, Workman; *Messrs.* Bryce, Downie, Gemmill, Pringle.

THEOLOGY.

Professors Hastie, Stewart, Story; *Dr.* Foster.

ST. ANDREWS, Fife, Scotland.

THE UNIVERSITY AND COLLEGE OF ST. ANDREWS.

The University of St. Andrews gives instruction and confers degrees in Arts, Science, Law, Medicine and Theology. In it are incorporated the United Colleges of St. Salvator and St. Leonard, restricted to the teaching of Arts, Science, Law and Medicine, and the College of St. Mary, which is restricted to the teaching of Theology. Degrees are conferred on candidates who have attended certain classes for specified times and passed certain examinations.

All classes are open, without restrictions, to women, as are also degrees in Arts, Science and Medicine. In special cases graduates of foreign universities are excused from the preliminary examinations for the degrees.

The University of St. Andrews holds a special examination for women only and grants to all who pass this examination a diploma and the title of L.L.A.

The academic year is divided into two sessions: a winter session of twenty weeks, beginning early in October, and a summer session of ten weeks, beginning in the fourth week of April.

The fees are £3 3s. ($15.75) for each class for the winter session and £2 2s. ($10.50) for the summer session. The matriculation fee is £1 1s. ($5.25).

Several bursaries (scholarships) varying in value from £15 to £30 ($75 to $150) yearly are open for competition to women students only. The question of opening more of the bursaries and fellowships to women is under consideration.

There is a hall of residence for women students (University Hall, St. Andrews). The charge for board and residence is from £30 ($150) for the winter session and from £15 ($75) for the summer session. Enquiries should be addressed to the warden of the hall, MISS LOUISA INNES LUMSDEN.

Further particulars in regard to the university may be found in the St. Andrews University Calendar, and further information may be obtained from the registrar, the University of St. Andrews, Scotland.

Professors and Lecturers.

ARTS.

LANGUAGES.—SEMITIC: *Professor* Birrell.
  CLASSICAL: *Professors* Burnet, Roberts.
  ENGLISH: *Professor* Lawson.
  MODERN GREEK: *Dr.* Jannaris.
PHILOSOPHY: *Professors* Knight, Ritchie.
HISTORY: *Dr.* Mackinnon.
PEDAGOGY: *Professor* Meiklejohn.

SCIENCE.

MATHEMATICS: *Professor* Lang.
PHYSICS: *Professor* Butler.
CHEMISTRY: *Professor* Purdie.
BIOLOGY: *Professor* William M'Intosh; *Mr.* Robertson.

MEDICINE.

Professor Pettigrew; *Dr.* Musgrove; *Mr.* Wytt; *Miss* Umpherston.

THEOLOGY.

Professors Herkless, Menzies, Stewart.

GREECE.

The only educational institutions of any importance in Greece are the National University in Athens, and the American, English, French and German Schools of Archæology, also situated in Athens. The University of Athens was opened to women in December, 1895. The other schools, which give no degrees, are founded principally for the purposes of research and exploration, and in general admit women.

ATHENS, Greece.
THE UNIVERSITY OF ATHENS.

This university was founded in 1837 on the same general plan as that of the German universities. It was opened to women, in spite of great opposition, in December, 1895, and there have been a number of women students at the university several of whom have obtained the Doctor's degree. All the libraries, reading rooms and laboratories are open to women students and a library and reading room have been established specially for women students. The university consists of the four Faculties of Philosophy (Arts and Science), Law, Medicine and Theology, and confers the degree of Doctor in each of these faculties.

The academic year is divided into the winter semester, beginning on September 15th and ending on February 1st, and the summer semester, lasting from February 1st till June 15th.

The tuition fees for the year are 160dr. ($19.20), and there is a fee of 100dr. ($12) for the Diploma of Doctor.

The number of professors is very large, and on this account the list is omitted. It may be found in the Minerva Jahrbuch der Gelehrten Welt. For further information apply to the secretary, MR. PETROS BRYZAKIS.

THE AMERICAN SCHOOL OF CLASSICAL STUDIES.

This school was founded by the Archæological Institute of America in 1881 and is supported by the coöperation of leading American universities and colleges. Its object is to furnish an opportunity to study classical Literature, Art and Antiquities and to aid in conducting the exploration and excavation of classical sites.

All the courses and privileges of the school are open to women as to men. Bachelors of Arts of coöperating colleges, and Bachelors of Arts who have been graduate students at coöperating colleges, are admitted to membership on presenting a certificate from the classical department of the college in which they last studied. American students, resident or travelling in Greece, may be enrolled as special students at the discretion of the director.

The applicant for admission to the school should fill out a registration blank (which may be obtained from the chairman of the managing committee or from the director), and send this with his credentials to the chairman, Prof. Thomas Day Seymour, Yale University, New Haven, Conn.

Two fellowships, of the value of $600, are awarded yearly, mainly on the result of a written examination, held in March, but other evidences of ability and attainments will be considered. A third fellowship, the "Agnes Hoppin Memorial Fellowship," of the value of $1,000, is available for the years 1899 and 1900, and will be awarded to a woman who, in the opinion of the committee, shall seem to be worthy of receiving it. Particulars may be obtained from the chairman of the committee on fellowships, PROF. BENJAMIN I. WHEELER, Ithaca, N. Y.

The director and professors reside in Athens during the school year, from October 1st to June 1st.

Members pay no fees; other persons admitted to the school pay $25 a year for tuition. At large hotels in Athens board and lodging can be obtained for $14 per week; at small hotels and in private families for $5.50.

Director, Rufus Byam Richardson; Professor of the Greek Language and Literature for 1899-1900, Herbert Weir Smyth, Professor of Greek, Bryn Mawr College; for 1900–1901, Edward Delavan Perry, Professor of Greek, Columbia University.

THE BRITISH SCHOOL AT ATHENS.

This school, founded in 1886 by the University of Oxford and the Society for the Promotion of Hellenic Studies, has for its object the study of Greek Art, Archæology, Language and Literature.

Students holding fellowships or scholarships from any British university, or belonging to the Royal Academy of Art or the Royal Institute of British Architects, and other persons of British nationality who can give satisfactory proof of their ability to profit by the courses of the school, are admitted as students. Every student must stay at least three months. Women are admitted on the same conditions as men.

The director resides in Athens from the beginning of November until the end of June.

There are no fees for tuition or for the use of the library. Men students are expected to reside in the hostel, paying 15dr. ($1.80) a week for their rooms.

Director, DAVID GEORGE HOGARTH, ESQ., The British School at Athens. Hon. secretary, WILLIAM LORING, ESQ., 2 Hare Court, Temple, London, E. C.

KAISERLICH DEUTSCHES ARCHÄOLOGISCHES INSTITUT.

The German schools at Athens and Rome were founded in 1829 and are under the control of the *Central-Direktion* in Berlin. They have for their object the furthering of archæological studies.

Women are allowed on the same conditions as men to attend the lectures, libraries and reading-rooms, and to take part in the excursions.

Secretaries in Athens: PROFESSOR DR. WILHELM DÖRPFELD, DR. PAUL WOLTERS.

ÉCOLE FRANÇAISE D'ATHÈNES.

The school was founded in 1847, and has for its object archæological research and exploration.

Members must hold the degree of *Docteur ès Lettres* or *Agrégé des Lettres, de Grammaire, de Philosophie, d'Histoire* or *des Sciences.*

The number of members of the school is fixed at six, and admission depends on the results of a competitive examination, both oral and written.

Women are allowed to attend the public lectures given in the school and to use the library on application to the Director.

Director, M. HOMOLLE; honorary directors, MM. BURNOUF and FOUCART.

HUNGARY.

The universities of Hungary are similar to those of Germany and Austria in general plan; see pp. 1–3, 62–64. They are three in number, namely, the universities of Agram, Budapest and Klausenberg. Of these the University of Budapest is the oldest and the most important; it comprises the four Faculties of Theology, Law, Medicine and Philosophy (Arts and Science), while the University of Agram has no Faculty of Medicine and that of Klausenberg no Faculty of Theology. It has not been thought necessary to give the list of professors at these universities; it may be found in the Minerva Jahrbuch der Gelehrten Welt.

In December, 1895, the philosophical, medical and pharmaceutical departments in the universities of Hungary were formally opened to women by a decree of the Hungarian Minister of Education. In his decree to the universities the Minister gave in detail the reasons which induced him to take the step. Briefly summarised they are: that the conditions of society have so changed that women are now more often obliged to undertake remunerative labor; that they are well-fitted for scientific and educational work, and that, therefore, facilities for study should be offered to them.

In order to enter the universities women have, however, to fill the same requirements as men, that is, to pass the *Maturitätsprüfung*, and the severity of the test shall, the decree states, be in no case relaxed. They are also obliged to take part in the dissecting, practical work, etc.

The fee charged for admission to all lectures for one semester is 30 florins ($15).

For dates of semesters and general particulars, see under Germany and Austria.

IRELAND.

See pp. 114–117.

ITALY.

There are in Italy seventeen state universities, four free universities and two institutions similar to universities, the *R. Istituto Superiore di studi practici e di perfezionamento* at Florence, and the *R. Accademia Scientifico-litteraria* at Milan, the first giving courses in Arts, Science and Medicine, and the latter courses in Philosophy and Philology. There are American, French and German schools of Archæology in Rome similar to those in Athens, and there is a zoological station at Naples at which many Americans study.

The universities as a rule provide instruction and confer degrees in Arts, Science, Law and Medicine. The candidate for the degree of Doctor (*laurea*) must attend a definitely specified series of courses for a specified number of years (from three to six years, according to the faculty).

The courses, degrees, laboratories and libraries at these universities are all open to women on the same conditions as to men. Two classes of students are admitted, regular students and hearers (*uditori*).

Regular students must have obtained, before entering, the certificate of a secondary school (*licenza liccale* or *tecnica*) or, if foreigners, must satisfy the Faculties of Arts and Science that the education they have received would have enabled them to obtain this *licenza*. In the case of students who have studied at a foreign university the faculty in which the student desires to attend courses decides on the admittance of the student. Such students should present certificates or diplomas from their former college or university, and also their certificate of birth.

Hearers have to fulfil no special requirements beyond presenting a certificate of birth. They are not admitted to degrees, but if they take the examinations they may in some cases receive certificates to the effect that they have studied in the university.

Students and hearers must matriculate and pay the matriculation fees for the ensuing year between August 1st and October 30th. The academic year is not divided into semesters; it begins on October 15th and ends on July 30th. Lectures begin in the first week of November and end on June 15th.

Regular students pay their fees (*tassa d' imatricolazione, tassa d' iscrizoni* and *tassa di diploma*) to the state treasury through the *ufficio demaniale*. The matriculation fee varies from 20 lire ($3.90) to 40 lire ($7.80), according to the faculty; the inscription fees cover all the courses which have to be taken for a degree and amount to from 50 lire ($9.75) to 165 lire ($32.18) yearly. Fees for examinations, from 10 lire ($1.95) to 25 lire ($4.88) yearly, and laboratory fees are paid to the *economato* of the university. Hearers pay a matriculation fee of 40 lire ($7.80) and a fee of 8 lire ($1.56) for each hour per week of lecture in the courses which they enter. They pay these fees to the same officials as the regular students.

Scholarships are open to women as to men and take the form, in general, of an exemption from fees. There are also fellowships open for competition to students that have obtained the degree of Doctor.

Information concerning the general university regulations is given in a pamphlet entitled Regolamento Universitario; information concerning a particular university, in the Annuario Accademico of the university in question, which, with the Regolamento Universitario may be obtained from the secretary of the university.

BOLOGNA, Italy.

REGIA UNIVERSITÀ DEGLI STUDI DI BOLOGNA.

This university, founded in the 12th century, was renowned in the past for the number of celebrated women counted among its students and professors.

The regulations are similar to those of all Italian universities; see pp. 132, 133.

Enquiries may be addressed to the *direttore di segretaria*, SIGNOR LUIGI BONA.

Professors and Lecturers.

ARTS.

LANGUAGES. — CLASSICAL: *Professors* Albini, Gandino, Puntoni; *Signors* Levi, Michelangeli, Olivieri.

ROMANCE: *Professor* Carducci; *Signors* Ferrari, Morpurgo, Restori, Solerti.

COMPARATIVE PHILOLOGY: *Professor* Turrini.

PHILOSOPHY: *Professors* Acri, Barbera, Valdarnini; *Signors* Ambrosini, DeNardi, Pilo.

POLITICAL ECONOMY: *Professor* Martello; *Signors* Barbieri, D'Apel, Gemma, Rossi.

HISTORY: *Professors* Bertolini, Falletti; *Signors* Vittorio Fiorini, Rossi.

ARCHÆOLOGY: *Professor* Brizio; *Signor* Szedlo.

ARCHITECTURE: *Professors* Benetti, Canevazzi, Stabilini, Venturi, Zannoni; *Signors* Ballarini, Berti, Bombicci, Muggia.

ENGINEERING: *Professors* Cavani, Cavazzi, Donati, Masi; *Signors* Gemelli, Gorrieri, Maganzini, Regnoli, Silvani.

SCIENCE.

MATHEMATICS AND ASTRONOMY: *Professors* Arzelà, Donati, Enriquez, Matteo Fiorini, Pincherle, Saporetti; *Signors* Razzaboni, Vivanti.

PHYSICS: *Professors* Righi, Ruffini; *Signor* Dessau.

CHEMISTRY: *Professor* Ciamician; *Signors* Angeli, Magnanini, Zanetti.

MINERALOGY: *Professor* Bombicci.

GEOLOGY: *Professor* Capellini; *Signor* Simonelli.

GEOGRAPHY: *Professor* Peroglio; *Signor* Sensini.

BIOLOGY: *Professors* Ciaccio, Emery, Mattirolo; *Signor* Coggi.

LAW.

Professors Brini, Costa, Gaudenzi, Giusti, Manfredini, Mantovani-Orsetti, Regnoli, Rossi, Salvioni, Vanni, Vivante; *Signors* Ballarini, Berardi, Conti, Diena, Lanza, Malagola, Ramponi, Trovanelli.

MEDICINE.

Professors Albertoni, Calderini, Calori, Fusari, Maiocchi, Martinotti, Murri, Novaro, Novi, Pellacani, Poggi, Roncati, Rovighi, Tartuferi, Tizzoni; *Signors* Belmondo, Bordè, Bozzi, Cattani, Gurrieri, Monti, Panzeri, Pinto, Pinzani, Respighi, Righi, Ruggi, Sabbatani, Salaghi, Testi.

CAGLIARI, Sardinia, Italy.

REGIA UNIVERSITÀ DEGLI STUDI DI CAGLIARI.

This university, founded in 1596, is under the same regulations as all the universities of Italy; see pp. 132, 133.

Enquiries may be addressed to the secretary, SIGNOR GIUSEPPE LOY-ISOLA.

Professors and Lecturers.

ARTS.

POLITICAL ECONOMY: *Professor* Masè-Dari.
ARCHITECTURE: *Signor* Fais.

SCIENCE.

MATHEMATICS AND ASTRONOMY: *Professors* Fais, Usai, Vivanet.
PHYSICS: *Professors* Guglielmo, Odde.
MINERALOGY AND GEOLOGY: *Professor* Lovisato.
BIOLOGY: *Professor* Lovisato; *Signor* Mazza.

LAW.

Professors Angioni-Contini, Barcaredda, Borgna, Careddu, Lanza, Loy-Isola, Porcu-Giua, Orrù, Soro; *Signors* Atzeri, Guzzoni, Picinelli.

MEDICINE.

Professors Biondi, Carbone, Fasola, Fenoglio, Gonella, Guzzoni degli Ancarani, Legge, Marfori, Mazza, Sabbatani, Sanfelice, Tonnini.

CAMERINO, Italy.

LIBERA UNIVERSITÀ DEGLI STUDI DI CAMERINO.

This university, founded in 1727, is under the same regulations as all the universities of Italy; see pp. 132, 133.

Enquiries may be addressed to the secretary, SIGNOR MARIO MANNUCCI.

Professors and Lecturers.

LAW.

Professors Arnó, Lorini, Marsili, Palumbo, Ranelletti; *Signors* D'Ajano, Claps, Mircoli, Ricci, Vighi.

MEDICINE.

Professors Berlese, Casali, Catterina, Fabrini, Gallerani, Kazzander, Mircoli, Pacinotti, Sartori.

CATANIA, Sicily.

UNIVERSITÀ DEGLI STUDI DI CATANIA.

This university, founded in 1444, is under the same regulations as all the universities of Italy; see pp. 132, 133.

Enquiries may be addressed to the *direttore di segretaria*, PROFESSOR MARIS MANDALARI.

Professors and Lecturers.

ARTS.

LANGUAGES. — CLASSICAL: *Professor* Sabbadini; *Signors* Biuso, Bruno.
ROMANCE: *Professors* Rapisardi, Sabbadini.
PHILOSOPHY: *Professor* Marino; *Signor* Taverni.

POLITICAL ECONOMY: *Professor* Giuseppe Maiorana-Calatabiano; *Signor* Marletta.
HISTORY: *Professor* Casagrandi.
ARCHÆOLOGY: *Signors* Bruno, Orsi.
ARCHITECTURE: *Signor* Fichera.

PEDAGOGY: *Professor* Taverni; *Signor* Catalano.

SCIENCE.

MATHEMATICS AND ASTRONOMY: *Professors* Chizzoni, Lauricella, Mollame, Pennacchietti, Riccò, Zurria; *Signor* Catania.
PHYSICS: *Professor* Grimaldi.
CHEMISTRY: *Signor* Grassi-Cristaldi.
MINERALOGY AND GEOLOGY: *Professor* Bucca.
GEOGRAPHY: *Signor* Giardina.
BIOLOGY: *Professors* Baccarini, Mingazzini; *Signors* Aloi, Calandruccio.

LAW.

Professors Abate-Longo, Carnazza-Amari, Carnazza-Puglisi, Ciccaglione, Coviello, Delogu, De Luca-Carnazza, De Mauro, La Rosa, Angelo Maiorana, Guiseppe Maioranna, Vadalà Papale, Zocco-Rosa; *Signors* Amabile, Blandini, Aprile di Cimia, Carnazza, Carnevale, Cavallaro, Cimbali, Fiorentino, La Monaca, Majorana, Mangano, Marino, Marletta, Pantano, Paternò-Castello, Peratoner, Politi, Rapisardi, Wrzi.

MEDICINE.

Professors Berretta, Capparelli, Clementi, Cosentino, Curci, D'Abundo, Di Mattei, Feletti, Francaviglia, Petrone, Tomaselli, Ughetti, Valenti; *Signors* Addario, Alonzo, Ardini, Condorelli, Coniglione, De Luca, Galvagno, Grimaldi, Guzzardi, Marchese, Maugeri, Misuraca, Pennino, Ronsisvalle, Sanfilippo.

FERRARA, Italy.

LIBERA UNIVERSITÀ DI FERRARA.

This university, founded in 1391, is under the same regulations as all the universities of Italy; see pp. 132, 133.

Enquiries may be addressed to the secretary, SIGNOR ENRICO BASSANI.

Professors and Lecturers.

ARTS.
POLITICAL ECONOMY: *Professor* Sitta.
ARCHITECTURE: *Signor* Duprà.
ART: *Signor* Ravegnani.

SCIENCE.
MATHEMATICS: *Professors* Borgatti, Vignocchi; *Signor* Roccella.
PHYSICS: *Professor* Bongiovanni.
CHEMISTRY: *Professors* Costa, Garelli.
MINERALOGY: *Signor* Costa.
BIOLOGY: *Professors* Cavazzani, Massalongo, Sala; *Signor* Zuffi.

LAW.
Professors Bennati, Giura, Martinelli, Pasqualini, Carabelli, Sitta, Turbiglio, Weiss De-Welden, Zeni; *Signor* Marchesini, Ruffoni.

MEDICINE.
Professors Bongiovanni, Cavazzani, Garelli, Ludovisi, Marfori, Massalongo, Morpurgo, Sala, Trambusti, Zuffi.

FLORENCE, Italy.

REGIA ISTITUTO DI STUDI SUPERIORI PRACTICI E DI PERFEZIONAMENTO.

This school, founded in 1321, is under the same regulations as all the universities of Italy; see pp. 132, 133.

Enquiries may be addressed to the secretary, SIGNOR TITO FIASCHI.

Professors and Lecturers.

ARTS.

LANGUAGES.—SEMITIC: *Professors* Castelli, Lasinio; *Signor* Scerbo.
  INDO-IRANIAN: *Professors* Pavolini, Severini; *Signor* Donati.
  CLASSICAL: *Professors* Festa, Paoli, Ramorino, Vitelli; *Signors* Nencini, Rasi.
  GERMANIC: *Professor* Parodi; *Signors* Fasola, Weile.
  ROMANCE: *Professors* Mazzoni, Rajna; *Signors* Bacci, Barbi, Parodi, Volpi.
PHILOSOPHY: *Professors* Conti, Tocco.
HISTORY: *Professors* Coen, Puini, Del Vecchio, Villari; *Signor* Franchetti.
ARCHÆOLOGY: *Professors* Fesri, Milani, Paoli; *Signors* Bertolotto, Schiaparelli, Teloni.

SCIENCE.

ASTRONOMY: *Professor* Abetti.
PHYSICS: *Professor* Roiti; *Signors* Marangoni, Salvioni.
CHEMISTRY: *Professor* Schiff.
MINERALOGY: *Professor* Grattarola; *Signor* D'Achiardi.
GEOLOGY AND GEOGRAPHY: *Professors* De Stefani, Marinelli; *Signor* Ristori.
BIOLOGY: *Professors* Fano, Giglioli, Mantegazza, Mattirolo, Targioni-Tozzetti; *Signors* Baroni, Batelli, Bottazzi, Danielli, Marchi, Oddi, Regalia.

MEDICINE.

Professors Bajardi, Banti, Bufalini, Chiarugi, Colzi, Filippi, Grocco, Lustig, Mya, Paoli, Pellizzari, Pestalozza, Roster, Tanzi; *Signors* Acconci, Agostini, Baquis, Barbacci, Bargellini, Bonardi, Borri, Celoni, Centanni, Coronedi, Ferruta, Flora, Gabbi, Galeotti, Giarrè, Grazzi, Del Greco, Grilli, Lumbroso, Mantegazza, Profeta, Rossi, Silvestri, Silvestrini, Simi, Staderini, Tedeschi, Toti, Trambusti.

GENOA, Italy.

REGIA UNIVERSITÀ DEGLI STUDI DI GENOVA.

This university, founded in 1812, is under the same regulations as all the universities of Italy; see pp. 132, 133.

Enquiries may be addressed to the *direttore di segretaria*, SIGNOR GIOVANNI OXILIA.

Professors and Lecturers.

ARTS.

LANGUAGES.—SEMITIC: *Signor* Dall'-Orto.
  CLASSICAL: *Professors* Cerrato, Eusebio, Fumi; *Signor* Pais.
  GERMANIC: *Signor* Dall'Orto.
  ROMANCE: *Professors* Barrili, De Lollis; *Signors* Guarnerio, Mango, Novara.
COMPARATIVE PHILOLOGY: *Professor* Bariola.
PHILOSOPHY: *Professors* Asturaro, Benzoni, Ferrari; *Signors* Cecchi, Chinazzi.
POLITICAL SCIENCE: *Professors* Asturaro, Drago, Ponsiglioni.
HISTORY: *Professor* Manfroni; *Signors* Cecchi, Oberziner, Rosi.
PEDAGOGY: *Professor* Benzoni.
ARCHÆOLOGY: *Signor* Eusebio.
ARCHITECTURE: *Professor* Resasco.

SCIENCE.

MATHEMATICS AND ASTRONOMY: *Professors* Garbieri, Loria, Monteverde, Piuma, Pizzetti; *Signors* Giudice, Morera, Perroni.

PHYSICS: *Professors* Pietro Maria Garibaldi, Morera.

CHEMISTRY: *Professor* Pellizzari.

MINERALOGY: *Professor* Negri.

GEOLOGY AND GEOGRAPHY: *Professor* Issel; *Signor* Squinabol.

BIOLOGY: *Professors* Cattaneo, Grossi, Parona, Penzig.

ENGINEERING: *Professors* Morera, Pizzetti; *Signors* Garbieri, Pellizzari, Rombo.

LAW.

Professors Paolo Emilio Bensa, Bigliati, Castellari, Cogliolo, Del Vecchio, De Murtas-Zichina, Drago, Grasso, Manara, Manenti, Mecacci, Roncali, Rossello, Ruffini, Severi, Traverso, Wautrain-Cavagnari; *Signors* Enrico Bensa, Berlingieri, Antonio Castellari, Cereseto, Civoli, Flora, Grego, Martinelli, Pipia, Porrini, Restano.

MEDICINE.

Professors Acconci, Brigidi, Canalis, Caselli, Pietro Maria Garibaldi, Giovanni Garibaldi, Griffini, Lachi, Livierato, Maragliano, Giulio Masini, Morisani, Morselli, Mosso, Oddi, Parona, Pellizzari, Profeta, Secondi, Severi; *Signors* Basso, Bossi, Cantù, Capranica, Casini, Cioja, Devoto, Ferrari, Giuria, Jemma, Levi, Livierato, Lucatello, Arturo Masini, Andrea Mazza, Giuseppe Mazza, Motta, Perrando, Poli, Polimanti, Sacchi, Staderini, Verdese.

MESSINA, Italy.
REGIA UNIVERSITÀ DEGLI STUDI DI MESSINA.

This university, founded in 1838, is under the same regulations as all the universities of Italy; see pp. 132, 133.

Enquiries may be addressed to the secretary, SIGNOR GIUSEPPE CARACCIOLO.

Professors and Lecturers.

ARTS.

LANGUAGES. — CLASSICAL: *Professors* Michelangeli, Pascoli; *Signors* Consoli, Crivellari.

ROMANCE: *Professors* Cian, Restori; *Signor* Cesareo.

COMPARATIVE PHILOLOGY: *Professor* Michelangeli.

PHILOSOPHY: *Professors* Cesca, Fisichella.

POLITICAL SCIENCE: *Professor* Supino; *Signor* Fleres.

HISTORY: *Professors* Romano, Tropea; *Signor* Porena.

ARCHÆOLOGY: *Professor* Tropea.

ARCHITECTURE: *Signors* Di Bella, Quèriau.

SCIENCE.

MATHEMATICS AND ASTRONOMY: *Professors* De Berardinis, Marcolongo, Martinetti, Vivanti; *Signors* Cacopardo, Visalli.

PHYSICS: *Professor* Salvioni.

CHEMISTRY: *Professor* Errera; *Signor* Giannetto.

MINERALOGY AND GEOLOGY: *Professor* La Valle.

GEOGRAPHY: *Professor* Bertacchi.

BIOLOGY: *Professor* Ficalbi; *Signor* Lessona.

LAW.

Professors Ascoli, Buscemi, Cesareo, De Cola-Proto, Faranda, Lilla, Macri, Manenti, Oliva, Sraffa, Ugo, Venezian; *Signors* Carnazza, Fulci, Puglia, Sciacca, Segrè.

MEDICINE.

Professors Colella, Crisafulli, Ferraro, Gabbi, Gaglio, Giuseppe, G. Pugliatti, R. Pugliatti, Rosario Salomoni, Scimemi, Trombetta, Weiss, Ziino, Zincone; *Signors* Cambria, Cammareri, Fusari, Melle, Terni, Testa, Tornatola.

MILAN, Italy.
REGIA ACADEMIA SCIENTIFICO-LITTERARIA DI MILANO.

This school, founded in 1859, is under the same regulations as all the universities of Italy: see pp. 132, 133.

Enquiries may be addressed to the secretary, SIGNOR EMILIO DE MARCHI.

Professors and Lecturers.

ARTS.

LANGUAGES.—CLASSICAL: *Professor* de Inama, Giussani.
GERMANIC: *Professor* Friedmann; *Signora* Schiff.
ROMANCE: *Professors* Dupuy, Novati, Scherillo; *Signors* Emilio, De Marchi, Ferrieri.
COMPARATIVE PHILOLOGY: *Professor* Ascoli.
PHILOSOPHY: *Professors* Jandelli, Luciano, Zuccante; *Signor* Vignoli.
HISTORY: *Professor* Rolando.
PEDAGOGY: *Signor* Martinazzoli.
ARCHÆOLOGY: *Signors* Ambrosoli, Ceriani, Attilio De Marchi, Serafino.
GEOGRAPHY: *Professor* Savio; *Signor* Ricchieri.

MODENA, Italy.
REGIA UNIVERSITÀ DEGLI STUDI DI MODENA.

This university, founded in 1683, is under the same regulations as all the universities of Italy; see pp. 132, 133.

Enquiries may be addressed to the secretary, SIGNOR ACHILLE CAMPIOLE.

Professors and Lecturers.

ARTS.

POLITICAL SCIENCE: *Professor* Valenti; *Signor* Franchi.
ARCHITECTURE: *Signor* Cavazzuti.

SCIENCE.

MATHEMATICS: *Professor* Nicoletti, Del Re; *Signors* Nicoli, Valeri.
PHYSICS: *Professor* Chistoni.
CHEMISTRY: *Professor* Magnanini; *Signor* Maissen.
GEOLOGY AND MINERALOGY: *Professor* Pantanelli.
BIOLOGY: *Professors* Monticelli, Mori; *Signors* Macchiati, Roncaglia.

LAW.

Professors Borri, Brandoli, Franchi, Melucci, Morelli, Olivi, Petrone, Sabbatini, Serafini, Strani, Triani; *Signors* Borciani, Conigliani, Ferrarini, Marchetti, Pacchioni.

MEDICINE.

Professors Albertotti, Berti, Borri, Casarini, Cesari, Fabbri, Fusari, Galvagni, Maggiora, Puglia, Tamburini, Ruggi, Vanni, Vassale; *Signors* Belmondo, Bertacchini, Casciani, Govi, Guicciardi, Levi, Monari, Nasi, Petrazzani, Ravaglia, Riccardi, Roncaglia, Saltini.

NAPLES, Italy.
REGIA UNIVERSITÀ DEGLI STUDI DI NAPOLI.

This university, founded in 1224, is under the same regulations as all the universities of Italy; see pp. 132, 133.

For the zoological station at Naples see p. 149.

Enquiries may be addressed to the secretary, SIGNOR ODOARDO SANTORO.

Professors and Lecturers.

ARTS.

LANGUAGES.—SEMITIC: *Professor* Buonazia.
INDO-IRANIAN: *Professor* Kerbaker.
CLASSICAL: *Professors* Cocchia, Flores, Kerbaker; *Signors* De Gennaro, D'Ovidio, Pascal.
ROMANCE: *Professors* D'Ovidio, Zumbini; *Signors* Agresti, Pèrcopo, Prudenzano, Zingarelli.
PHILOSOPHY: *Professors* Chiappelli, Masci; *Signors* Bosurgi, Fimiani, Maturi, Memola, Tarantino.
POLITICAL SCIENCE: *Signors* Betocchi, Colaianni, D'Ippolito, Lioy, Mazzola, Miraglia, Nitti, Tammeo.
HISTORY: *Professors* De Blasiis, Holm, Mariano; *Signors* Biamonte, Correra, Faraglia, Schipa.
ARCHÆOLOGY: *Professors* De Petra, Sogliano; *Signor* Patroni.
ARCHITECTURE: *Professor* Capocci; *Signors* Bellini, Curri, Fischetti, Folinea, Giuliani, Laneri, Tango.
PEDAGOGY: *Professor* Fornelli; *Signor* Vecchia.

SCIENCE.

MATHEMATICS AND ASTRONOMY: *Professors* Capelli, Cesàro, Cua, Del Pezzo, Fergola, Montesano, Nobile, Pinto, Raucci, Salvatore-Dino, Siacci; *Signors* Amanzio, Amodeo, Angelitti, Avena, Bellini, Brambilla, Campanile, Isé, Masoni, Nicodemi, Rinonapoli.
PHYSICS: *Professors* Palmieri, Villari; *Signors* Campanile, Ciccone, Del Gaizo, Guiliani, Mercalli, Palazzo, Semmola.
CHEMISTRY: *Professor* Oglialoro-Todaro; *Signors* Forte, Januario, Napolitano, Sardo, Zinno.
MINERALOGY: *Professor* Scacchi; *Signor* Franco.
GEOLOGY: *Professor* Bassani; *Signors* De Loreffzo, Johnston-Lavis, Matteuci.
GEOGRAPHY: *Professor* Porena.
BIOLOGY: *Professor* Costa, Della Valle, Delpino, Nicolucci, Paladino, Trinchese; *Signors* Balsamo, Berlese, Colosi, Comes, Geremicca, Lucarelli, Mazzarelli, Monticelli, Palma, Pasquale, Raffaele.

LAW.

Professors Arcoleo, Bovio, Fadda, Fiore, Emmanuele Gianturco, Lomonaco, Marghieri, Milone, Miraglia, Napodano, Pepere, Persico, Pessina, Scaduto, Viti; *Signors* Abignente, Alimena, Amellino, Arangio Ruiz, Betocchi, Biondi, Campese, Cannada-Bartoli, Carnevale, Ciccaglione, Ciccarelli, Contuzzi, Coviello, De Cillis, Di Maio, De Marinis, Di Martino, De Roberto, Gagliardi, Gargiulo, Girardi, Grippo, Guariglia, Guarracino, Lanza, Lombardi, F. Longo, M. Longo, Manenti, Marino, Masucci, Minutillo, Napodano, Perrone, Petroni, Pisapia, Rubino, Salvia, Scalamandrè, Schiappoli, Semmola, Sorgente, Squitti, Summonte, Tuozzi, Varcasia, Vigliarolo.

MEDICINE.

Professors Albini, Antonelli, Armanni, Bianchi, Boccardi, Cardarelli, Chirone, Corrado, Cozzolino, D'Ambrosio, D'Antona, De Amicis, De Giaxa, De Martini, De Renzi, De Vincentiis, Frusci, Gallozzi, Malerba, Massei, Morisani, Rummo, Schrön, Semmola, Vizioli; *Signors* Aiello, Ajevoli, Amoroso, Antonelli, Arena, Baculo, Bernabei, Biondi, Brancaccio, Breglia, Buonomo, Cacciapuoti, Caccioppoli, Cagnetta, Calabrese, Campione, Cantarano, Capozzi, Caruso, Ciaramelli, Ciccone, Cirìncione, Colella, Conca, Costabile, Cotronei, D'Amore, D'Evant, De Bisogno, De Bonis, De Dominicis, De Grazia, De Luca, De Michele, De Paolis, De Sanctis, De Simone, Del Gaizo, Del Vecchio, Di Giacomo, Di Lorenzo, Ducrey, Falcone, Fasano, Eugenio Fazio, Ferdinando Fazio, Fede, Ferrajolo, Ferrannini, Ferrara, Folinea, Fornario, Franco, Gauthier, Gianturco, Gioffredi, Greco,

Gregoraci, Guarino, Jacontini, Jappelli, Jennaco, Laccetti, Lauro, Leocata, Lobello, Lupó, Magnarapa, Manfredi, Marsiglia, Masucci, Maturi, Mazziotti, Melle, Meola, Miranda, Moauro, Montefusco, Morano, Morelli, Morra, Ninni, Novi, Oro, Pane, Pianese, Pansini, Paolucci, Parascandolo, Alessandro Pascale, Giovanni Pasquale, Patroni, Pecoraro, Pedicini, Pellecchia, Penta, Petteruti, Piccinino, Piretti, Polignani, Radice, Raffaele, Reale, Renzone, Ria, Romanelli, Romano, Rubino, Salvati, Salvi, Salvia, Scalese, Scervini, Scibelli, Scotti, Senise, Sgobbo, Sgrosso, Spatuzzi, Spinelli, Squillante, Stanziale, Tamburrini, Tedeschi, Tortora, Traversa, Tria, Vetere, Virgilio, Vitone, Vizioli, Volpe, Zagari, Zuccarelli.

PADUA, Italy.

REGIA UNIVERSITÀ DEGLI STUDI DI PADUA.

This university, founded in 1222, is under the same regulations as all the universities of Italy; see pp. 132, 133.

Enquiries may be addressed to the *direttore di segretaria*, SIGNOR ——— ———.

Professors and Lecturers.

ARTS.

LANGUAGES —SEMITIC : *Signor* Lolli.
INDO-IRANIAN : *Professor* Teza.
CLASSICAL : *Professors* Cortese, E. Ferrai, Gnesotto, Setti ; *Signor* Ercole.
GERMANIC : *Professor* Baragiola ; *Signor* Weigelsperg.
ROMANCE : *Professors* Crescini, Flamini, Galanti, Medin.
PHILOSOPHY : *Professors* Ardigò, Bonatelli, Ferrari, Ragn'sco ; *Signors* Dandolo, Morando.
HISTORY : *Professors* L. A. Ferrai, Gloria, De Leva, Pinton ; *Signors* Callegari, Musatti, Raulich.
GEOGRAPHY : *Professor* Pennesi ; *Signor* Biasiutti.
ARCHITECTURE : *Professor* Hesse.

SCIENCE.

MATHEMATICS AND ASTRONOMY : *Professors* D'Arcais, Bordiga, Favaro, Gazzaniga, Legnazzi, Levi-Civita, Lorenzoni, Padova, Ricci, Salvotti, Veronese ; *Signor* Chiri.
PHYSICS : *Professor* Vicentini ; *Signor* Lussana.

CHEMISTRY : *Professor* Nasini ; *Signors* Anderlini, Carrara, Spica-Marcataio.
GEOLOGY AND MINERALOGY : *Professors* Omboni, Panebianco.
GEODESY : *Signor* Miari-Fulcis.
BIOLOGY : *Professors* Berlese, Canestrini, Saccardo ; *Signors* Arrigoni, Crevatin, Fiori, Tedesch. de Toni.

LAW AND POLITICAL SCIENCE.

Professors Brugi, Cavagnari, Ferraris, Franceschini, Landucci, Levi-Catellani, Loria, Polacco, Sacerdoti, Giov. Tamassia, Tuozzi ; *Signors* Armanni, Besta, Castori, Conigliani, Contento, Fedozzi, Leoni, Luzzatti, Monte-Martini, Norsa, Sitta, Dalla Volta.

MEDICINE.

Professors Bassini, Belmondo, Bonome, Breda, Castellino, Cervesato, Chirone, De Giovanni, Gradenigo, Inverardi, Marfori, Salvioli, Schwarz, Serafini, Stefani, A. Tamassia, Tricomi, Vlacovich ; *Signors* Alessio, Bolzoni, Bonuzzi, Borgherini, Bosma, Catterina, Cavazzani, Ceconi, Cordaro, Dalle Ore, Ferrari, Lussana, Maggia, Manca, Massalongo, Ovio, Penzo, Querenghi, Righi, Stefani, Tedeschi, Zaniboni.

PALERMO, Italy.

REGIA UNIVERSITÀ DEGLI STUDI DI PALERMO.

This university, founded in 1779, is under the same regulations as all the universities of Italy; see pp. 132, 133.

Enquiries may be addressed to the *direttore di segretaria*, SIGNOR B. BRUNO.

Professors and Lecturers.

ARTS.

LANGUAGES.—SEMITIC: *Signor* Lagumina.
CLASSICAL: *Professor* Giri; *Signor* Cosentino.
ROMANCE: *Signors* Amico, Di Gregorio, Mango, Pipitone.
PHILOSOPHY: *Professors* Di Giovanni, Faggi.
HISTORY: *Professors* Columba, Siragusa.
ARCHÆOLOGY: *Professor* Salinas.
ARCHITECTURE: *Professors* Almeyda, Basile, Salemi-Pace; *Signors* Gemmellaro, Romano.

SCIENCE.

MATHEMATICS AND ASTRONOMY: *Professors* Angelitti, Gerbaldi, Guccia, Maisano, Torelli, Venturi; *Signors* Albeggiani, Paternò, Soler, Zona.
PHYSICS: *Professors* Caldarera, Macaluso, Pagliani; *Signors* Cantoni, Gebbia.
CHEMISTRY: *Professor* Peratoner; *Signors* Leone, Minunni, Oddo.
MINERALOGY AND GEOLOGY: *Professor* Gemmellaro.
GEOGRAPHY: *Professor* Richieri; *Signors* Battista, Siragusa, Zona.
BIOLOGY: *Professors* Borzì, Kleinenberg; *Signors* Lo Jacono, Ross, Terracciano
AGRICULTURE: *Signor* Ziino.

HYGIENE: *Signor* Leone.
ENGINEERING: *Professors* Caldarera, Capitò, Pagliani, Pintacuda, Venturi; *Signors* Albeggiani, Cusumano, Gebbia, Rotigliano.

LAW AND POLITICAL SCIENCE.

Professors Agnetta di Gentile, Cusumano, Guarneri, Gugino, Impallomeni, Orlando, Maggiore-Perni, Papa D'Amico, Paternostro, Ricca-Salerno, Riccobono, Salvioli, Sampolo, Schiattarella; *Signors* G. D'Aguanno, De Cola Proto, Di Bernardo, Leto-Silvestri, Li Donni, Longo, Merenda, Pagano, Scherma, Siciliano, Alfonso Siragusa, Todaro.

MEDICINE.

Professors Angelucci, Argento, Cervello, Chiarleoni, Giuffrè, Manfredi, Marcacci, Marchesano, Mondino, Montalti, Monti, Randaclo, Rummo, Sirena, Tansini, Tommasoli; *Signors* Acquisto, Ajello, Alessi, Brancaleone, Carini, Caruso-Pecoraro, A. D'Aguanno, De Bono, De Grazia, Di Blasi, Dotto, Faraci, Ferrannini, Ficano, Foderà, Giglio, Giliberti, Lazzaro, Lipari, Lo Jacono, Mannino, Mirto, Misuraca, Piazza-Martini, Pernice, Bernardo Salemi-Pace, Salomone-Marino, Scardulla, Spallitta, Rosolino Tusa, Salvatore Tusa.

PARMA, Italy.

REGIA UNIVERSITÀ DEGLI STUDI DI PARMA.

This university, founded in 1422, is under the same regulations as all the universities of Italy; see pp. 132, 133.

Enquiries may be addressed to the *direttore di segretaria*, SIGNOR ANTONIO PIGORINI.

Professors and Lecturers.

SCIENCE.

MATHEMATICS: *Professors* Lavaggi, Raschi, Vecchi.
PHYSICS: *Professor* Cardani.
CHEMISTRY: *Professor* Mazzara.
GEOLOGY: *Professor* Uzielli.
MINERALOGY: *Signor* Simonelli.
BIOLOGY: *Professor* Avetta; *Signors* Binna, Coggi, Negrini.
ARCHITECTURE: *Signors* Bartoli, Marini.

LAW AND POLITICAL SCIENCE.

Professors Arduini, Bolaffio, Bonfante, Brandileone, Laghi, Laviosa, Malgarini, Perozzi, De Pirro, Redenti, Tommasini, Zanzucchi; *Signors* Berenini, Costa, Fornasari, Riccobono, Tartufari.

MEDICINE.

Professors Ceccherelli, Corona, Cugini, Ferrari, Gallenga, Inzani, Mibelli, Molina, Rattone, Riva, Tenchini, Truzzi, Ughi; *Signors* Baistrocchi, Bocchi, Caprara, Colucci, Coulliaux, Crosti, Guizzetti, Monguidi, Pozzoli, Sacchi, Verdelli, Zoja.

PAVIA, Italy.

REGIA UNIVERSITÀ DEGLI STUDI DI PAVIA.

This university, founded in 1361, is under the same regulations as all the universities of Italy; see pp. 132, 133.

Enquiries may be addressed to the *direttore di segretaria*, SIGNOR CARLO FELICE RESTAGNO.

Professors and Lecturers.

ARTS.

LANGUAGES. — CLASSICAL: *Professors* Canna, Rasi.
GERMANIC: *Signor* Schiff.
ROMANCE: *Professors* Gorra, Rossi; *Signor* Restori.
COMPARATIVE PHILOLOGY: *Professor* Salvioni.
PHILOSOPHY: *Professors* Cantoni, Credaro; *Signors* De Domenicis, Iuvalta, Mantovani.
POLITICAL ECONOMY: *Professor* Benini; *Signor* Gobbi.
HISTORY: *Professors* Lazzarini, Merkel; *Signor* Romano.
PEDAGOGY: *Professor* De Dominicis.
ARCHÆOLOGY: *Professor* Mariani.
ARCHITECTURE: *Professor* Brusotti.

SCIENCE.

MATHEMATICS AND ASTRONOMY: *Professor* Aschieri, Belcredi, Pascal, Platner, Somigliana; *Signors* Berzolari, Formenti, Pannelli, Vivanti.
PHYSICS: *Professors* Bartoli, Cantone, Formenti; *Signors* Gerosa, De Marchi.

CHEMISTRY: *Professor* Tullio Brugnatelli; *Signor* Purgotti.
MINERALOGY: *Signors* Artini, Luigi Brugnatelli.
GEOLOGY: *Professor* Taramelli; *Signors* Mariani, Salomon, Tommasi.
GEOGRAPHY: *Professor* Bellio.
BIOLOGY: *Professors* Briosi, Maggi, Pavesi.

LAW.

Professors Buzzatti, Cattaneo, Civoli, Del Giudice, Ferrini, Longo, Mariani, Mazzola, Minguzzi, Simoncelli, Vidari; *Signors* Eliseo, Majno, Nulli, Vacchelli.

MEDICINE.

Professors Baldi, Bottini, Falchi, Filomusi Guelfi, Golgi, Maggi, Mangiagalli, Mazzucchelli, Mouti, Oehl, Orsi, Pavesi, Raggi, Sangalli, Scarenzio, Silva, Sormani, Zoia; *Signors* Cantu, Clivio, Ferrari, Gorini, Jemoli, Levi, Maggi, Mazza, Pestalozza, Platschik, Rampoldi, Resinelli, Staurenghi, Stefanini, Zambianchi.

PERUGIA, Italy.
UNIVERSITÀ LIBERA DEGLI STUDI DI PERUGIA.

This university, founded in 1266, is under the same regulations as all the universities of Italy; see pp. 132, 133.

Enquiries may be addressed to the secretary, SIGNOR VITTORIO MARINI.

Professors and Lecturers.

POLITICAL SCIENCE: *Professor* Benini.

LAW.
Professors Brunamonti, Carusi, Cuturi, Innamorati, Miceli, Puviani, Scalvanti, Tarducci; *Signors* Giannantoni, Tancetti.

MEDICINE.
Professors Adriani, Axenfeld, Batelli, Bellucci, Coggi, De Paoli, Madruzza, Patella, Pisenti, Rossi, Ruata, Salvioni, Va'enti; *Signors* Agostini, Badaloni, Cecchini, Kruch, Zanetti.

PISA, Italy.
REGIA UNIVERSITÀ DEGLI STUDI DI PISA.

This university, founded in 1343, is under the same regulations as all the universities of Italy; see pp. 132, 133.

Enquiries may be addressed to the *direttore di segretaria*, SIGNOR GIACOMO ENRICO ROSSETTI.

Professors and Lecturers.

ARTS.
LANGUAGES.—INDO-IRANIAN: *Professor* Pullé.
CLASSICAL: *Professor* Tartara, Zambaldi; *Signor* Nencini.
ROMANCE: *Professors* Biadene, D'Ancona, Flamini.
COMPARATIVE PHILOLOGY: *Professor* Pullé.
HISTORY OF LITERATURE: *Signor* Barbi.
PHILOSOPHY: *Professors* Jaja, Paoli, Rossi.
HISTORY: *Professors* Crivellucci, Pais; *Signor* Lupi.
POLITICAL SCIENCE: *Professor* Toniolo.
ARCHÆOLOGY; *Professor* Ghirardini; *Signor* Lupi.
AGRICULTURE: *Professor* Calderini; *Signor* Ristori.

SCIENCE.
MATHEMATICS: *Professors* Bertini, L. Bianchi, Dini, Finzi, Nardi-Dei; *Signors* Bettazzi, Biagivi, Ciani, Enriquez, Lazzeri.
PHYSICS: *Professors* Battelli, Maggi, Pacinotti; *Signors* Faè, Lauricella, Stefanini.
CHEMISTRY: *Professor* Tassinari; *Signors* Antony, Garbasso.
GEOLOGY AND MINERALOGY: *Professors* D'Achiardi, Canavari, Zaccagna.
GEOGRAPHY: *Professor* Sottini; *Signor* Zaccagna.
BIOLOGY: *Professors* Arcangeli, Richiardi; *Signors* Bonardi, Bottini.

LAW.
Professors E. Bianchi, Buonamici, Calisse, Codacci-Pisanelli, Corsi, Gabba, Mortara, Napodano, Pampaloni, Sadun, Supino, Vacchelli; *Signors* Anzilotti, Baisini, Brunetti, Giannini, Lessona, Magri, Petrone, Sighele, Tiranti, Zerboglio.

MEDICINE.
Professors Aducco, Ceci, Ducrey, Fedeli, Fubini, Grazzi, Guarnieri, Maffucci, Manfredi, Paci, Pinzani, Queirolo, Romiti, Sadun, Di Vestea; *Signors* Battelli, Bertelli, Burci, D'Abundo, Frascani, Marchionneschi, Minati, Sonsino.

ROME, Italy.

REGIA UNIVERSITÀ DEGLI STUDI DI ROMA.

This university, founded in 1303, is under the same regulations as all the universities of Italy; see pp. 132, 133.

Enquiries may be addressed to the secretary, SIGNOR TELESFORO DARETTI.

Professors and Lecturers.

ARTS.

LANGUAGES.—SEMITIC: *Professors* Guidi, Schiaparelli.
  INDO-IRANIAN: *Professors* De Gubernatis, Valenziani.
  CLASSICAL: *Professors* Cugnoni, Halbherr, Monaci, Piccolomini, De Ruggiero; *Signors* Albini, Levi, Vaglieri.
  ENGLISH: *Signor* Garlanda.
  ROMANCE: *Professors* Ceci, De Gubernatis, Monaci; *Signors* Castagnola, Cesareo, Martini, Salvadori.
COMPARATIVE PHILOLOGY: *Professor* Ceci; *Signor* Cima.
HISTORY OF LITERATURE: *Signor* Zannoni.
PHILOSOPHY: *Professors* Barzellotti, Labriola, Turbiglio; *Signors* D'Alfonso, Gizzi, Tarozzi.
HISTORY: *Professors* Beloch, Labanca, Monticolo, Pigorini; *Signors* Cantarelli, De Sanctis, Tomassetti, Zannoni.
ART AND ARCHÆOLOGY: *Professors* Lanciani, Loewy, Pigorini, de Ruggero; *Signors* Vaglieri, Venturi.
ARCHITECTURE: *Professors* Calderini, Gui, Rosso; *Signor* Manfredi.

SCIENCE.

MATHEMATICS: *Professors* Beltrami, Biolchini, Castelnuovo, Ceradini, Cerruti, Cremona, Nagy, Pittarelli, Reina, Tonelli; *Signors* Bortolotti, Fano, Di Legge, Sella.
PHYSICS: *Professors* Ascoli, Beltrami, Blaserna, Saviotti; *Signor* Banti.
CHEMISTRY: *Professors* Cannizzaro, Giorgis, Paterno di Sessa; *Signors* Miolati, Montemartini.
MINERALOGY: *Professor* Strüver.
GEOLOGY: *Professors* Meli, Portis; *Signors* De Angelis, Viola.
GEOGRAPHY: *Professor* Dalla Vedova.
BIOLOGY: *Professors* Carruccio, Grassi, Magini, Marro, Pirotta, Sergi; *Signors* Brizi, Buscalioni, Carruccio, Colini, Grossi, Kruch, Lanzi, Magini, Marchesini, Mingazzini, Moschen, Tedeschi, Todaro, Vinciguerra.
ENGINEERING: *Professors* Ceradini, Favero, Giorgis, Nazzani, Savrotti.

LAW AND POLITICAL SCIENCE.

Professors Galluppi, Galluzzi, Filomusi Guelfi, De Marco, Messedaglia, Meucci, Nocito, Pierantoni, Schupfer, Scialoja, Semeraro; *Signors* Brunialti, Caporali, Carusi, Facelli, Ferri, Lessona, Lorini, Manna, Mari, Martini, Orano, Petrone, Racioppi, Salandra, Schanzer, Tangorra, Trincheri, Valenti.

MEDICINE.

Professors Baccelli, Businelli, Campana, Celli, Colasanti, Durante, d'Urso, Luciani, Marchiafava, Mingazzini, Occhini, Pasquali, De Rossi, Rossoni, Sciamanna, Todaro, Toscani, Tommasi-Crudeli, Valenti, Versari; *Signors* Albanese, Arcangeli, Ascoli, Bastianelli, Bignami, Concetti, Curatulo, D'Anna, De Sanctis, De Semo, Dutto, Faraci, Fermi, Ferraresi, Ferreri, Fortunati, La Torre, Leoni, Lomonaco, Manara, Marocco, Mazzoni, Mingazzini, Padula, Parisotti, Pensuti, Postempski, Rho, Rossi, Scalzi, Scellingo, Tarulli, Tassi, Versari.

AMERICAN SCHOOL OF CLASSICAL STUDIES IN ROME.

This school, which was opened in 1894, has the same general objects as the American School of Classical studies at Athens; see p. 128.

All the courses and privileges of the school are open to women on the same conditions as to men. Bachelors of Arts of American colleges of good standing and persons who are able to submit satisfactory proof that their studies have been such as to enable them to pursue advanced courses of work at the school may become members. Americans residing or travelling in Italy who are not members of the school may, at the discretion of the directors, be admitted to its privileges.

Application for admission should be addressed to Casino dell' Aurora, via Lombardia, Rome, or to PROFESSOR MINTON WARREN, Harvard University, Cambridge, Mass.

The academic year begins on October 15th and ends on June 1st.

No charges are made for tuition.

Two fellowships of the value of $600 and one of the value of $500, for the study of Christian Archæology, are usually awarded in each year on the result of an examination held about the middle of March. They are open to all Bachelors of Arts of universities and colleges in the United States and to other American students of similar attainments.

All particulars may be obtained from PROFESSOR MINTON WARREN, Johns Hopkins University, Baltimore, Md.

Director of the school in 1898–99, PROFESSOR TRACY PECK, Professor of Latin Language and Literature, Yale University; Director of the School from 1899 to 1904, MR. RICHARD NORTON.

KAISERLICHE DEUTSCHES ARCHÄOLOGISCHES INSTITUT.

For particulars see p. 129.

ÉCOLE FRANÇAISE DE ROME.

Similar in organisation to the École Française d' Athénes; see p. 130. Director, M. L'ABBÉ DUCHESNE; honorary director, M. LE BLANT.

ITALY.

SASSARI, Sardinia.

REGIA UNIVERSITÀ DEGLI STUDI DI SASSARI.

This university, founded in 1556, is under the same regulations as all the universities of Italy; see pp. 132, 133.

Enquiries may be addressed to the secretary, SIGNOR MICHELE COSSU.

Professors and Lecturers.

POLITICAL SCIENCE: *Professor* Pinna-Ferrà.

LAW.

Professors Besto, Bibbiana, Demurtas-Zichina, Dettori, De Villa, Manunta-Manca, Mariotti, Piras, Soro Delitala; *Signors* Castiglia, Manca Leoni, Mossa, Pitzolo.

MEDICINE.

Professors Binna, Conti, Fiori, Mazzotto, Nicotra, Patrizi, Pitzorno, Ravà, Roth, Sclavo, Simula, Traversa, Valente, Vincenzi.

SIENA, Italy.

REGIA UNIVERSITÀ DEGLI STUDI DI SIENA.

This university, founded in the 14th century, is under the same regulations as all the universities of Italy; see pp. 132, 133.

Enquiries may be addressed to the secretary, SIGNOR TEMISTOCLE MOZZANI.

Professors and Lecturers.

LAW.

Professors Ciacci, Civoli, Diena, Graziani, Leporini, Lessona, Moriani, Patetta, Rossi, Virgilii, Vitali, Zanichelli; *Signors* Castellari, Falaschi, Giannantoni, Ottolenghi, Ranelletti, Zdekauer.

MEDICINE.

Professors Barbacci, Barduzzi, Bernabei, Bianchi, Bocci, Cantieri, Falaschi, Funaioli, Guaita, Gucci, Morisani, Morpurgo, Ottolenghi, Raimondi, Sanquirico, Spediacci, Tassi; *Signors* Bianchi, Bordoni, Borgiotti, Cattaneo, Colombini, Ficalbi, Gasparrini, Giacomini, Lussano, Mibelli, Morpurgo, Nanotti, Remedi, Ruffini, Sanarelli, Scarlini, Tassi.

TURIN, Italy.

REGIA UNIVERSITÀ DEGLI STUDI DI TORINO.

This university, founded in 1412, is under the same regulations as all the universities of Italy; see pp. 132, 133.

Enquiries may be addressed to the *direttore di segretaria*, SIGNOR EMILIO LUCIO.

148   URBINO.

Professors and Lecturers.

ARTS.

LANGUAGES.—SEMITIC AND INDO-IRANIAN: *Professor* Pizzi; *Signor* Nazari.
CLASSICAL: *Professors* Fraccaroli, Stampini; *Signors* Garizio, Valmaggi, Zuretti.
ROMANCE: *Professors* Graf, Renier; *Signors* Camus, Cian, Gabotto, Gorra.
COMPARATIVE PHILOLOGY: *Professor* Pezzi.
PHILOSOPHY: *Professors* Bobba, D'Ercole; *Signors* Billia, Zuccante.
POLITICAL ECONOMY: *Professors* Cognetti, De Martiis; *Signors* Einaudi, Iannaccone, Masè-Dari.
HISTORY: *Professor* Cipolla; *Signors* Garizio, Manfroni, Merkel.
PEDAGOGY: *Professor* Allievo.
ARCHÆOLOGY: *Professors* Ferrero, Rossi; *Signor* Schiaparelli.
ARCHITECTURE: *Professor* Ceppi.

SCIENCE.

MATHEMATICS AND ASTRONOMY: *Professors* Berzolari, D'Ovidio, Jadanza Peano, Segre; *Signors* Bettazzi, Guarducci, Pieri, Porro, Zanotti-Bianco.
PHYSICS: *Professors* Naccari, Volterra; *Signors* Campetti, Garbasso, Rizzo.
CHEMISTRY: *Professor* Fileti; *Signor* Ponzio.
MINERALOGY: *Professor* Spezia.

GEOLOGY: *Professor* Parona; *Signors* Sacco, Piolti.
BIOLOGY: *Professors* Camerano, Mosso; *Signors* Belli, Buscalioni, Giglio-Tos, Rosa, Voglino.

LAW.

Professors Bertolini, Brondi, Brusa, Carle, Castellari, Chironi, Ferroglio, Fusinato, Germano, Mattirolo, Mosca, Nani, Ronga; *Signors* Amar, Arno, Ballerini-Velio, Brezzo, Cattaneo, Dusi, Frassati, Garelli, Gariazzo, Lombroso, Pasquali, Righini, Tedeschi.

MEDICINE.

Professors Bizzozero, Bozzolo, Bruno, Carle, Foà, Fusari, Giacosa, Giovannini, Gradenigo, Lombroso, Angelo Mosso, Pagliani, Perroncito, Reymond, Silva, Tibone; *Signors* Bajardi, Belfanti, Benedicenti, Bergesio, Bono, Bordoni-Uffreduzzi, Caponotto, Carbone, Carbonelli, Carrara, Cavallero, Cesaris-Demel, Ciartoso, Cognetti De-Martiis, Corradi, Dionisio, Ferri, Ferria, Fileti, Gosio, Grandis, Martinotti, Marro, Mo, Motta, Muscatello, Monari, Musso, Naccari, Negro, Oliva, Ottolenghi, Patrizi, Pellizzi, Peroni, Pescarolo, Peschel, Raineri, Resegotti, Riva-Rocci, Roncoroni, Sacerdotti, Salvioli, Sansoni, Sclavo, Scofone, Secondi, Sperino, Varaglia, Vicarelli, Vinay.

URBINO, Italy.

LIBERA UNIVERSITÀ PROVINCIALE.

This university, founded in 1671, is under the same regulations as all the universities of Italy, see pp. 132, 133.

Enquiries may be addressed to the secretary, SIGNOR CAMILLO BARDOVAGNI.

Professors and Lecturers.

POLITICAL SCIENCE: *Signor* Vecchiotti-Antaldi.

LAW.

Professors Budassi, Dusi, Meriggioli, Mircoli, Fiocchi-Nicolai, Siotto-Pintor, Vanni; *Signors* Valenti, Vecchiotti-Antaldi.

MEDICINE.

Professor Bedeschi.

NAPLES, Italy.

STAZIONE ZOÖLOGICA.

This morphological and physiological laboratory, founded in 1872 and arranged for independent research in zoology, botany and physiology, is open to women on the same conditions as to men. Permission to use a table in the laboratory may be obtained, according to the nationality of the applicant, from the Ministers of Education of Germany, Austria, Hungary, Russia, Holland, Belgium, Italy, Switzerland; from the Universities of Oxford and Cambridge, England; or in the United States from the authorities of the Smithsonian Institute, from the Association for Maintaining an American Women's Table, or from Columbia University. For the student who thus obtains permission the laboratory is open for the whole year free of charge; private persons who take a table for their own use pay 2,500 francs ($500) per year or fraction of a year.

In 1898 an association was formed for maintaining an American Women's table at the station. Permission to use this table is granted by the executive board of the association and preference is given to well qualified women applicants, but if no suitable women present themselves men are eligible in their stead. The appointments are made for a longer or shorter period as may seem expedient, and the scholars may be given financial aid if necessary. As many as three scholars may be elected at one time. The application should be addressed to the Secretary of the Executive Board, Miss Ida H. Hyde, 1 Berkeley Street, Cambridge, Mass., from whom all particulars may be obtained. The remaining members of the Executive Board are: President M. Carey Thomas, chairman, Bryn Mawr College, Bryn Mawr, Pa.; Mrs. Alice Freeman Palmer, treasurer, 11 Quincy Street, Cambridge, Mass.; Miss Florence Cushing, 8 Walnut Street, Boston, Mass.; Miss Laura D. Gill, 26 Prospect Street, Northampton, Mass.; Miss Agnes Irwin, Dean of Radcliffe College, Cambridge, Mass.; Mrs. John H. Westcott, Princeton, N. J.

Director, PROFESSOR ANTON DOHRN; Assistant Director, PROFESSOR KARL SCHÖNLEIN.

THE NETHERLANDS.

There are in the Netherlands, in addition to the municipal university of the city of Amsterdam, three state universities—Leyden, Utrecht and Groningen. The state universities are under the supervision of the Minister of the Interior of the Netherlands and the affairs of each are regulated by a *Curatorium* of five members; the University of Amsterdam is under the authority of the Common Council (*Gemeenteraad*) of the city of Amsterdam. There is also a small free university in Amsterdam with only six professors. The universities provide instruction in Arts, Science, Law, Medicine and Theology, and give in each of these departments the degree of Doctor.

No distinction is made between women and men, women being allowed to matriculate and to take degrees on exactly the same conditions as men.

The academic year usually begins in the middle of September and extends to the first week of July though the lectures close about the middle of June; 200 fl. ($80) a year is charged by the universities for instruction, and whoever pays this sum may matriculate as a regular student. Students who do not desire to attend more than two courses are exempt from the regular fee, but must pay 30 fl. ($12) a year for each course they attend.

In order to be admitted to a university examination the candidate is required to produce a certificate stating that he has passed either the final examination of a gymnasium or an equivalent examination held every year by the state.* Any

---

* In the case of foreigners certain examinations of other countries are considered by law equivalent to these examinations and are accepted as a sufficient substitute by the universities, as, for instance, the final examination of a German gymnasium.

student who produces such a certificate has a right to take the university examinations whether he has attended the university or not. The fee to be paid upon taking any examination, except the final one for the degree of doctor, which is free, is 50 fl. ($20).

AMSTERDAM, The Netherlands.
UNIVERSITEIT TE AMSTERDAM.

This university, founded in 1632, is under the same regulations as the other universities of the Netherlands; see pp. 150, 151.

Enquiries may be addressed to the secretary, PROFESSOR HECTOR TREUB.

Professors and Lecturers.

ARTS.

LANGUAGES.—SEMITIC: *Professor* Matthes.
 CLASSICAL: *Professors* Karsten, Uhlenbeck; *Docent* Beck.
 GERMANIC: *Professors* Uhlenbeck, te Winkel; *Docent* Frantzen.
 MALAYAN: *Docent* Forker.
PHILOSOPHY: *Professors* Spruitt; *Docent* Jelgersma.
HISTORY: *Professors* Rogge, Valeton.
ART AND ARCHÆOLOGY: *Professors* Van den Es, Six.

SCIENCE.

MATHEMATICS AND ASTRONOMY: *Professors* D. J. Korteweg, Van Pesch.
PHYSICS: *Professors* Sissingh, van der Waals; *Reader* Zeeman.
CHEMISTRY: *Professors* de Bruyn, Gunning, Roozeboom, van 't Hoff; *Docents* Boldingh, Cohen, Reicher.
MINERALOGY AND GEOLOGY: *Professor* Molengraaff.

BIOLOGY: *Professors* Bos, De Vries, Weber; *Reader* Sluiter.
GEOGRAPHY: *Professor* Kan.
PHARMACY: *Professor* Stoeder.

LAW AND POLITICAL SCINCE.

Professors Conrat, Van Hamel, De Hartog, Houwing, Jitta, M.W. F. Treub; *Docents* Lioni, Miseroy, Cohen Stuart.

MEDICINE.

Professors Bolk, Da Costa, Guye, J. A. Korteweg, Kuhn, Pel, Place, Rotgans, Ruge, Saltet, Stokvis, Straub, H. Treub, Van Rees, Winkler; *Docents* Bruin, Burger, De Leon, van Deventer, Graanboom, Grevers, van Hoorn, Jelgersma, Meyjes, Rijnberk, Salomonson, Tilanus.

THEOLOGY.

Professors Brandt, de Bussy, Chantepie de la Saussaye, Cramer, Völter; *Reader* Westhoff.

GRONINGEN, Holland.
RIJKS-UNIVERSITEIT TE GRONINGEN.

This university, founded in 1614, is under the same regulations as the other Dutch universities; see pp. 150, 151.

Enquiries may be addressed to the secretary, PROFESSOR P. G. WILDEBOER.

LEYDEN.

Professors and Lecturers.

ARTS.

LANGUAGES.—SEMITIC: *Professors* van den Ham, Wildeboer.
CLASSICAL: *Professors* Polak, Speijer.
ENGLISH: *Professor* Bülbring.
GERMANIC: *Professors* Symons, van Helten; *Docent* Boer.
ROMANCE: *Professor* van Hamel.
COMPARATIVE PHILOLOGY: *Professor* Symons.
PHILOSOPHY: *Professor* Heymans.
HISTORY: *Professors* Boissevain, Bussemaker.
ARCHÆOLOGY: *Professors* Boissevain, Polak.

SCIENCE.

MATHEMATICS AND ASTRONOMY: *Professors* de Boer, Kapteijn, Schoute.

PHYSICS: *Professor* Haga; *Reader* Wind.
CHEMISTRY: *Professors* Eijkman, Holleman.
MINERALOGY AND GEOLOGY: *Professor* van Calker.
BIOLOGY: *Professors* Moll, van Ankum.

LAW.

Professors Krabbe, Land, Nieuwenhuis, Pet, Reiger; *Docent* van der Tuuk.

MEDICINE.

Professors Fokker, Huizinga, Koch, Kooyker, Middendorp, Mulder, Nijhoff, Reddingius, van Wijhe; *Docents* Ranneft, Schutter, Wiersma; *Reader* Kooij.

THEOLOGY.

Professors van Dijk, Kruyf, Meyboom, Reitsma, van Rhijn, Valeton, Wildeboer,

LEYDEN, Holland.

RIJKS-UNIVERSITEIT.

This university, founded in 1575, is under the same regulations as the other Dutch universities; see pp. 150, 151.

Enquiries may be addressed to the secretary, PROFESSOR P. J. COSTJN.

Professors and Lecturers.

ARTS.

LANGUAGES.—SEMITIC: *Professors* De Goeje, Oort, Tiele.
CLASSICAL: *Professors* Bolland, Hartman, van Leeuwen; *Docent* Hesseling.
MODERN GREEK: *Docent* Hesseling.
GERMANIC: *Professors* ten Brink, Cosijn, Verdam.
ROMANCE: *Docent* de Grave.
JAPANESE: *Reader* Serrurier.
MALAYAN: *Professor* de Groot; *Reader* Klinkert.
JAVANESE: *Professor* Vreede.
SUDANESE: *Reader* Grashuis.
TURKISH: *Reader* van Gelder.
CHINESE: *Professor* Schlegel.
COMPARATIVE PHILOLOGY: *Professor* Kern.

PHILOSOPHY: *Professor* Bolland.
HISTORY: *Professors* Blok, Muller.
ARCHÆOLOGY: *Professor* Holwerda.
ETHNOGRAPHY: *Professor* de Groot; *Reader* Serrurier.
HISTORY OF MOHAMMEDANISM: *Reader* Van Gelder.

SCIENCE.

MATHEMATICS AND ASTRONOMY: *Professors* H. G. van de S. Bakhuyzen, Kluyver, Van Geer; *Docent* E. F. van de S. Bakhuyzen.
PHYSICS: *Professors* Lorentz, Onnes; *Docents* Molenbroek, Siertsema.
CHEMISTRY: *Professors* Franchimont, Van Bemmelen, Wijsman; *Reader* Schreinemakers; *Docent* Stortenbecker.
MINERALOGY AND GEOLOGY: *Professor* Martin.

THE NETHERLANDS.

BIOLOGY: *Professors* Hoffmann, Suringar.
PHARMACY: *Professor* Wijsman.

LAW AND POLITICAL SCIENCE.
Professors Andreae, Asser, Drucker, Greven, Oppenheim, Tichelaar, Van der Hoeven, Van der Lith, Van der Vlugt.

MEDICINE.
Professors Einthoven, Koster, MacGillavry, Nolen, Rosenstein, Treub, Van Heukelom, Van Iterson, Veit, Zaaijer; *Docents* Dekhuyzen, Nijkamp.

THEOLOGY.
Professors Eerdmans, Gooszen, Gunning, van Manen, Offerhaus, Pijper, Tiele.

UTRECHT, Holland.
RIJKS-UNIVERSITEIT.

This university, founded in 1636, is under the same regulations as the other Dutch universities; see pp. 150, 151.

Enquiries may be addressed to the secretary, PROFESSOR H. W. BETTINK.

Professors and Lecturers.

ARTS.

LANGUAGES.—SEMITIC: *Professor* Houtsma.
  CLASSICAL: *Professors* Van der Vliet, Van Herwerden.
  GERMANIC: *Professors* Gallée, Kalff; *Docents* Hettema, Wirth.
COMPARATIVE PHILOLOGY: *Professor* Gallée.
PHILOSOPHY: *Professor* Freiherr Van der Wyck.
HISTORY: *Professor* Krämer; *Docent* Van Gelder.
ART AND ARCHÆOLOGY: *Professor* Van Herwerden; *Docent* Morell.
ETHNOLOGY: *Docent* Steinmetz.

SCIENCE.

MATHEMATICS AND ASTRONOMY: *Professors* V. A. Julius, Kapteijn, Nyland, de Vries; *Docents* Mounier, Snellen.
PHYSICS: *Professor* W. H. Julius.

CHEMISTRY: *Professors* Bettink, Dibbits, Mulder; *Docent* Couvée.
MINERALOGY: *Professor* Wichmann.
GEOLOGY: *Docent* Lorié.
BIOLOGY: *Professors* Hubrecht, Went; *Reader* Vosmaer.

LAW AND POLITICAL SCIENCE.
Professors De Bourouill, De Louter, Hamaker, Molengraaff, Naber, Pols Simons; *Docents* Kooiman, Rijke.

MEDICINE.
Professors Narath, Pekelharing, Rosenberg, Snellen, Spronck, Talma, Zraardemaker; *Readers* Brondgeest, Dentz, Van der Meulen; *Docents* Boekelman, Gutteling, Huysman, Woltering.

THEOLOGY.
Professors Baljon, Cannegieter, Kleyn, Lamers, Valeton, Van Leeuwen, Van Veen.

NORWAY.

CHRISTIANIA, Norway.
KONGELIGE FREDERIKS UNIVERSITET.

There is only one university in Norway, that of Christiania, founded in 1811. Women have been admitted since 1884 to all the courses, degrees, and, where there is no special regulation to the contrary, to the scholarships and prizes.

Instruction is given and degrees are conferred in Arts, Science, Law, Medicine and Theology. The highest degree conferred is that of Doctor.

Students that have matriculated at a foreign university are admitted on presenting a certificate of having passed an examination equal in difficulty to that required from candidates from a Norwegian gymnasium.

Women are admitted to the libraries and laboratories on the same conditions as men.

The first semester begins in the middle of January, the second in the beginning of September.

All lectures are free. Foreigners pay a matriculation fee of 20 kr. ($5.40) and there are laboratory fees of 12 to 32 kr. ($3.24 to $8.64).

Professors and Lecturers.

ARTS.

LANGUAGES.—SEMITIC: *Professors* Blix, Seippel.
  INDO-IRANIAN: *Professors* Bugge, Torp.
  CLASSICAL: *Professors* Schjott, Stenersen.
  ENGLISH: *Professor* Joh. Storm.
  SLAVONIC: *Docent* Broch.
  GERMANIC: *Professors* Falk, Friis, Moe.
  ROMANCE: *Professor* Joh. Storm; *Docent* Loseth.
HISTORY OF LITERATURE: *Docent* Collin.
PHILOSOPHY: *Professor* Mourly Vold.
HISTORY: *Professors* Daae, J. E. Sars, Gustav Storm.
GEOGRAPHY: *Professor* Nielsen.
ART AND ARCHÆOLOGY: *Professors* Dietrichson, Lieblein, Rygh.

SCIENCE.

MATHEMATICS: *Professors* Bjerknes, Guldberg, Sylow; *Docent* Holst.
ASTRONOMY AND METEOROLOGY: *Pro-*

fessors Geelmuyden, Mohn.
PHYSICS : *Professors* Birkeland, Schiotz.
CHEMISTRY : *Professors* Hiortdahl, Waage.
MINERALOGY AND GEOLOGY : *Professors* Brogger, Helland, Vogt.
BIOLOGY : *Professors* Collett, Nansen, G. O. Sars, Wille.

LAW.

Professors Aschehoug, Hagerup, Ingstad, Morgenstierne, Platou, Stang, Taranger ; *Docent* Gjelsvik.

MEDICINE.

Professors Boeck, Guldberg, Hjort, Holst, Johannessen, Laache, Leegaard, Nicolaysen, Poulsson, Schonberg, Strom, Torup, Uchermann ; *Docent* Holst.

THEOLOGY.

Professors Brandrud, Brun, Michelet, Odland, Petersen.

RUSSIA.

No account is given here of the numerous Russian universities. Full particulars of the courses and professors may be found in the Minerva Jahrbuch der Gelehrten Welt.

All the universities in Russia are now closed to women; a few grant diplomas to women in Dentistry and Pharmacy.

In St. Petersburg there are classes in History, Languages, Philosophy, Mathematics and Physics for the higher education of women, distinct from the university, but under the supervision of the Ministry of Public Instruction. These are attended by large numbers of women. Foreign subjects who have attended certain courses at a gymnasium for women are admitted as special students with the permission of the Curator.

SCOTLAND.

See pp. 118–126.

SPAIN.

The universities in Spain have since 1857 been under the control of the General Director of Public Education.

The country is divided, for the purpose of university instruction, into ten departments: Madrid, Barcelona, Granada, Oviedo, Salamanca, Santiago, Seville, Valencia, Valladolid and Saragossa. The universities consist as a rule of the five faculties of Arts, Science, Law, Medicine and Pharmacy. They have always been open to women on the same conditions as to men, but women have availed themselves in very few cases of the opportunity of studying at the universities.

The courses of lectures were arranged in 1857 and have not since been changed. Students have no liberty of choice as to the lectures they attend. The degrees of Bachelor, Licentiate and Doctor are conferred by each of the faculties.

The academic year begins in October. There are no fees for lectures. The matriculation fee is 16 milreis ($17.20).

On account of the small number of foreigners attending the Spanish universities, the lists of professors are not given here. They may be found in the Minerva Jahrbuch der Gelehrten Welt.

SWEDEN.

There are in Sweden two State universities, the universities of Lund and Upsala, each comprising faculties of Philosophy (Arts and Science), Law, Medicine and Theology; the high schools of Gothenburg and Stockholm, the first of which devotes itself to Arts only and the second to Science, and the Medical and Surgical Institute of Stockholm, which is a state institution.

In 1870 a royal decree was issued giving to women the right to become regular students and to take degrees in the medical faculties of the State universities on the same conditions as men, and in 1873 this right was extended to the faculties of Law and Philosophy. The high schools of Gothenburg and Stockholm were not founded until after 1870, and have from the first been open to women.

The faculty of Theology is not yet open to women.

In order to be admitted as a student to one of the universities or high schools the candidate must have passed the final examination or *mogenhets examen* of an elementary school. Candidates who have not passed this examination may in some cases become "hearers" in the university courses by special permission of the faculty and the individual professor, but are not permitted to take degrees.

The academic year is divided into the autumn semester, beginning on September 1st and ending on December 15th; and the spring semester, beginning on January 15th and ending on June 15th.

The matriculation or registration fee varies from 10 to 12 crowns ($2.70 to $3.24) and a fee of 10 or 20 crowns ($2.70 or $5.40) is paid each semester. All public courses are open

SWEDEN.

free of charge; these are sometimes supplemented by private lectures costing from 20 to 40 crowns ($5.40 to $10.80) a semester.

There are numerous scholarships and prizes, which, though no special statement is made to the effect, are not in general open to women.

The Fredrika-Bremer-Förbundet at Stockholm is an association whose object is to be a medium for collecting information of interest to educated women. The secretary, 54 Drottninggattan, Stockholm, has kindly offered to answer questions in regard to Swedish universities that may be addressed to her by readers of the Handbook.

GOTHENBURG, Sweden.
GÖTEBORGS HÖGSKOLA.

This school, founded in 1887, consists as yet of the faculty of Arts only, but has power to confer degrees.

The general regulations are the same as those of the Swedish universities; see pp. 158, 159.

Enquiries may be addressed to the secretary, HERR ERIC BÖKMAN.

Professors and Lecturers.

ARTS.

LANGUAGES.—SEMITIC: *Professor* Lindberg.
CLASSICAL: *Professor* Paulson; *Docents* Janzon, Wåhlin.
ENGLISH: *Reader* Westall.
GERMANIC: *Professors* Cederschiöld, Ho'thausen; *Docent* Bååth.

ROMANCE: *Professor* Vising; *Docent* Mortensen; *Reader* Avenard.
PHILOSOPHY: *Professor* Norström; *Docent* Liljeqvist.
POLITICAL SCIENCE: *Professor* Stavenow; *Docent* Kjellén.
HISTORY: *Docent* Stavenow.
ART: *Professor* Warburg.

LUND, Sweden.
KAROLINSKA UNIVERSITETET.

This university, founded in 1666, comprises faculties of Arts Science, Law, Medicine and Theology, and is under the same general regulations as all Swedish universities; see pp. 158, 159.

Enquiries may be addressed to the rector, PROFESSOR QUENNERSTEDT.

STOCKHOLM.

Professors and Lecturers.

ARTS.

LANGUAGES.—CLASSICAL: *Professors* Alexanderson, Wide, Zander; *Docents* Linde, Lindskog.
ENGLISH: *Docents* Kock, Rodhe; *Reader* Harvey.
GERMANIC: *Professors* Lidforss, Söderwall; *Docents* Beckman, Hjelmqvist, Kjederqvist, Söderberg; *Reader* Freund.
ROMANCE: *Professor* Wulff; *Reader* Philipot.
ORIENTAL: *Professors* Flensburg, Tegnér; *Docent* Zetterstéen.
PHILOSOPHY: *Professors* Borelius, Leander; *Docents* Boström, Herrlin, Larsson, Strömberg.
POLITICAL SCIENCE: *Professor* Fahlbeck; *Docent* Andersson.
HISTORY: *Professors* Fahlbeck, Freiherr v. Schwerin, Weibull; *Docents* Stille, Wimarson.
ART AND ARCHÆOLOGY: *Docent* Söderberg.
ÆSTHETICS AND HISTORY OF LITERATURE: *Docents* Mortensen, Sylwan, Wrangel.

SCIENCE.

MATHEMATICS AND ASTRONOMY: *Professors* Björling, Charlier, Engström; *Docents* Brodén, Delin, Möller, Psilander, Strömgren, Wiman.
PHYSICS: *Professor* Bäcklund; *Docents* Granqvist, Rydberg.
CHEMISTRY: *Professor* Loven; *Docents* Löndahl, Wallin.
GEOLOGY: *Professor* Torell; *Docents* Hennig, Moberg, Törnqvist.
BIOLOGY: *Professors* Bergendal, Berggren, Quennerstedt, Thomson, Torell; *Docents* Jönsson, Lidforss, Ljungström, Murbeck, Ohlin, Wallengren.

LAW.

Professors J. A. Ask, Björling, Graf Hamilton, Kallenberg, Thyrén, Winroth; *Docents* Antell, Broomé, Hellner, Livijn.

MEDICINE.

Professors Bendz, Blix, Fürst, Hildebrand, Lang, Lindgren, Löwegren, Ödman, Ribbing; *Docents* Forssman, Gadelius, Hedin, Petren, Wadstein.

THEOLOGY.

Professors Ahnfelt, Eklund, Holmström, Johansson, Rosenius; *Docents* Hammar, Lundborg, Pfannenstill.

STOCKHOLM, Sweden.
STOCKHOLMS HÖGSKOLA.

This school, founded in 1878, consists as yet of a Mathematical and Scientific section only, but it is hoped that it will shortly be enlarged by the addition of a faculty of Law and Political Science.

The general regulations are the same as those of the Swedish universities; see pp. 159, 159.

The matriculation fee is 25 crowns ($6.75) and the fee for lectures (which is remitted in the semester in which the matriculation fee is paid) is the same.

Enquiries may be addressed to the secretary.

Professors and Lecturers.

ARTS.

SWEDISH: *Professor* Ljungstedt.

HISTORY OF LITERATURE: *Professor* Levertin.
POLITICAL SCIENCE: *Professor* Leffler.

SWEDEN.

SCIENCE.
MATHEMATICS AND ASTRONOMY: *Professors* Bendixson, Bohlin, Gyldén, Mittag-Leffler, Phragmén; *Docents* Kobb, v. Koch.
PHYSICS: *Professors* Arrhenius, Bjerknes.
CHEMISTRY: *Professor* Pettersson.
MINERALOGY AND GEOLOGY: *P. ofessor* De Geer; *Docents* Bäckström, Hamberg.
BIOLOGY: *Professors* Lagerheim, Leche; *Docents* Anderson, Carlgren, af Klercker, Klinckowström.

UPSALA, Sweden.
KONGL. UNIVERSITETET I UPSALA.

This university, founded in 1477, comprises faculties of Arts, Science, Law, Medicine and Theology, and is under the same regulations as all the Swedish universities; see pp. 158, 159.

Enquiries may be addressed to the secretary, HERR J. VON BAHR.

Professors and Lecturers.

ARTS.
LANGUAGES.—SEMITIC: *Professor* Almkvist.
SLAVONIC: *Professor* Lundell.
CLASSICAL: *Professors* Danielsson, Persson; *Docents* Knös, Lagercrantz, Lundström, Odelberg.
ENGLISH: *Reader* Harlock.
GERMANIC: *Professors* Erdmann, Läffler, Noreen; *Docents* v. Friesen, Lange, Tamm, Wadstein, Wiklund; *Reader* Meyer.
ROMANCE: *Professor* P. A. Geijer; *Docents* Linder, Rydberg, Staaff, Wahlund; *Reader* Lévy-Ullmann.
SANSKRIT AND COMPARATIVE PHILOLOGY: *Professor* Johansson; *Docent* Lidén.
PHILOSOPHY: *Professor* K. R. Geijer; *Docents* Bager-Sjögren, Burman, Edfeldt, Hägerstrom, von Scheele.
POLITICAL SCIENCE: *Professor* Alin; *Docents* Nyström, Varenius.
HISTORY: *Professor* Boëthius, Hjärne; *Docents* Ahlenius, Clason, Hallendorff, Hildebrand.
ART: *Professor* Schück; *Docents* Kjellberg, Petrini.
EGYPTOLOGY: *Professor* Piehl.
HISTORY OF LITERATURE: *Docents* Levertin, Meyer, Staffen.

SCIENCE.
MATHEMATICS AND ASTRONOMY: *Professors* Dunér, Falk, Hildebrandsson; *Docents* Berger, Ericsson, Holmgren Malmborg, Söderberg, Westman.
PHYSICS: *Professors* Ångström, Lundquist; *Demonstrator* Granqvist; *Docents* Josephson, Petrini.
CHEMISTRY: *Professors* Cleve, Widman; *Docents* Bladin, Langlet, Palmaer.
MINERALOGY AND GEOLOGY: *Professor* Hogbom; *Docents* Holmquist, Munthe, Nordenskjöld, Wiman.
BIOLOGY: *Professors* Fries, Kjellman, Lundström, Tullberg, Wirén; *Docents* Aurivillius, Hedlund, Jägerskiöld, Johansson, Juel, Lönnberg, Sernander.
GEOGRAPHY: *Docent* Lönborg.

LAW AND POLITICAL SCIENCE.
Professors Blomberg, Dahlberg, Davidson, Hagströmer, Sjögren, Trygger; *Docents* Almén, Eschelsson, Reuterskiöld.

MEDICINE.
Professors Clason, Elfstrand, Gullstrand, Hammar, Hammarsten, Henschen, Lennander, Lindfors, Mörner, Nerander, Nordlund, Petersson, Sundberg; *Demonstrators* Öhrwall, Vestberg; *Docents* Bolin, Dahlgren, Floderus, Schuldheis.

THEOLOGY.
Professors Berggren, Danell, Ekman, Lundström, Martin, Quensel, Rudin, Tottie; *Docents* Eklund, Kolmodni, Stave.

SWITZERLAND.

There are in Switzerland seven universities—Basle, Berne, Fribourg, Geneva, Lausanne, Neuchatel and Zurich. These are all open to women. At Basle, Berne and Zurich the language used is German, and the only degree given is that of Doctor, as in German universities. In Geneva, Lausanne and Neuchatel, on the other hand, the language used is French and the degrees are similar to those of French universities, the *baccalauréat*, *licence* and *doctorat*. In Fribourg both languages are used, but the university organisation is German.

BASLE, Switzerland.
UNIVERSITÄT BASEL.

The university of Basle, consisting of the four faculties of Philosophy (Arts and Science), Law, Medicine and Theology, was founded in 1460.

Every one wishing to become a regular student must present a certificate of good character and satisfactory testimonials in regard to his previous education and must register (matriculate) both with the rector of the university and with the dean of the faculty in which he is to study. This must be done before the end of the first fortnight of the semester. The fees for matriculation amount to 14 francs ($2.80) and are paid to the pedell.

Before the end of the first three weeks of the semester the student must present himself to the quæstor and pay the fees for lectures, and finally must obtain the signatures of the different lecturers in his course book. When leaving the university the student must again present himself to the rector and obtain the *Abgangszeugniss*.

Hearers must be over seventeen years of age and are permitted to attend lectures on paying the fees.

The degree of Doctor is conferred in all the faculties except that of Theology, which grants the degree of Licentiate only.

Women have been allowed to study in the university since 1890, under certain conditions. In order to be admitted as a regular student a woman must be of Swiss nationality, or, if a foreigner, must have received her education in the canton of Basle. To be admitted as a hearer to the lectures of the Philosophical faculty she must hold a certificate entitling her to teach in the primary or secondary schools of the canton. Women who satisfy the above requirements have all the privileges of men students as regards the holding of scholarships and the use of libraries, laboratories, museums, etc.

The winter semester extends from October 15th to the end of March; the summer semester from April 15th to the end of July.

The lecture fees for all lectures which are not free are, in the Theological Faculty, 3 francs ($0.60) a semester for each hour weekly, and in the other faculties 5 francs ($1.00). Laboratory fees are in general 5 francs ($1.00) per hour weekly for the semester.

Further information and the *Verzeichniss der Vorlesungen* can be obtained from the pedell, HERR VIKTOR HOFER.

Professors and Lecturers.

ARTS.

LANGUAGES.—SEMITIC: *Professor* Mez.
INDO-IRANIAN: *Professor* Misteli.
CLASSICAL: *Professors* Bethe, Groos, Hagenbach, Misteli, Wackernagel; *Docent* Münzer.
ENGLISH: *Professor* Soldan; *Docent* Binz.
GERMANIC: *Professors* Koegel, Meyer; *Docent* Trog.
ROMANCE: *Professor* Soldan.
COMPARATIVE PHILOLOGY: *Professor* Socin.
PHILOSOPHY: *Professors* Heman, Heussler, Joël.
POLITICAL SCIENCE: *Professor* Kozak; *Docent* Geering.
HISTORY: *Professors* Baumgartner, Boos, Albert Burckhardt, Thommen; *Docents* Haller, Luginbühl, Mez, Schneider.
PEDAGOGY: *Professor* Heman; *Docent* Largiadèr.

ART AND ARCHÆOLOGY: *Professors* J. J. Bernoulli, D. Burckhardt, Dragendorff, Meyer, Wölfflin; *Docent* Daniel Burckhard.

SCIENCE.

MATHEMATICS AND ASTRONOMY: *Professors* Kinkelin, Riggenbach, Von der Mühll; *Docents* Flatt, Hurwitz.
PHYSICS: *Professors* Hagenbach-Bischoff, Kahlbaum; *Docent* Veillon.
CHEMISTRY: *Professors* Kahlbaum, Niezki, Piccard; *Docents* Fichter, Kreis, Nienhaus, Osann.
MINERALOGY: *Professor* Carl Schmidt; *Docent* Kraatz.
GEOLOGY: *Professor* Carl Schmidt; *Docent* Tobler.
BIOLOGY: *Professors* Rudolph Burckhardt, Zschokke; *Docent* Griesbach.
HYGIENE: *Professors* Albrecht Eduard Burckhardt.

LAW.

Professors Karl Chr. Burckhardt, Fleiner, Heusler, Speiser, Teichmann, Wieland; *Docents* Peter, Stehlin.

MEDICINE.

Professors Bumm, Bunge, A. Burckhardt, E. Burckhardt, Corning, Courvoisier, Dubler, Gönner, Hagenbach-Burckhardt, Hägler, Hosch, Immermann, Jaquet, Kauffman, Kollmann, Massini, Mellinger, Metzner, Schiess, Siebenmann, August Socin, Wille; *Docents* Buri, Egger, Feer, Hosch, Leopold Rütimeyer, Schwendt, Streckeisen, Wolff.

THEOLOGY.

Professors Böhringer, Bolliger, Bornemann, Duhm, von Orelli, Overbeck, W. Schmidt, Stähelin; *Docents* Bertholet, Bruckner, Goetz, Handmann, Megger, Riggenbach, Vischer, Wernle.

BERNE, Switzerland.
UNIVERSITÄT BERN.

The University (*Hochschule*) of Berne, consisting of the faculties of Philosophy (Arts and Science), Law, Medicine and Theology (Catholic and Protestant), was founded in 1834 and opened to women in 1874. In 1898–99 the number of women matriculated students was 117 and the number of hearers 55. A women docent lectures on Drama in the 19th Century.

Every one wishing to enter as a student must be over eighteen years of age, must present a certificate of good character to the rector, and must pay the matriculation fee of 15 francs ($3.00). A woman, in addition, is required to prove that she is independent, or to present a certificate signed by her guardian giving her permission to attend the university. A fee of 5 francs ($1.00) paid to the rector at the time of matriculation gives the student permission to use the library.

Any one is permitted to attend the lectures as a hearer on buying from the pedell an *Auskultanten Karte*, costing 20 cents.

Regular students and hearers must register with the professors and lecturers whose course they wish to attend, and show their matriculation or auskultanten cards.

They are also obliged, under penalty of a fine, to register their addresses with the pedell within the first fortnight of the semester, and to inform him of any subsequent change of address.

The degree of Doctor is conferred in all the faculties under slightly varying conditions. The candidate for the degree of Doctor of Philosophy must, as in the German universities, present a satisfactory dissertation and pass an oral examination in three subjects.

The winter semester begins on October 15th and the summer semester on April 15th, lasting till August 15th.

Lists of lecturers and other official pamphlets may be procured at any bookshop and enquiries may be addressed to the pedell.

Professors and Lecturers.

ARTS.

LANGUAGES.—SEMITIC: *Professor* Kurz.
  INDO-IRANIAN: *Professor* Müller-Hess.
  CLASSICAL: *Professors* Haag, Praechter; *Docent* Jahn.
  ENGLISH: *Professor* Müller-Hess; *Docent* Künzler.
  GERMANIC: *Professors* Hirzel, Singer, Sutermeister, Vetter, Walzel.
  ROMANCE: *Professors* Freymond, Michaud; *Docents* Bessire, Gauchat, Niggli, Thormann.
PHILOSOPHY: *Professor* Stein; *Docent* Tumarkin.
POLITICAL ECONOMY: *Professor* Oncken.
HISTORY: *Professors* von Mülinen, Tobler, Woker; *Docent* Geiser.
ART: *Professors* Auer, Volmar.
ARCHITECTURE: *Professor* Auer.
PEDAGOGY: *Professor* Haag.

SCIENCE.

MATHEMATICS AND ASTRONOMY: *Professors* Graf, Huber, Ott; *Docents* Benteli, Moser.
PHYSICS: *Professor* Forster; *Docents* Gruner, Moser.
CHEMISTRY: *Professors* Friedheim, Kostanecki, Rossel; *Docents* Mai, Schaffer, Schmidt, Tambor.
MINERALOGY: *Professor* Balzer; *Docent* Kissling.
GEOLOGY AND GEOGRAPHY: *Professors* Baltzer, Brückner; *Docent* Kissling.
BIOLOGY: *Professors* Eduard Fischer, Ludwig Fischer, Studer.
HYGIENE: *Professor* Girard.

LAW

Professors Gretener, Hilty, Huber, Lauterburg, Lotmar, Marcusen, Oncken, Reichel, Reichesberg, Rossel, v. Salis, Stooss, Zeerleder; *Docents* Kebedgy, Opet, Schmidt, Sieber.

MEDICINE.

Professors C. Emmert, Girard, Heffter, Jadassohn, Kocher, Kronecker, Langhans, Müller, Pflüger, Sahli, Stooss, Strasser, Tavel, Tschirch, Valentin, Zimmermann; *Docents* Asher, Bueler, Collon, Conrad, Deucher, Dubois, Dumont, Dutoit, Emmert, Howald, Lindt, Lüscher, Niehans, Walthard.

THEOLOGY.

Professors Barth, Blösch, Herzog, Lauterburg, Lüdemann, Marti, Michaud, Müller, Steck, Thürlings, Woker.

MUSIC.

Docent Hess-Rüetschi.

FRIBOURG, Switzerland.

UNIVERSITÉ DE FRIBOURG.

The University of Fribourg, founded in 1889, consists of the three faculties of Philosophy (Arts and Science), Law and Theology. Women are not admitted as regular students, but they are allowed to attend the courses as hearers, and in the faculty of Philosophy they may take the same examinations and obtain the same diplomas as men students on the same conditions.

The French and German languages are both used, but the university organisation resembles that of German universities in all essential points. Foreigners are as a general rule admitted, provided they possess the qualifications which would admit them to universities in their own countries. The rector decides all doubtful and exceptional cases.

The degree of Doctor is conferred by the Philosophical faculty on candidates who, having studied for three years at a university and having satisfactory testimonials as to character and education, present a dissertation that is approved by the faculty and pass an oral examination in three subjects.

The winter semester begins in the middle of October and the summer semester in the middle of April.

The fee for the first matriculation is 30 francs ($6.00) and for the second 20 francs ($4.00).

Professors and Lecturers.

ARTS.

LANGUAGES.—SEMITIC: *Professor* Grimme.
CLASSICAL: *Professors* Jüthner, Michaut.
GERMANIC: *Professor* Detter.
SLAVONIC: *Professor* Kallenbach.
ROMANCE: *Professors* Giraud, Marchot.
PHILOSOPHY: *Professors* Bartijn, Michel.
POLITICAL SCIENCE: *Professors* Büchel, Jaccoud, Rubland.
HISTORY: *Professors* Büchi, Schnürer, Reinhardt, Steffens; *Docent* Holder.
ART AND ARCHÆOLOGY: *Professors* Hess, Steffens, Zemp.
PEDAGOGY: *Professor* Horner.

SCIENCE.

MATHEMATICS: *Professors* Daniels, Lerch.

PHYSICS: *Professor* von Kowalski.
CHEMISTRY: *Professors* Baumhauer, Bistrzycki, Thomas-Mamert.
GEOLOGY: *Professor* de Girard.
GEOGRAPHY: *Professor* Brunhes.
BIOLOGY: *Professors* Arthus, Kathariner, Westermaier.

LAW.

Professors Bise, Büchel, Clerc, Favre, Fietta, Gottofrey, Hauptmann, -Jaccoud, Koschembahr-Lyskowski, Lampert, Lenz, Oser, Pedrazzini, Perrier, Zycha.

THEOLOGY.

Professors Beck, Berthier, Coconnier, Fei, Frankenstein, Kirsch, Mandonnet, del Prado, Rose, Speiser, Weiss, Zapletal.

MUSIC.

Professor Wagner.

GENEVA, Switzerland.
UNIVERSITÉ DE GÈNEVE.

The University of Geneva, founded in 1559, consists of the five faculties of Arts (*Lettres*), Science, Law, Medicine and Theology. Women are admitted on the same conditions as men. There are now about 170 women students, the majority attending courses in sociology, medicine and natural science. The French language is used and the organisation of the university is similar to that of French universities.

Any person over eighteen years of age is admitted as a hearer to all lectures, but not to the hospitals or the practical courses of the Medical faculty.

Persons who have obtained the *certificat de maturité* in one of the sections of the gymnasium of Geneva or who can prove by certificates or diplomas that they have received an education equal in standard to that implied by the *certificat de maturité* are allowed to matriculate as regular students. The faculty in which the student desires to study decides upon the equivalence of the certificates, and the entrance requirements vary considerably in the different faculties. In some (the department of Social Science, for instance), a knowledge of Greek and Latin is not considered necessary; in others it is essential.

The university confers the following degrees: *Bachelier ès lettres, ès sciences, ès sciences médicales, en théologie; Licencié ès lettres, ès sciences sociales, en droit, en théologie, Docteur ès lettres, en sociologie, en philosophie, ès sciences, en droit, en médecine, en théologie; Diplôme de chimiste, Diplôme de pharmacien.*

For the degrees of *Bachelier* and *Licencié* the candidate must pass an oral and a written examination, for the degree of *Docteur*, he must in general pass an oral examination and sustain a thesis. The requirements as to time, etc., vary in the different faculties. In Arts the candidate can enter for the degree of *Bachelier* on beginning his work in the university. To enter for the degree of *Licencié* he must already hold the *baccalauréat* and have studied in a university for four semesters after obtaining it. Equivalent degrees are in general accepted in place of the *baccalauréat* or *licence* of Geneva.

Persons desiring to matriculate as students should apply to *M. le secrétaire-caissier de l'Université* and present their certificates and testimonials to him for the consideration of the faculty. Students and hearers must register during the first fortnight of the semester for each course they desire to attend, and must procure a course book and present it for signature each semester to the rector, the dean of the faculty and the professors whose courses they attend.

Women are admitted to all the libraries, reading-rooms and laboratories. The laboratories are of two kinds, those in which the students work every day more or less independently, and those known as *répétitoires*, in which the work is merely complementary to the courses, and which are attended only once weekly for about three hours.

The first semester begins on October 15th. The lectures begin on October 22nd and end on March 22nd; the second semester begins on April 8th and ends on July 15th. A summer course in French language and literature, consisting of about eleven lectures a week, is given from the middle of July to the end of August and a shorter course is given in the first three weeks of October.

The fees are: for matriculation, 20 francs ($4.00); for course book, 1 franc ($0.20); for each hour per week of lecture for the semester, 5 francs ($1.00); for exmatriculation, 10 francs ($2.00). There are fees of from 50 francs to 200 francs ($10 to $40) for the different diplomas.

Further information may be found in the Règlement de l'Université de Genève, and in the Programme des Cours de l'Université de Genève, which may be obtained from the *secrétaire-caissier*.

Enquiries may be addressed to *M. le Secrétaire-caissier de l'Université*.

There is an association of women students—the *Société Internationale des Étudiantes de l'Université de Genève*.

Professors and Lecturers.

ARTS.

LANGUAGES.—SEMITIC: *Professor* Montet.
INDO-IRANIAN: *Professor* de Saussure.
CLASSICAL: *Professors* Paul Oltramare, Nicole, de Saussure; *Docents* Courvoisier, Vulliéty.
ENGLISH: *Docent* Roget.
GERMANIC: *Professor* Émile Redard; *Docent* Vogel.
ROMANCE: *Professors* Bouvier, Duproix, Muret, Ritter; *Docents* Bally, Mercier, Paris, Schneegans, Thudichum, Vulliéty, Zbinden.
COMPARATIVE PHILOLOGY: *Professors* Muret, Wertheimer.
PHILOSOPHY: *Professors* Flournoy, Gourd, Adrien Naville; *Docent* Briquet.
POLITICAL SCIENCE: *Professors* Favon, Pantaleoni, Wuarin; *Docents* de Girard, Wiede, Winiarski.
HISTORY: *Professors* Borgeaud, Fazy, Edouard Naville; *Docent* Dunant.
PEDAGOGY: *Professor* Duproix.
ART AND ARCHÆOLOGY: *Professors* de Crue, Montet, Nicole; *Docent* Vulliéty.

SCIENCE.

MATHEMATICS AND ASTRONOMY: *Professors* Caillier, Galopin, R. Gautier, G. Oltramare; *Docents* Fehr, Lyon.
PHYSICS: *Professors* Rilliet, Soret; *Docent* Dutoit.
CHEMISTRY: *Professors* Graebe, Guye, Monnier, Pictet; *Docents* Bonna, Crépieux, Kehrmann, Lauch, Rüst, Ullmann, Welt.
MINERALOGY: *Professor* Duparc.
GEOLOGY AND GEOGRAPHY: *Professors* Duparc, Sarasin; *Docent* Ritter.
BIOLOGY: *Professors* Bedot, Chodat, Laskowski, Monnier, Thury, Yung; *Docents* Briquet, Fuhrmann, Hochreutiner, Rodrigue.
HYGIENE: *Professor* Vincent.

LAW.

Professors Bridel, Brocher, Alfred Gautier, Gentet, Gosse, Martin, Moriaud, Rehfous, Roguin; *Docents* Combothecra, Dunant, Odier, Sacopoulo.

MEDICINE.

Professors Brun, Chodat, d'Espine, Eternod, Haltenhoff, Julliard, Martin, Mayor, H. Oltramare, Prevost, Auguste Reverdin, J. Reverdin, Revilliod, Vaucher, Vincent, Zahn; *Docents* Audéoud, Bétrix, Beuttner, Bourcart, Braun, Buscarlet, Cordès, Christiani, Dupraz, Froelich, Keser, Kummer, Ladame, Ed. Martin, Mégevand, Patru, Ruel, Seigneux, Thomas, Wyss.

THEOLOGY.

Professors Balavoine, Chantre, Doret, Frommel, Martin, Montet, Nicole.

MUSIC.

Docent Roehrich.

LAUSANNE, Switzerland.

UNIVERSITÉ DE LAUSANNE.

In 1890 the Academy of Lausanne, founded in 1537, was formed into a university.

Women are admitted to this university on exactly the same conditions as men. All students who have been matriculated students of any other university and have not been expelled from it are eligible for admission.

The degrees given in the different faculties are the *licence* and *doctorat* and only matriculated students may obtain degrees. In the engineering school the *diplôme d'ingénieur* is given. The time required to obtain the *licence* is, in general, four years in theology, three in law and two in science or arts.

The student is free to arrange his courses as he chooses and is not obliged to complete his work in a specified time.

Three kinds of lectures are given:—the *cours publics* which are free of charge; the *cours universitaires* for which the fee is five francs ($1.00) a semester for each hour weekly; and the *cours particuliers* which are specially arranged for.

There is a special fee for laboratory courses.

The matriculation fee is 20 francs ($4.00).

The winter semester lasts from October 15th to March 25th, the summer semester from April 8th to July 25th.

Holiday courses in French and German language and literature are held from July 17th to August 26th.

Further information may be obtained from the secretary, M. J. BONZEN.

Professors and Lecturers.

ARTS.

LANGUAGES—ORIENTAL: *Professors* Goergens, Spiro.
CLASSICAL: *Professors* Baudat, Besançon, Vallette; *Docents* Chatelanat, Delburbe.
ENGLISH: *Professor* Maurer; *Reader* Neilson.
GERMANIC: *Professor* Maurer; *Docents* Stilgebauer, Taverney.
ROMANCE: *Professors* Bonnard, Muret, Renard; *Readers* André, Parander.
PHILOSOPHY: *Professor* Millioud.
HISTORY: *Professors* Maillefer, Renard, Rossier.
ART AND ARCHÆOLOGY: *Docent* de Molin.
PEDAGOGY: *Professor* Guex.
HYGIENE: *Professor* Galli-Valerio.

SCIENCE.

MATHEMATICS AND ASTRONOMY: *Professors* Amstein, Charles Dufour, Joly.
PHYSICS: *Professors* Dapples, Henri Dufour, Mayor, Palaz; *Docents* Amann, Gross.
CHEMISTRY: *Professors* Brélaz, Brunner, Chuard; *Docents* Dutoit, Kunz-Krause, Pelet, Seiler.
GEOLOGY AND MINERALOGY: *Professors* Golliez, Lugeon, Renevier.
BIOLOGY: *Professors* Blanc, Jean Dufour, Wilczek; *Docents* Bieler, Jaccard.
ENGINEERING: *Professors* Chenaud, Gaudard, Grenier, Mayor, Melley.
AGRICULTURE: *Professor* Chuard; *Docent* Martinet.

LAW AND POLITICAL SCIENCE.

Professors Burckhardt, Erman, Favey, de Félice, Brocher de la Fléchère, Grenier, Larguier, Pareto, Roguin, Spiro; *Docents* Herzen, Jaquemot, Soldan.

MEDICINE.

Professors Bourget, Bugnion, de Cérenville, Combe, Demiéville, Dind, Dufour, Herzen, Larguier, Lowenthal, Mahaim, Nicolas, Rabow, Rapin, Roux, Secretan, Stilling, Valerio; *Docents* Berdez, Dufour, Eperon, de la Harpe, Muret, Perret, Rossier, Verrey, Vulliet.

THEOLOGY.

Professors Chapuis, Combe, Dandiran, Emery, Fornerod, Paschoud, Vuilleumier; *Docent* Rapin.

NEUCHATEL, Switzerland.
ACADÉMIE DE NEUCHATEL.

This university, founded in 1866, consists of the four faculties of Arts, Science, Law and Theology. Women are admitted as students and hearers on the same conditions as men, and at present about twenty are attending the university courses. The constitution of the university is similar to that of the University of Geneva, and all the details given above (pp. 167, 168) apply, with a few exceptions, to Neuchatel.

Students and hearers must be over eighteen years of age. Hearers are not allowed to attend more than ten hours of lectures weekly, and they are not granted any certificate. Entrance examinations are held by all the faculties, but any student holding a certificate equivalent to the certificate of a Swiss or German gymnasium is admitted as a regular student without examination.

The first semester begins on October 14th and ends in the middle of March. The second semester begins on April 4th and ends in the middle of July. Students must register on the first day of the semester.

From July 10th to September 2nd a holiday course in modern French is held for foreigners.

The fees are: for matriculation, 10 francs ($2.00); for each hour per week of lectures for the winter semester 2.50 francs ($0.50), and for the summer semester 2 francs ($0.40); (hearers pay double this sum); for the different laboratories, 5 francs to 30 francs ($1.00 to $6.00) for the semester.

Prizes of 100 francs ($20) are open for competition to registered students.

Further information may be found in the *Programme des Cours* which can be obtained from the *Recteur de l' Académie de Neuchatel.*

Professors and Lecturers.

ARTS.

LANGUAGES. — CLASSICAL : *Professors* Dessoulavy, Le Coultre.
ENGLISH : *Professor* Nippel ; *M.* Swallow.
GERMANIC : *Professor* Domeier.
ROMANCE : *Professors* Amici, Dessoulavy, Le Coultre, Piaget, Warnery ; *MM.* Dubied, Piaget, Ragonod.

COMPARATIVE PHILOLOGY: *Professor* Perrochet.
PHILOSOPHY: *Professor* Murisier.
POLITICAL SCIENCE: *Professor* Junod.
HISTORY: *Professor* de Chambrier; *MM.* Diacon, Farny.
ART AND ARCHÆOLOGY: *Professor* Wavre; *M.* Dessoulavy.

SCIENCE.

MATHEMATICS AND ASTRONOMY: *Professors* Arndt, Hirsch, Isely, Weber.
PHYSICS: *Professor* Weber.
CHEMISTRY: *Professor* Billeter; *MM.* Berthoud, Rivier.

MINERALOGY: *Professor* de Tribolet.
GEOLOGY AND GEOGRAPHY: *Professor* Du Pasquier, Knapp, Schardt.
BIOLOGY: *Professors* Beraneck, Châtelain, Tripet.
HYGIENE: *Professor* Châtelain.

LAW.

Professors Béguelin, Courvoisier, Jeanhenry, Meckenstock, Mentha.

THEOLOGY.

Professors DuBois, Dumont, Ladame, Morel, Perrochet, Quartier-la-Tente.

ZURICH, Switzerland.
UNIVERSITÄT.

The University (Hochschule) of Zurich, founded in 1832, was formally opened to women in 1872 on precisely the same conditions as to men, and women are even permitted to hold professorial chairs. In 1898–99 there were 169 women students, 126 of whom were studying medicine. The university consists of the four faculties of Philosophy (Arts and Science), Law and Political Science, Medicine and Theology; the language used is German and the general organisation is similar to that of a German university.

Inhabitants of Zurich desiring to enter the university must hold the Maturitätszeugniss of a school in the canton; foreigners must hold certificates equivalent to this, or pass an entrance examination, and must prove that they possess an adequate knowledge of the German language. Students must register in the week before the beginning of the semester, and no student is admitted under eighteen years of age. These regulations apply to hearers as well as to regular students.

The degree of Doctor is conferred by each of the faculties under slightly different conditions; in general the candidate must pass an oral examination and present a satisfactory thesis.

There are six libraries open to regular students; hearers are allowed to use these libraries when introduced by a professor.

The semesters begin in the middle of October and the middle of April, and end in March and August respectively.

The fees are: for matriculation 12 francs ($2.40), with other fees amounting to 7 francs ($1.40); for lectures, 5 francs ($1.00) a semester for each hour weekly; for the Doctor's degree, 310 to 420 francs ($62 to $84).

For further information see the *Verzeichniss der Vorlesungen* and the different *Promotions-Ordnungen*. Enquiries may be addressed to the pedell of the university, HERR RUEGGER.

Professors and Lecturers.

ARTS.

LANGUAGES. — CLASSICAL: *Professors* Blümner, Hitzig, Kægi; *Docents* Bloch, Schulthess.
INDO-IRANIAN: *Professor* Ryssel.
ENGLISH: *Professor* Vetter; *Docent* Schirmer.
GERMANIC: *Professors* Bachmann, Frey, Stiefel; *Docents* Betz, Hoffmann.
ROMANCE: *Professors* Morf, Ulrich; *Docents* Gauchat, Morel.
SANSCRIT AND COMPARATIVE PHILOLOGY: *Professor* Kægi.
PHILOSOPHY: *Professors* Kym, Meumann; *Docents* Eleutheropulos, Kreyenbühl, Willy.
HISTORY: *Professors* Dändliker, v. Knonau, Oechsli, Schweizer; *Docents* Caro, Häne, Heierli.
ART AND ARCHÆOLOGY: *Professors* Blümner, Rahn; *Docents* Bloch, Brun, Stückelberg.
PEDAGOGY: *Professor* Hunziker.

SCIENCE.

MATHEMATICS AND ASTRONOMY: *Professors* Burkhardt, Meyer, Wolfer; *Docents* Gubler, Kraft, Weiler.
PHYSICS: *Professor* Kleiner; *Docent* von Wyss.
CHEMISTRY: *Professor* Abeljanz, Werner; *Docents* Bischler, Feist, Schall.
GEOLOGY AND MINERALOGY: *Professors* Mayer-Eymar, Grubenmann, Heim.
GEOGRAPHY: *Professors* Stoll; *Docent* Früh.
BIOLOGY: *Professors* Dodel, Lang, Schinz; *Docents* Hescheler, Heuscher, Kündig, Martin, Overton, Standfuss.

LAW AND POLITICAL SCIENCE.

Professors Cohn, Herkner, Hitzig, F. Meili, Schneider, Schollenberger, Treichler, Vogt, Zürcher; *Docents* Goldstein, Wächter.

MEDICINE.

Professors Billeter, Bleuler, Eichhorst, Felix, v. Frey, Gaule, Goll, Haab, Huguenin, Krönlein, von Monakow, Müller, Ribbert, Ruge, Wyder, Oskar Wyss, Hans von Wyss; *Docents* Bernheim, Gustav Brunner, Bühler, Cloetta, Fick, Hitzig, Höber, Huber, Kaufmann, Kreis, Lüning, Hans Meyer, Rohrer, Schlatter, Schulthess, Seitz, Silberschmidt, Suchannek.

THEOLOGY.

Professors Christ, Egli, Furrer, Kesselring, Ryssel, Schmiedel, von Schulthess-Rechberg; *Docents* Kappeler, E. Meili, Rüegg.

EIDGENÖSSISCHE POLYTECHNISCHE SCHULE.

This school, founded in 1855, though under different administration from the *Hochschule*, has its classes in the same building, and students of one school are at liberty to attend the lectures of the other. The polytechnic school gives instruction in technical work and the applied sciences, engineering, pharmacy, etc.

The requirements for entrance, fees, etc., are similar to those of the *Hochschule*, and women are admitted on the same conditions as men. Application for admission to the courses should be sent in about three weeks before the beginning of the semester. Candidates for admission either as regular students or hearers must satisfy the authorities that they have had the necessary preparation, or must pass a preliminary examination in the subjects they desire to study.

Enquiries should be addressed to the *Direktion des Eidgenössischen Polytechnikums in Zürich* and should be written in German, French or Italian.

There is an association of women students, the *Studentinnen Verein*.

Professors and Lecturers.

ARTS.

LANGUAGES.—ENGLISH: *Professor* Vetter.
   GERMANIC: *Professors* Baumgartner, Stiefel; *Docent* Saitschick.
   ROMANCE: *Professors* Pizzo, Seippel.
PHILOSOPHY: *Professor* Stadler.
POLITICAL SCIENCE: *Professors* Charton, Platter, Roelli; *Docent*———
HISTORY: *Professors* Guilland, Oechsli, Stern.
HISTORY OF WAR AND TACTICS: *Professors* Affolter, Becker, Rothpletz, Schweizer; *Docent* E. Fiedler.
ART: *Professors* Bluntschli, Graf, Rahn.
LITERATURE: *Docent* Saitschik.
PEDAGOGY: *Professors* Stadler, Zurcki; *Docent* Hunziker.

SCIENCE.

MATHEMATICS AND ASTRONOMY: *Professors* Decher, W. Fiedler, Franel, Geiser, Hirsch, Hurwitz, Lacombe, Minkowski, Rudio, Wolfer; *Docents* Beyel, E. Fiedler, J. Keller, Kraft, Rebstein, Weilenmann, Weiler.
PHYSICS: *Professors* Pernet, H. F. Weber; *Docents* Guye, Kawalki, Kopp, v. Wyss.
CHEMISTRY: *Professors* Bamberger, Barbieri, Gnehm, Hartwich, Lorenz, Lunge, Schulze, Treadwell; *Docents* Bosshard, Constam, Feist, Grete, Winterstein.
MINERALOGY: *Professor* Grubenmann.
GEOLOGY: *Professor* Heim.
BIOLOGY: *Professors* C. Keller, Lang, Roth; *Docents* Heuscher, Martin, Standfuss.
BOTANY: *Professors* Cramer, Schröter.
GEOGRAPHY: *Professor* Guilland; *Docent* Früh.
HYGIENE: *Professor* Roth.
ENGINEERING AND ARCHITECTURE: *Professors* Becker, Decher, Escher, Fliegner, Gerlich, Herzog, Lasius, Löhle, E. Meyer, Prásil, Recordon, Ritter, Stodola, Tetmajer, Tobler, A Weber, Wyssling, K. Zschokke, Zwicky; *Docents* Denzler, Gentilli, Kraft, Messerschnitt, Nachtweh.
AGRICULTURE: *Professors* Bourgeois, Bühler, Engler, Felber, Krämer, Nowacki; *Docents* Baechler, Bosshard, Burri, Grete, Krauer, Mertens, Stebler.

THE MEANING OF EDUCATION
WITH OTHER ESSAYS AND ADDRESSES

BY

NICHOLAS MURRAY BUTLER
Columbia University

CLOTH. 12MO. $1.00

HAMILTON W. MABIE
"I do not recall any recent discussion of educational questions which has seemed to me so adequate in knowledge and so full of genuine insight."

REVIEW OF REVIEWS
"We are sure that the teachers of the country will be glad to have these articles and addresses brought together in a single volume. On all that pertains to the science of education no writer more readily commands assent than Dr. Butler."

HARTFORD POST
"The book is an extremely sensible and practical contribution to its subject, and should be well received both for its merits and timeliness of topic."

PAUSANIAS' DESCRIPTION OF GREECE
TRANSLATED WITH A COMMENTARY

BY

J. G. FRAZER, M.A., LL.D. (Glasgow)
Fellow of Trinity College, Cambridge

PRICE, IN SET ONLY, $30.00 NET

Vol. I.   Introduction. Translation. Critical Notes on the Greek Text.
Vol. II. Commentary on Book I. (Attica.)
Vol. III. Commentary on Books II.-V. (Argolis, Laconia, Messenia, Elis I.)
Vol. IV. Commentary on Books VI.-VIII. (Elis II., Achaia, Arcadia.)
Vol. V.   Commentary on Books IX., X. (Bœotia, Phocis.) Addenda.
Vol. VI. Indices. Maps.

THE MACMILLAN COMPANY

66 Fifth Avenue   New York City

The
Development of English Thought

A STUDY IN ECONOMIC INTERPRETATION OF HISTORY

By SIMON N. PATTEN
Professor of Political Economy, University of Pennsylvania

Cloth Extra, Crown 8vo. $3.00

THE CHURCHMAN

"Full of interest and suggestion, usually clearly and often cleverly written, at once an evidence of and an incitement to thought."

CHICAGO TRIBUNE

"What is, perhaps, most remarkable about the general treatment of the subject is the breadth of view kept in mind, the writer having constant regard to the higher moral, religious, and intellectual aspects of English life quite as much as its more material characteristics."

The German Universities

THEIR CHARACTER AND HISTORICAL DEVELOPMENT

By FRIEDRICH PAULSEN
Professor of Philosophy and Pedagogy in the University of Berlin

Translated with the sanction of the Author by EDWARD DELAVAN PERRY, Professor in Columbia College, New York, with an Introduction by NICHOLAS MURRAY BUTLER.

12mo. Cloth. $2.00

"A book which will be found extremely useful by all Americans who are interested in the higher education." — *The Sun*, New York.

"An instructive and entertaining review of the character and development of the German universities written by a professor of the University of Berlin. It will be found of great value to educators and all those interested in educational matters." — *Troy Times*.

THE MACMILLAN COMPANY

66 Fifth Avenue   New York City

www.ingramcontent.com/pod-product-compliance
Lightning Source LLC
Chambersburg PA
CBHW032151160426
43197CB00008B/860